In the Archive of Longing

In the Archive of Longing

Susan Sontag's Critical Modernism

Mena Mitrano

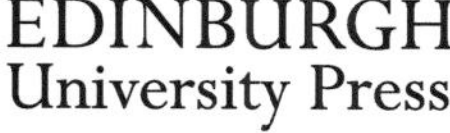

Edinburgh University Press is one of the leading university presses in the UK. We publish academic books and journals in our selected subject areas across the humanities and social sciences, combining cutting-edge scholarship with high editorial and production values to produce academic works of lasting importance. For more information visit our website: www.edinburghuniversitypress.com

Edinburgh University Press Ltd
The Tun – Holyrood Road,
12(2f) Jackson's Entry,
Edinburgh EH8 8PJ

First published in hardback by Edinburgh University Press 2016

Typeset in 11/13 Adobe Sabon by
IDSUK (DataConnection) Ltd, and
printed and bound in Great Britain by
CPI Group (UK) Ltd, Croydon CR0 4YY

A CIP record for this book is available from the British Library

ISBN 978 1 4744 1434 0 (hardback)
ISBN 978 1 4744 2560 5 (paperback)
ISBN 978 1 4744 1435 7 (webready PDF)
ISBN 978 1 4744 1436 4 (epub)

Contents

Illustrations

Acknowledgements

First and foremost I would like to express my gratitude to David Rieff for granting permission to quote from his mother's papers and to reproduce the images included in this book. His generosity has made a difference; it is an honour to acknowledge it publicly.

I also thank the following individuals and institutions: Pierre Alferi, his brother and his mother (Derrida Estate) for permission to quote and reproduce details from Jacques Derrida's correspondence with Susan Sontag; Gloria Steinem and her office staff, for permission to quote from the Gloria Steinem Papers; Tony Burke and Michael Burke (the Kenneth Burke Literary Trust) for permission to quote from Kenneth Burke's correspondence with Susan Sontag; Sandra Stelts, for putting me in touch with Tony Burke; Peggy Kamuf for putting me in touch with Pierre Alferi; Noah Khoshbin, Robert Wilson and the Watermill Center (Paul Thek Estate) for permission to quote from Paul Thek's correspondence with Susan Sontag; the Manuscripts and Archives Division of the New York Public Library and the Astor, Lenox, and Tilden Foundations for permission to quote from the Berenice Abbott Papers.

This book owes to the assistance of librarians, to the wisdom of colleagues, and to the loyalty of friends.

Special thanks to Genie Guerard, at the Department of Special Collections of the Charles E. Young Research Library, UCLA, for her valuable and decisive help. The Department of Special Collections at UCLA is home to Collection 612, Susan Sontag Papers; I thank Amy Wong and all the staff for their assistance over time, especially Simon Elliott who scanned and transferred the images included here. I wish to express my gratitude to the entire 'gang' at the Sophia Smith Collection, Smith College, for the marvelous time I spent in their library in the earlier stages of the project, a time of freedom of experiment and insight, and my fond appreciation to the entire staff of the New Public Library and its Manuscripts and Archive Division for unfailingly recreating for me every single time that magic atmosphere needed for productivity. At the John Felice Rome Center of Loyola University Chicago, I was able to rely on the assistance of Elise Aversa and Anne Wittrick.

A Research Associateship at the Five College Women's Studies Research Center, South Hadley, Massachusetts, in the spring of 2010, enabled me to make headway on the project. The friendship and conversation with our Director at the time, Laura Lovett, with my tutor at the Center, Mary Russo, with the other research associates, and with colleagues at the Weissman Center for Leadership, Mount Holyoke College, have been a true gift for the development of the project. During my time in Massachusetts, I benefited from the wisdom and guidance of Daniel Horowitz who shared his notes on the Susan Sontag archive before I visited it and provided encouragement and useful criticism to my work-in-progress. In the summer of 2011 I began research in the Susan Sontag papers at UCLA, where I also went back the following year. I first presented the results of my archival research at the Modernist Studies Association Conference in Buffalo (MSA 13), where I was inspired by the contact with a thriving international community of modernist scholars. I went on to present early drafts of parts of the manuscript at the 3rd Derrida Today Conference at Irvine (2012), at a roundtable on 'Weak Theory' at the Modernist Studies Association Conference at the University of Sussex (MSA 15), at two different editions of the Critical Theory Conference of Rome (2012, 2014), and at the Center for American Studies in Rome (2014). I wish to acknowledge the contribution of the audiences at these venues and of the colleagues I talked to, especially Marie-Rose Logan for conversations on the Sontag and Derrida connection.

David Ayers first read parts of the early version of the manuscript. Tyrus Miller read the manuscript at its early and later stages; his advice and criticism helped me refine the slant of the study. Andrew Cutrofello, from the Philosophy Department at Loyola, has read different drafts of large parts of the manuscript both at the early and final stage, offering important comments and suggestions for revision. Our exchanges have accompanied the making of this book. When the time came of choosing a title, Andrew played his part in the ritual of naming. Peter Carravetta has also been generous with his time. He has gone through the final typescript and helped me with revisions. His unique command of critical thought and his great erudition have turned the process into a learning adventure, sparking questions that cannot be settled easily but are left for future conversation.

The positive responses from the two anonymous readers have been a gift at the revision stage; their suggestions for expansion and revisions have made this into a better book. Jackie Jones believed in the project as soon as she saw it; I found in her the caring publisher that I had been looking for. Special thanks to her, to Adela Rauchova, Rebecca Mackenzie, James Dale, to whom I am indebted for all his hard work and for his patience, Andrew Kirk, who copyedited the typescript, and to the entire team at Edinburgh University Press for turning my manuscript into the book that is now in your hands.

I thank my loyal friends, especially Michele Huddleston, who has made my two stays in L. A. memorable, Moe Angelos, for sharing her work and for our conversations in New York and about New York, Susan Jahoda and Stephen Korns, for being there and offering various kinds of support.

Finally, I thank MF, the best public intellectual that I know, for enabling me to complete my work, and Paul for his presence in the final stage of the work.

Introduction

The Archival Relation

> My ideal, when I write about an author, would be to write nothing that could fill him with sadness, or if he is dead, that would make him weep in his grave: think about the author on whom you are writing. Think about him so hard that he can no longer be an object, and likewise so that you cannot identify with him. Avoid the double shame of the scholar and the familiar. Return to an author a little of that joy, that energy, that amorous and political life that he knew how to give and invent.
>
> Gilles Deleuze and Claire Parnet, *Dialogues* (1987)

1

Interest in Susan Sontag has grown in recent years. As I complete this book, two new books on her have just come out: the first, an intimate portrait, the second, a biography translated from the German.[1] Not surprisingly, her life draws attention. It is a fascinating example of the formation of the public intellectual in modernity. With the publication of two volumes of her journals we have been given access to an extraordinary document of that formation.[2] The conflicting desires for knowledge and experience, which for Sontag the woman translated into a constant oscillation between the mind and the body, writing and life; the use of the body and sexuality to accede to intellectual illumination; the city as the new topography of philosophical truth; the vertiginous overlap of being and seeming, of individual self and self-fashioned public identity – all these motifs are woven together in an absorbing story that is not Sontag's alone but is representative of many. She has never appeared more as a public intellectual than in her journals, in that representative struggle to create herself.

This book, however, is neither an intimate portrait nor a biography. It is an in-depth study of Susan Sontag's thought, concentrating on her contribution to literary criticism. Her career as a public intellectual parallels the transformation of contemporary literary criticism and the rise of theory. Sontag was a pioneer in proposing a new critical theory. Strangely, however, her intervention remains largely understudied.[3] While her slogan 'against interpretation' has become part and parcel of her celebrity persona, the meaning of that project seems to remain peripheral – even foreign – to the movement we have come to call 'theory', where, instead, it fully belongs. I take my cue from the great René Wellek who famously dismissed Sontag (pairing her with Roland Barthes) as a destroyer of criticism, someone who wanted to transform it into writing (*History* 151). That was an early reception, and since then, as I have mentioned, work on Sontag has flourished. The Sontag I present here has contributed to transform literary criticism into a privileged space of reflection.

Far from being a rejection of all interpretation, Sontag's first collection of essays, *Against Interpretation* (1966), claimed a more ample scope for the critical act. She proposed a 'critical theory' ('On Style' 20) that would no longer be limited to the exegesis of individual texts considered in isolation but would reach to 'a substratum of hidden thoughts and feelings' ('Nathalie Sarraute' 106). Her aim was a critical theory that reconstructed the order of things in which individual artefacts are situated. Her rise paralleled Barthes' *écriture*, which she considered as a modernist practice – 'irresponsible, playful, formalist' ('Remembering Barthes' 170), and Jacques Derrida's *différance*, the opening of communication to 'non-semantic movements' and to the freedom of every sign from every given context. When, in the title essay of her book, 'Against Interpretation', originally written in 1964, she proposed that the task of criticism was 'to cut back content so that we can see the thing at all' and rejected the depth of hermeneutic meaning in favour of an 'erotics of art' ('Against Interpretation' 14), Derrida echoed with a similar disposal of hermeneutic depth, advocating, with particular voluptuousness in 'Signature Event Context' (1971), a flat plane of writing 'cut off from all absolute responsibility, from consciousness as the authority of the last analysis' (316). Their performances are two sides of the same sensibility (the word Sontag would probably use). In a letter to her, the French philosopher himself called his early project on grammatology 'against interpretation'.[4] Although her career spans the life of the critical movement we loosely designate with the name of theory, Sontag is not part of its genealogy. However, from her position outside of something she rightly belongs to, she inevitably addresses theory: the question of her contribution to the transformations of criticism raises the question of what theory really means.

Her archive may be seen as a testimony (a preserved documentary trace) of her persisting engagement of theory. Her journals show that at the same time that she read the critical theory of the early Frankfurt School, the semiology of Barthes and Derrida was very much on her mind.[5] Apart from Barthes and Derrida, the long list of theorists with whom she was in dialogue includes Fredric Jameson, whom she read with an eye to his reparative idea that art 'allow[s] us to be reborn to the world in its existential freshness and horror';[6] it includes Michel Foucault, whose notion of power probably impacted on her inquiry into fascist aesthetics; it includes Gilles Deleuze, whose schizoanalysis she saw as a new wave of her against interpretation.[7] She was aware of theory, read it, but did not join in – at least not overtly.

The subterranean dialogue with theory would probably be enough to justify pursuing the question of Sontag's connection to it, but there is more. The striking feature of her journals is that modernism and theory seem to happen at the same time. Some of her reading lists place in visual proximity titles that we would associate with modernism and titles that we would associate with theory. The proximity creates the impression of a mutual influence; it is highly suggestive of a confusion of tongues in which established chronologies are altered. The impression is strong, indelible. Drawing on Paul Ricoeur's terminology, I call it a psychical trace (Ricouer 427) and discuss it in a core chapter of this book (Chapter 4). From it my inquiry has radiated and settled in the form you are reading.

If Sontag raises the question of an archival relation to theory – of theory, too, as an archival relation, something 'unwritten', in excess of her published work – this is only the symptom, if you will, of another important relation which consists in the conjoining of modernism and theory suggested in her archive. The unfolding of this relation in the silence and shadow of the archive, in the raw form of the journal, serves to forge anew Sontag's well-known interest in modernism. She no longer seems belated, melancholic, or even anachronistic, a modernist in a time of theory; rather, her tie to modernism, which amounts to a devotion and a fidelity, becomes a force in and of theory, in fact, *her* style of theory.

2

The connection between modernism and theory is not new. It was the Hungarian critic Peter Szondi who first looked upon the protagonists of the new theory of literature – especially Barthes and Derrida – as

Mallarmeans of our age (Szondi 159). More recently the debate has grown, especially within the expanding field of modernist studies, and scholars affirm 'wide, deep, and pervasive' affinities between modernism and theory that remain to be explored (Ross 2).[8] Sontag's archive is one of the best places for the study of this intimate link, and the study may cast new light on her published work as well.

Once she wrote: 'Only ideas which are a means of transport are my concern.'[9] Modernism was for Sontag such an idea. Her early association of the term is with the life of the mind as a living practice, a living writing without genre, except, possibly, for the rawness of the journal, 'a peculiarly modern literary genre' ('Artist as Exemplary Sufferer' 53). Modernism is a primordial impression of the joy of writing, of a thinking-writing continuum, its trace a fingerprint to match. Neither personal nor anachronistic, this impression is substantiated by philosophy, in particular by the turn that philosophy had taken with critical theory. Adorno and the early Frankfurt School had passed on to her an awareness of the limits of concepts, an alertness to the claim of conceptual knowledge to describe and understand reality. Her fidelity to the modernist value of the autonomy of art is inseparable from the search for a different thought that would not occlude the rich complexity of reality. Shifting her position in the proximity of art, she insisted on reflection that does not usurp the work of art, that does not try to put its feet in art's boots – as she wrote in her notes to Derrida's Columbia lecture on Heidegger's essay 'The Origin of the Work of Art'.[10] Her critical theory refrains from the grasp of the concept or, in a world that appears as a surface of reproduced images, withdraws from the 'rough grip' of interpretation ('Against Interpretation' 10). Against the grain, in *On Photography* (1977), when others spoke of the decline of modernism, she championed a broadening of modernism. From an aesthetics of abstraction, the term began to indicate a much wider sensibility closer to the values of the present, a *pensiero debole* or weak thought attuned to the fragility and vulnerability of being.

In a contribution to the debate on the link between modernism and theory, Susan Stanford Friedman reminds us that there often is a 'metonymic slide' between the critical theory of the earlier Frankfurt School and later theory ('Theory' 237). With Sontag, it is hard not to address that metonymic slide. As I have suggested, although Sontag is not part of theory's genealogies, it is precisely from a position of foreignness that she keeps alive the question of theory, reminding us moreover that 'we ought to understand what "theory" means and presumably what it excludes' (Friedman, 'Theory' 237).

This book discusses Sontag's affiliation to the critical theory of the early Frankfurt School, and shows how the modernism which that theory inevitably carries with it impacted on Sontag's proximity to art and to its promise, by virtue of its claim to autonomy, to be the site of a 'real thinking' that would elude the constrictions of the finished concept. Against the grain and under the guidance of Walter Benjamin, this modernism became her own 'later' theory, leading her to question the performance of the critic in ways that resonate with our present.

3

We cannot begin to glimpse Sontag's connection with later theory if, besides her affiliation to critical theory, we do not also consider the fundamental importance of philosophy in her career. The first person we encounter in Sontag's archives is someone trained in philosophy. Her papers amplify the importance of her philosophical training and her journals, in particular, bring to the foreground the quest for 'the texture of a forgotten mode of thought'.[11] They make her abandonment of traditional philosophy and her increasing proximity to art seem less like a chancy biographical circumstance and more like a choice in the name of her philosophical quest. She gives the impression of having departed from philosophy without turning her back on it; she appears to have left it only to take it elsewhere. The archive gives us instruments to read her published work in a new light; there, she talks openly of the impossibility of philosophy, that is to say, of its possibility only as an 'incomplete discourse'. For Sontag, who was an admirer of Nietzsche, aphoristic writing is the sign of a metamorphosis in 'traditional' philosophy, which has migrated in other forms ('Thinking Against Oneself' 78). It can also help us read her work on great thinkers – from Emil Cioran to Benjamin – as other than portraits of men she admired. Beyond the dynamic of plain autobiographical identification, certain essays can be read as active attempts by Sontag to inscribe herself in a post-philosophical tradition of critical thought.

The publication of the two volumes of her *Journals & Notebooks*, edited by her son David Rieff, allowed many readers to share the experience of the archive. This consists in the sense of marvel, of surprise, of joy at Sontag's enterprise: the desire to think; in her phrase – to 'move the world' ('The Idea of Europe' 286). In this enterprise, Walter Benjamin becomes Sontag's master, but her discipleship, far from obeying the logic of strict apprenticeship, is an active manifestation of Sontag's position *vis-à-vis* later theory. Benjamin allows her to move the modernism which critical theory inevitably carries in its bosom to the present and, from that vantage point, address theory with the imperative of a passionate life of the mind, of the pursuit of a thinking-writing continuum that exceeds form and the grip of the finished concept. With his principal motifs – the city, the passage, the labyrinth – Benjamin appears as a modern Ariadne, the thinker in the experimental position of the interpreter in an open, indiscriminate landscape of things where thinking comes as a pressure from the outside. In full grasp of the power of philosophical construction, Benjamin lingers before its exertion, under the almost philological spell of the spectacle of the material world. He enables her to see in the city what Le Corbusier discovered in nature: thinking's own 'law of the meander' which takes a slow winding path, then breaks into something and generates an idea. Benjamin shows Sontag the position of the observer who writes, as she puts it in 'Singleness' (1995), 'what's given' to her (259). Thus, with Benjamin, she can say that theory is no longer a matter of genealogies, but a certain kind of life.

Encountering Sontag in the archive means following her longing to withdraw from rhetoric, dogma and thinking imagined as 'possessing'.[12] She yearned to be united with a 'new idea' until thinking felt like a mood, rarified to a tone, and seemed just the ongoing pursuit of an elusiveness – pure activity and pure desire. At the centre of this book, against the background of her reading, which suggests a lively movement and exchange of ideas between modernism and theory, I would like you to see the fascinating enterprise of a descent towards 'the situation of thinking'.[13] Having turned away from philosophy, having taken it elsewhere, Sontag emerges, a figure taking up her place in the post-philosophical scenario of a broken and incomplete critical discourse, next to Benjamin and those other aphoristic writers who are sometimes referred to as anti-philosophers.[14]

4

This book weaves archival research and close readings of Sontag's essays. For reasons of space, the selection cannot be exhaustive. I focus on essays that help me relate the story of the critical act according to Sontag. The only exception I make to the rule of concentrating on her essays is in Chapter 6, which includes a discussion of her novel *The Volcano Lover* (1992).

Chapter 1, 'Thoughts about Thinking: Approaching Sontag', reintroduces the reader to Sontag's view of the critical act. It begins with her special concern with reproduction and its effects on thought and, relying on a reading of *Against Interpretation* (1966), discusses her emancipation from the New Critical milieu and her proposal of a different criticism with a larger scope that would contrast the regime of the ready-made. I show how at this stage Sontag explores ways in which, given the dominant values of reproduction, reflection on the work of art can still produce new ideas and not repeat the already done.

Chapter 2, 'Aesthetic Experience and Critical Theory', explores Sontag's affiliation to the critical theory of the earlier Frankfurt School, focusing on Adorno. It shows that Adorno's influence is inseparable from Sontag's realisation of the metamorphosis of traditional philosophy. Through a comparative reading of Sontag, Adorno and Hans Robert Jauss, it tracks Sontag's effort to overcome Adorno's prohibition of beauty and develop a less pessimistic view of meaning. Aesthetic experience becomes the possible domain of a thought that can elude both commodification and the repetition of the already done. Discussion is based on a close reading of key essays in her second collection, *Styles of Radical Will* (1969), combined with reflections on Sontag's annotated copy of Adorno's *Minima Moralia* and on fragments from Adorno glued into her journals.

Chapter 3, 'The Public Intellectual', focuses on silence and its importance in Sontag's work and in her image. Largely based on a close reading of Sontag's essay on the New York neo-avant-garde, 'The Aesthetics of Silence', this chapter continues to explore Sontag's awareness of the waning of philosophy in the modern world and her turn to the (modernist) autonomy of art for the promise of new meaning – of 'thought beyond thought'. The chapter puts the category of silence in historical perspective through an iconographic reading of Sontag's identity as a public intellectual and the feminist intellectuals of her time. In contrast to her colleagues, who embodied the newly found heroism of speech, Sontag appears as a silent muse, a dissident mind more interested in the interior, hidden aspects of the political tie.

Chapter 4, 'Modernism and Theory', is devoted to the co-emergent mutuality of modernism and theory in Sontag's archive. Against the background of the mutuality projected by her reading lists, we follow Sontag's descent into the situation of thinking. The mutuality in the archive is paralleled by a broadening of modernism in her essays on photography, inspired by Benjamin. No longer reduced to an aesthetics of abstraction ('the abstracting eye'), modernism broadens to a wider sensibility, a weaker thought concerned with the fragility and precariousness of Being.

Chapter 5, 'Iconologies', focuses on the decisive role of Sontag's proximity to art practice. The chapter begins with a discussion of her understudied collaboration with artist Paul Thek. The collaboration enhanced her defence of the autonomy of art further, encouraging her to construe aesthetic experience as the terrain for a different kind of thought which, in line with critical theory, eludes the constrictions of finished concepts. As she veered away from philosophy and closer to art, Sontag took other New York artists as her reference points. The chapter goes on to examine the role of Jasper Johns in reintroducing her to modernism and the influence of Robert Rauschenberg's fragmented surfaces, which became a correlative of the incomplete and broken philosophical-critical plane inhabited by the modern thinker.

The book culminates with two chapters on Sontag's special connection to Benjamin. Chapter 6, 'Aura, Dread and the Amateur', weaves together close readings from Benjamin's work – especially 'Little History of Photography', 'The Work of Art in the Age of Mechanical Reproduction' and a 1937 fragment on the aura – and Sontag's later work on photography, 'Certain Mapplethorpes' (2003) and *Regarding the Pain of Others* (2003), to discuss Sontag's reception of Benjamin's most popular idea, the loss of the aura, more in its psychoanalytic valence than in its dialectical one. It begins with a reading of Benjamin's Art Work essay to show how the celebration of reproduced images signals – theatrically and parodically – the loss of a hermeneutic depth and, with it, the loss of the co-implication of the act of understanding with the expectation of a returning gaze from the artefact/Other. I argue that this loss is celebrated because in fact it is a loss of history insofar as the narrative of the returning gaze, in Benjamin, sublimates the conflict-ridden, evil play of the gaze between condescending oppressor and resentful oppressed. The aim is to show that Sontag inherits from Benjamin an idea of photography as a locus of seduction and dread from which flows not only a basic capacity to think but also the potential of new, history-altering ideas (the event). Rejoining Benjamin, Sontag links her yearning for thought and her theoretical withdrawals to an ethical scope.[15]

Chapter 7, 'Interlocution', offers a detailed reconstruction of Benjamin's influence from the archival materials. It discusses their master/disciple relation, its unfolding and climax in Sontag's 'theft' of Benjamin's being when, at the completion of her work on him, she applies to herself his self-description: 'I was born under the sign of Saturn.' I call this fascinating event interlocution and suggest that, besides being representative of the reader–writer relation, it gives us new insight into her portrait of Benjamin, which became the title essay of her fourth collection *Under the Sign of Saturn* (1980). There, his 'theory of melancholy' is her own intervention in theory. In order to understand the meaningfulness of this move it is necessary to recall the context of the present revival of interest in Sontag. Why Sontag now?

5

A line of continuity could certainly be traced that united the early Frankfurt School, and especially Adorno's negative dialectics, to later movements like poststructuralism and deconstruction, whose shared aim is to salvage from philosophical construction and the concept those aspects of material reality that elude thought. Literary criticism, in the ampler form of theory, has attempted not so much to redress this profound lack of equality as to make the humanities more hospitable to it. It has enlisted in the task the aid of a philosophical tradition that rigorously resists abstraction but affirms the object – the concrete, the ontic, the material – in brief, what cannot be subsumed by the subject.[16] This continuum of critique, however, has come to a halt. Scholars in the humanities have grown increasingly uncomfortable with the acts of unmasking and dismantling typically associated with Adornian and Derridean critique. Fundamental questions about the critical gesture are being asked anew: some wonder whether the critical act has not become just 'a rote, ritualized' or even 'rootless act'.[17] The emergence of the notion of reparative criticism together with a widespread interest in concepts of affect, intimacy and tenderness suggest the search for a more affirming criticism.[18] It is at this junction that Sontag's work attracts.

Only now, perhaps, can we begin to appreciate the dissonance in her persona: while the public intellectual asserts, the mind longs for an unprecedented state of lightness. Pinned to her fidelity to the modernist autonomy of art, the dissonance carries over to the present. Sontag meets us divided. She must see herself as an eternal amateur, someone who does not build any systems but always remains at the beginning of an endless writing in excess of any single genre. At the same time she is also a thinker, who, following the model of the dramaturgical philosopher, changes identities: the beholder, the anthropologist, the artist, the dandy, or simply, as she calls herself in 'Singleness', '(literature's) servant' (259).

Only now perhaps can we begin to understand her pursuit of evanescence, of a thought made of moods and tones, that risks reducing itself to being a thinking about thinking – 'The only thoughts I have that seem to/ stay "true" are thoughts about thinking (and feeling) –/ their contours, methodology, dilemmas',[19] because only now do her archival withdrawals resonate with a critical practice of 'self-interruption' (Berlant 27), with the ever-growing 'need to invent new genres for the kind of speculative work we call "theory"' (Berlant 21). In our time, under the label of 'weak theory', a certain performance of the critic has been proposed: a critic without certainties who wishes for the interruption of 'sovereign knowingness' (Dimock 744). Criticism wants to retreat from strong claims and opt instead for the 'trying out' of 'a lower-level kind of theorizing' (Dimock 733), for 'lateral planes of meditation', 'wayward lines of association oblique to any existing system', 'dispersed episodic webs of association' (Dimock 737). There is an expectant mood of 'other meanings' in the humanities, the dream of a truly different critical gesture: 'What could be said for a critical practice that does not even clinch the case?' (Dimock 736).

Sontag, with her rejection of the forensic dimension of criticism based on asserting, convincing and presenting claims in a setting where 'aesthetic judgments make sense as part of disputes between individuals and social groups' (Ngai 44), where the interpreter is like a judge in front of his or her questioners, becomes a reference point. Like the weak theorist, she oscillates between the strong claim and the 'mood' of thinking, between assertion and descent, between 'noetic prehension' and 'the situation of thinking', books and notebooks.

Despite the deconstructive passion applied to the centre–margin master paradigm – perhaps one of the most popular objects of intellectual desire in the past decades – the weak theorist seems left with melancholy before a persisting 'invariance of power' (Dimock 734), before a landscape of non-communing peripheries that remain 'in the peripheral vision of those not at home with them' (Dimock 752). Again, Sontag's work resonates with this sense of parallel temporalities, missed encounters, impotent simultaneities. Her choice, in the heyday of theory, to side with what she termed Benjamin's 'theory of melancholia' was provocative. Apart from questioning theory's chronology and its genealogies, she raised unsettling questions about belonging and community that concern the weak theorist's landscape of monads.

Seen through her, community becomes a strange word; belonging comes in strange forms. Belonging to a thriving community may be a condition for anyone thinking and writing, perhaps the fundamental element of his or her well-being. Yet it is also problematic. Like other philosophers before her, Sontag knows about the (im)possibility of community.[20] The melancholia associated with her image is in fact the fundamental melancholia of community. She alludes to it in 'In Memory of Their Feelings', an essay whose title modifies 'In Memory of Our Feelings', a poem by Frank O'Hara which became the title of a painting by Jasper Johns, and celebrates friendship as artistic-intellectual collaboration:

> We meet. This could be at a dinner party (forks, knives, spoons, etcetera).
>
> We say things like, How lovely to see you. I've been busy. I think so. I don't know. That must have been very interesting. (Everything is interesting. But some things are more interesting than others.) Probably not. I've heard. In Frankfurt, in Illinois, in London. Next year. What a pity. He's gone away. He'll come back soon. They're organizing something. You'll get an invitation.
>
> We smile. We nod. We are indefatigable. I think I'm free next week. We say we wish we saw more of each other.
>
> We eat, we savor.
>
> Meanwhile, each harbors a secret idea of ascending, of descending. We go on. The plane's edge beckons. ('In Memory of Their Feelings' 186).[21]

Sontag's community is made up of thinkers and artists who commingle but are alone together. They take from each other the bread that they eat alone. The polite instruments of nourishment – forks and spoons – distract us from the central aporia in the warm idea of community, its impossibility.[22]

In *Regarding the Pain of Others*, her last essay on photography, the melancholy existence of non-communicating peripheries and worlds invites 'a reflection on how our privileges are located *on the same map* as [other people's] suffering, and may – in ways we might prefer not to imagine – be linked to their suffering, as the wealth of some may imply the destitution of others' (102–3, my emphasis).[23] Resuming the narrative of the aura, she is concerned here with a gaze that can no longer be returned. Signs no longer lend themselves to productive allegory but harden into distant, almost hostile, marks. The distance keeps widening, until, in the extreme example of photographs of atrocities, the tragic hiatus dividing perpetrator and victim illustrates a new metaphysical silence between observer and observed.

Once democratising, the surfaces of technological reproduction now simplify the world: on the one hand, those who lie safe and huddled in themselves, on the other, those who are reduced to naked life. Symbolic distance from reality – space for thought – is Sontag's theme. She belongs with those thinkers who remind us not to cohere around ideas as if they were 'totems of causes' (*Regarding* 84).

6

We are drawn to certain writers not because they are the best in the absolute but because they give us something. They act as transformational objects; they usher us into the world. They render unto us our sense of being, that moment in which we *are*, that is to say, we are – boldly – part of the world, in a posture similar perhaps to Raphael's *Donna Velata*, '[a]bsolutely restricted to her own existence', the symbol of an equilibrium of forces, 'a rounded-off microcosm, comparable to a star revolving around its own axis' (Panofsky, *Three* 51); or, like Benveniste's linguistic subject dynamically coming forward, designating himself a first person: part of the world, in front of the world. Perhaps it is such moments that Virginia Woolf called moments of being, when, as she writes in a passage about her memories of St Ives, '[t]he buzz, the croon, the smell, all seemed to press voluptuously against some membrane; not to burst it; but to hum round one such a complete rapture of pleasure' (66).[24] From the distance of memory she can relive thought as the experience of a pressure from the outside, as a vertiginous merging of reflection and aesthetic bliss which mounts into rapture, or ecstasy. She does not know which. The uncertainty is key. For these moments in which our being is exalted can for the thinker and writer wane in solipsistic exercise, in isolated raptures of the self. Hence Woolf's indecision. At first she writes: 'It was rapture rather than pleasure' (66). Later, she is no longer sure: 'I am only the container of the feeling of ecstasy, of the feeling of rapture' (67).

Sontag, more decisively, speaks of ecstasy: 'Indeed, one might spend a lifetime apologizing for having found so many ways of acceding to ecstasy' ('About Hodgkin' 159). Ecstasy refers not only to her lifetime defence of the modernist autonomy of art (beauty) but also to her aboriginal idea of modernism as the infinite notebook of moments of being; it recalls the joy of the thinking-writing continuum as a technique of life, the living thought of the cosmophage – world eater – as she has been called by those who admire her (see Koestenbaum), another name for the observer unremittingly before the world, exposed to the hum and buzz of the environment.

Sontag was very visible in New York; she went to places but she cannot be associated with any specific privileged site. Just as we can imagine her at MoMA, as if it were her second home, the Strand Bookstore, where they called her by first name, at the Japan Society, where she was invited to be the curator of a film festival (see Castle), or at Lincoln Center, studiously underdressed, we can just as well imagine her taking the subway at the corner of 103rd and Broadway, waiting for the train as the street performer bends over his guitar singing something in Spanish about *la conciencia*. We can always imagine her writing what's given to her, an I-skin, the membrane against which 'all seemed to press voluptuously'. Perhaps the *promesse du bonheur* in this model is far from diminished as we, too, eat the world through the ear buds of our beautiful cell phones and tablets.

Chapter 1

Thoughts about Thinking: Approaching Sontag

> The only thoughts I have that seem to stay 'true' are thoughts about thinking (and feeling) – their contours, methodology, dilemmas –
>
> Susan Sontag, *Journals & Notebooks*

The beholder and the ready-made

Susan Sontag's critical production shows a preference for unfinished form, for notes and fragments ('Notes on Camp', 'Fragments of an Aesthetic of Melancholy') or for the cumulative sequence of meditations on or regarding a topic (*On Photography*, *Regarding the Pain of Others*). What has become known as her 'epigrammatical mode' (Sayres, 'Susan Sontag' 595) combines with a tendency to protect the object of inquiry rather than explicate. The combination of unfinished form and opacity has fascinated her readers.

For her most perceptive readers, silence is a key term in Sontag's critical canon. Cary Nelson first noticed the 'deep, sweet silence' with which Sontag surrounds the artefacts she examines, as if to signal the encounter with an otherness that she consistently tries to preserve ('Soliciting' 720).[1] Sohnya Sayres followed up: 'the work itself is bracketed off in a language of untouchability' (*Elegiac Modernist* 82). Like Nelson, like Sayres, anyone approaching Sontag must reckon with her paradoxical silence as a critic and a writer: 'Meaning glints off its surface. The silence of a work that Sontag repeatedly asks be respected, resounds' (Sayres, *Elegiac Modernist* 82–3). Nelson also usefully describes her style as 'written reverie' ('Soliciting' 720), a phrase that alludes to the image of the writer lost in thought at the same time that it evokes the attempt to capture a stream of thoughts that remains somehow in excess of the written and, in any case, does not settle into finished concepts. Sontag was a philosopher by formation who liked to call herself a writer. Approaching her means finding words for this fact. Nelson's phrase conveys something uneasy about the fusion of the two identities of thinker and writer. A 'written reverie' suggests a certain turbulence in the passage from thinking to writing. It poses the problem whether thought might be written into finished concepts, whether, in fact, thought can be transferred into writing or whether it lingers before the concept's threshold – exactly like a reverie. For this reason the phrase is useful to introduce what appears to be a central question of Sontag's work, that is to say, the clash of faculties – thinking and writing, seeing and thinking – with the consequence of an incomplete (impossible?) crossing of thought towards its full expression.

Sontag proclaimed her longing for an 'absolute integrity of thought', for 'disavowals of mind' ('Thinking Against Oneself' 80, 82). Thought must be capable of a certain self-cannibalism – Prometheus and the 'remorseless eagle who consumes his perpetually regenerated entrails' – if it is to go on and renew itself (81). Even though she preferred the humbler title of writer, her ideal was a philosophical attitude beyond the limits of cultural identity and beyond the will to self-preservation and self-interest. She favoured the stance of the thinker in open resistance to her society, constantly interrogating her motives for mental activity. In *Regarding the Pain of Others* (2003), her second book on photography, the genealogy of that peculiar philosophical stance, which she identified as European, goes back to William Wordsworth. Sontag marvels at the continuity between our globalised world, with its daily 'diet of horrors', and the Romantic poet's industrialised society in which, similarly, 'a craving for extraordinary incident' combined with growing urban crowds and mass culture to 'blunt the discriminating powers of the mind', reducing it to 'a savage torpor' (*Regarding* 107). She imaginatively redraws the world – from modernism and Virginia Woolf (*Three Guineas*) to the violence of Abu Ghraib – as a cultural continuum of 'shock-pictures' which launch more urgently than ever the question of thinking. She is concerned about the transformation of thought into 'common ideas of significance'; thinking seems to have been reduced to the act of 'trigg[ering] predictable thoughts, feelings' (*Regarding* 86).

Photography, because of its uses, becomes the most advanced outpost of the question of thinking in a world of total reproduction. Benjamin had realised that in modernity the work of art *is* technological reproduction. Sontag realised that, as technological reproduction, art merges with an indiscriminate drive to exhibit and externalise something before a public, with the result that, as shown by the extreme case of photographs of atrocities, our capacity for moral response has been bleached out. Technological reproduction and images cannot be faulted for the waning of the capacity to transform being affected into effective action. The cause, for Sontag, is the waning of thinking. Thinking, she finds, has become 'stipulating' (*Regarding* 86); it amounts to crystallisations of predictable ideas, to the recognition of 'totems of causes' (84), to rites of assent and collective instruction. The world feels like a huge megastore (9); her concrete image recalls Alain Badiou's homogeneous surface of capital and market (Badiou 10–11).[2]

The impression, in *Regarding the Pain of Others*, is that of someone giving herself to the pressure of the surface: vulnerable, without theories, exposed, in the open of an oppressive vista or repetitive ready-made ideas. Thinking can only repeat previous thoughts. Discouraged, she appeals to her beloved Plato, insisting on the mind as inner receptacle or *chora* where we 'picture', that is to say, join present to past via memories and phantasms. 'Even in the era of cybermodels, what the mind feels like is still, as the ancients imagined it, an inner space – like a theatre' (*Regarding* 88–9). Plato and traditional philosophy notwithstanding, thinking cannot be a truth from within. The basic trait of philosophical discourse can no longer be the self-evidence of 'its inner quality'; it can no longer be the effect of its own 'inner structure . . . independent of its relation to the external world' (Groys ix).[3] Rather, like her colleague Gilles Deleuze, she experiences thinking as a pressure from the outside, as a passion she must endure.

In *Regarding the Pain of Others*, Sontag achieves the stance of the thinker as a vulnerable beholder. Over the years, the achievement had been prepared for by her investment in a favoured image of thought which consists in the clash *against* something – a clash attended by the prospect of a great impoverishment. Sontag, who felt the 'need to strip down',[4] experiences thinking as the point at which the mind fails against the rock-hard symbolic nakedness of an object. Accordingly, she portrays herself in public as a woman struggling to retain some basic mental power. In the essay 'The Idea of Europe (One More Elegy)', rather than assuming the role of ambassador between Europe and America, she opts for a disempowering intellectual fantasy. She wants to think – to 'move the world' – but 'cannot do it' ('The Idea of Europe' 286). The intellect is endangered, ensnared at every turn by a certain arbitrary nakedness, by an inexplicable subtraction. Genuine mental acts seem to arise from the conflict between seeing and thinking.[5] Her intellectual life is marked by such a basic conflict, which redoubles as the tension between art and thought, that is to say, between the bliss of aesthetic experience and the possibility of its legibility. It would not be possible to begin approaching Sontag without addressing this conflict.[6]

Is criticism thought or is it power?

After the avant-garde, art had become the privileged site of a new truth effect. Duchamp, in particular, with his readymades, may be seen as the emblem of what art critic and philosopher Carla Lonzi called 'an operation of truth' ('La solitudine' 356).[7] Truth is no longer certified from above, but dispersed and dependent on the new freedom of the individual from submission to authority. As Lonzi writes, 'free at last from the imperative to conform to pre-constituted formulas and ethical models dictated by social conditioning, the individual is put finally in the position of accepting as truth what proceeds from an unimpeded certification of consciousness' (356). 'It is no longer,' says Lonzi, 'a question of defending ideas on the basis of ideological struggles'; the point is to circulate ideas on the basis of what she terms their 'individual authenticity' (356). The individual is neither determined by his or her belonging to a social group, from which he or she borrows the vesture of meaning, nor defers to a superior authority (*patres*), an elite group of intellectuals who constitute themselves as the appointed guardians of standards of value and taste.[8] In the face of this plane of multiple and multiplying singularities, criticism, if it does not open up to the new truth effect, becomes either anachronistic or a forceful re-inscription of ideologies.

The new task of the critic is to be able to recognise those forms of artistic production that manifest as the 'creation of techniques of life through which the human subject reacts in a non-neurotic fashion to the fall of social myths and ideologies, of cultural dichotomies, to the overthrow of boundaries and, more generally, to a new cosmic condition' (Lonzi, 'La solitudine' 356). Not to fall into oblivion, criticism must seize a parallel freedom to the contemporary artwork after Duchamp (356).

Historically, Sontag is situated at this crossroads. Like Lonzi, Sontag does not ignore the consequences of the avant-garde. Lonzi started out as an art critic and her wish to produce a criticism of proximity to the artist's practice led her eventually to withdraw from criticism. Criticism dissolved into a new form of philosophical discourse and Lonzi became the founder of Italian feminist philosophy, which she inaugurated iconoclastically with her text against Hegel (*Sputiamo su Hegel*, 1970). Sontag, instead, follows the inverse path. She begins with philosophy but progressively leans towards art. Proximity to art, especially visual and performing arts, increasingly appears as the precondition for 'real thinking'.[9] If a greater proximity to art can guarantee the philosophical attitude of the thinker on a quest for unthought thought, her aphoristic and fragmentary mode, as erudite, seductively fast and omnivorous, delightfully 'jagged' as it might be (Maunsell 88),[10] reveals the problem of a thinking restlessly striving to settle into expression and form. The unique thing about Sontag is that 'criticism' comes to be the main battlefield of this restlessness.

The diasporic plane

The degree to which Sontag is concerned about reproduction in her first collection of essays, *Against Interpretation* (1966), should not be underestimated. She rejects 'ready-made ideas' about art ('Marat/Sade/Artaud' 166), especially the assumption that art can be reduced to its content: 'Another ready-made idea: a work of art is to be understood as being "about" or representing or arguing for an "idea"' (169). In challenging the dominant standard according to which the value of a work of art 'is the value of the ideas it contains, and whether these are clearly and consistently expressed' (169), she questions the function of the work of art to be the means for argumentative and linear critical discourse. Thus, to be 'against interpretation', as her lead essay proclaims, is to emancipate the artwork from being the vessel of ideas. The stance translates in a pronounced emphasis on style as a way of preserving a margin of autonomy. It is through style that the problem of the new enters criticism.

'On Style', the second essay in her first collection, dwells on reception. It takes on the problem of a more ample breadth and scope of criticism, a term which she prefers to 'critical theory': 'The great task which remains to critical theory is to examine in detail the formal function of subject-matter' ('On Style' 20). She adds: 'Until this function is acknowledged and properly explored, it is inevitable that critics will go on treating works of art as "statements"' (21). Defined as anything that deviates from a norm, style can prevent criticism from falling into oblivion in the regime of reproduction. Attention to the formal function of subject matter, therefore, is key. In the first collection she seems to be laying the premises of a criticism understood as reflection that is not condemned to repeat but that can produce the new.

This is why she talks of critical theory and of 'another use of ideas' ('Marat/Sade/Artaud' 171). Critical theory is less isolated than criticism. It is critical discourse that assumes an equal exchange and dialogue with the artwork, to the point of a mutuality. Not only can art give rise to criticism, but the latter's formulations can operate as 'sensory stimulants' for artworks to come: 'Often, the sensibility (the theory, at a certain level of discourse) which governs certain works of art is formulated before there exist substantial works to embody that sensibility' (172). She offers the example of 'writers and critics' like Roland Barthes, Michel Foucault and Alain Robbe-Grillet, whose theory has given rise to new literary forms (172).[11] Their work is theory in the sense that it does not illustrate single artworks, but is an 'anti-rhetorical aesthetic' that can itself generate art. Their work moves beyond criticism into the realm of theory because it does not limit itself to describing modern experience but has a stake in it; it is close to it and speaks about the sensibility which governs certain works of art. In fact, the kind of non-isolated interpretative practice which she calls theory serves to orient; it creates a whole in which certain works come to make sense (172).

Sontag proposes a model of resonance between artwork and critical discourse (theory that is against interpretation). She locks art and criticism in a genuine relation of mutuality which breaks down an ancient subordination of the latter to the former, and conceives both, in their mutual, sensory interlocution, as a reserve for unforeseen ideas. She thus manages to project a continuous diasporic plane of possible invention that defies the bleak prospect of total reproduction. In a regime of reproduction, if criticism limited itself to affirming the content of the work, it would simply end up repeating the same, already existing ideas; there would be no margin for invention for the thinker/critic. Sontag poses, therefore, an elusive something in reserve in the work of art, so that, by receiving it, criticism might not be a repetition of what has been already done and already said. The leitmotif of *Against Interpretation* is the possibility of criticism not to be reproduction, copy. At the time, she was making her way through the legacy of the critical theory of the early Frankfurt School thinkers she admired, especially Theodor Adorno and Walter Benjamin. She took her cue from their research which was premised on the idea that technological reproduction had superimposed on the world 'a spectral and mortuary cosmos' of images that simultaneously showed it and hid it from man's dulled receptive faculties.[12]

Some of the key essays from 1964 onwards bear the trace of an initial engagement with Benjamin, whose work, it appears, she began to read first hand in that year. At this early stage of her response to Benjamin, however, her use of his work is rather superficial, more an enthusiastic appropriation of images than the intellectual collaboration into which it would develop over time. At this stage she understands his idea of the destruction of the aura politically, as the celebration of reproduction: 'a pure power that equalizes everything and abolishes all differences' (Groys 104). Thus, the destruction of the aura enters her work under the name of 'camp'. 'Notes on "Camp"', one of her most popular essays, is explicitly devoted to the problem of the copy. Camp taste translates the decay of uniqueness, and the difference between the original and the copy. Camp, she writes, 'transcends the nausea of the replica'; it makes 'no distinction between the unique object and the mass-produced object' ('Notes on "Camp"' 289). In her vertiginous aphoristic accumulation, the lover of camp joins Benjamin's jubilant masses who hold copies close to them in the Art Work essay.

It is in the collection's lead essay, 'Against Interpretation', that, despite the basic appropriation of Benjamin, we hear something different from the celebration of reproduction as an exciting novelty. She envisions the space of an endless play of differences, suggesting the alternative kind of reproduction that Boris Groys calls 'diasporic' (102). Diasporic reproduction is reproduction that offers the opportunity of producing something new by way of the copy. When she affirms the parity between the primary art object and the secondary discourse of criticism, she is trying to open up a space for diasporic reproduction. When she talks of a sensibility that is formulated before there exists substantial works to embody it, she is saying something similar to Groys when he writes that we can expect 'from the diasporic copy that it departs from the original, that it shows the face of the Other, the new, the unexpected' (104). This means, says Groys, that even in conditions of total reproduction we can expect 'the philosophical attitude and wait for evidence of the new, unthought-of Other' (104). From early on, Sontag treats criticism in terms of the diasporic copy.[13]

Against interpretation

In 'Against Interpretation', Sontag attempts to open up as space for the unexpected, which she renders as the 'flight from interpretation' ('Against Interpretation' 10). Pop Art, because of its unremarkable, ordinary content, points to the new opening: it uses 'a content so blatant' that 'it ends by being uninterpretable' (10). She connects past and present. What she observes in the experimental painting around her can be traced, she argues, to earlier experiments in modern poetry (French Symbolism) and certainly to the modernism of Ezra Pound, whom she favours over T. S. Eliot because he escaped 'the rough grip of interpretation' (10). Pound's revolution consists in 'turning away from content in poetry in the old sense'; like Pop Art, his poetry resists being made 'prey to the zeal of interpreters' (10).

Sontag does not seize on the aesthetic encounter for the chance to do criticism. Her essay is a defence against the 'infestation of art by interpretation' (11), an exhortation to elude the interpreters for the sake of the life – that is the aliveness – of a particular art form (11). The surfaces of Pop Art,[14] like difficult modernist texts, prove particularly interesting because they confirm the landscape that, even at this early stage, she felt she had inherited from Benjamin: the world rearranged by the reproducibility of the work of art into an indiscriminate vista of things (works, objects, people) that lie at rest, self-enclosed, concealed in themselves, impermeable to understanding. She invokes the vista in her essay 'On Style': 'A work of art is a thing *in* the world, not just a text or a commentary *on* the world' (21). The challenge is to relocate thinking in this landscape. Not only do works of art multiply; as they multiply endlessly they confuse themselves 'in the conflicting tastes, odors, sights of the urban environment' ('Against Interpretation' 13); they become one with 'the material plenitude' and 'the sheer crowdedness' that constitute the conditions of modern life (13). As works of art blend in an environment where everything 'conjoin(s) to dull our sensory faculties' (13), the figure of the interpreter who judges and asserts disappears, to be superseded by another figure, that of the beholder. Sontag's beholder is significantly less self-possessed: she dwells in intellectual impotence, her faculties bombarded, dulled, her mind in reserve, held still before the rearrangement of the world as a heterogeneous whole on to which she can neither cast a commanding gaze nor exert intellectual mastery.

Quite wonderfully, in 'Against Interpretation' the critic is synonymous with this anonymous beholder bombarded by stimuli. Sontag writes: 'It is in the light of the condition of our senses, our capacities . . . that the task of the critic must be assessed' (14). Despite the numbness, a new grace sets in as the figure withdraws from a forensic setting ruled by the aim of asserting, presenting claims and convincing, like a judge before a public of questioners.

This is a good thing: 'What we decidedly do not need now is further to assimilate Art into Thought, or (worse yet) Art into Culture' (13). The aim is 'to see more, to hear more, to feel more' (14). As the beholder advances, a divide opens between art and thought. Is criticism thought or is it power? The question begins to make sense. Does criticism repeat social and cultural values or can it actually open up to reflection, to what Sontag calls 'the use of intelligence' ('Spiritual Style' 179). That is the point of her phrase 'against interpretation'. It does not mean a rejection of all interpretation; on the contrary, it champions a criticism open to reflection, closer, that is, to that 'operation of truth' which was the legacy of the avant-gardes and with regard to which the critic risked becoming an anachronistic figure.

In the essay on Lévi-Strauss, 'The Anthropologist as Hero' (1963), also included in *Against Interpretation*, the distance between the interpreter and the beholder widens; the first seems eclipsed by the 'eyewitness' and the gaze becomes the fulcrum of meaningfulness (75). Anthropology is brought about by the 'psychological revolution' of the ready-made and by the new truth effect (75). Like psychoanalysis, it is about knowledge that cannot be certified by an authority from above; it cannot be transmitted through exams and tests. It relies on the inner transformation of the knower, on that 'inner revolution that will make him into a new man' (75).

The uniqueness of the essay lies in Sontag's capacity to link the historical moment of transformation in critical thought to an interior dialectic of attraction and repulsion – 'coldness and pathos' (79) – which the thinker and his theoretical invention (structuralist anthropology) embody advantageously. A favourite embodiment of the beholder, Lévi-Strauss is aligned with a 'cult of aloofness' (79). He distances himself, for example, from the 'overrich style' of Genet, and is closer instead to the 'cool microscopic styles' of new French Cinema (Resnais) (79). His intellectual agnosticism allows him to destroy rites, myths, taboos. Through his formalism, these up to then stable social and historical signifiers, which one might define as the glue of societies, fall, only to re-emerge no longer as signs but as floating marks without meaning and relevance. Reassembled like a language, she writes, whose parts are 'meaningless in themselves' (80),[15] these fundamental signifiers are observed from a distance and drained of the capacity to touch and wound. The beholder gazes at the disappearance of pre-literate people but can erode the pathos, the personal affect, and so come to stand as 'the lucid and anguished observer . . . purged by the severity of theory' (80). Lévi-Strauss's theory proceeds from the play of distance and proximity initiated by an ambiguous intellectual object; it reacts to some cultural violence, which, as the anthropologist's object of inquiry, is simultaneously attractive and repulsive. It is the achievement of a distance without anguish.

In his reading of Lévi-Strauss, included in *Of Grammatology* (first published in French in 1967), Derrida would insist on the pathos. The philosopher criticised the anthropologist for producing knowledge by 'remorse' (*Of Grammatology* 114). He unmasked the thinker's scientific observation as 'empirical affect' (117). Differently, for Sontag, Lévi-Strauss's theory is criticism with a more ample breadth and directly ties in with the emphasis on style that runs through her first collection. She admires the distance of theory because it enables the denial of established meaning and the liberating altering of time, together with the utopian strain (freedom from need to enslave other men in order to make progress possible). The heroism of the anthropologist's theory has something in common with modernism's 'abstracting eye', which she would celebrate a few years later.

Material marks

The dialectic of 'coldness and pathos' that Sontag identifies in Lévi-Strauss is not extraneous to her own work. In his recent study of the public intellectual, Daniel Horowitz observes that Sontag chose topics towards which she held an 'explicitly ambivalent' attitude (327). Camp is a prime example of an intellectual object that simultaneously attracted and repelled her; she was 'strongly drawn' to it just as she was 'offended by it' (Sontag qtd. in Horowitz 327). In an earlier study, Cary Nelson noticed how the readers of her published work have to brave 'mutually sustained and countered impulses toward intimacy and abstraction' ('Soliciting' 720). It is as if the object first presented itself to the mind with the contours of something essentially hostile, withdrawn in a pre-symbolic rawness that repels the mind. Strangely, the mental act – 'the Archimedean point from which I can move the world' (Sontag, 'The Idea of Europe' 286) – is enabled by this balking of the mind, by this fundamental repulsion. Consider the short but important essay that introduces the volume *Italy: One Hundred Years of Photography* (1987). Here Sontag describes the labour of distancing given a repelling intimacy.

Photographic images of Italy become the occasion to mourn the depth of the past:

> The depth possessed by these images of an older Italy is not just the depth of the past. It is the depth of a whole culture, a culture of incomparable dignity and flavor and bulk . . . that has been thinned out, effaced, confiscated. To be replaced by a culture in which the notion of depth is meaningless. That is not meant to be sauntered through. That becomes an abstraction. To be seen as an image. To be seen from the air . . . ('One Hundred Years of Photography' 222)

The roving eye out of aesthetic absorption poses a reserve of meaning, a 'bulk' that has disappeared in the distance: the word 'effaced' suggests meaning that has been obliterated in its very forms, while 'confiscated' suggests that perhaps it is meaning that might have migrated to other forms. I single out this essay because the depth of Italian photography stands for the very depth of the aesthetic encounter (as it will be discussed in the next chapter). The anthology of photographs encourages a kind of absorption which, in turn, leads to the apprehension of a faculty (thinking as free, uninhibited sauntering through forms) and a reassuring sense of belonging ('dignity and flavor') which had vanished in the distance, hardened in thin marks, in abstract grids of an aerial view.

If we take the initiative and leaf through the same anthology of Italian photography, we realise that Sontag might have had little reason to mourn the past. Some of the images trigger distinctly uncomfortable feelings. *Poor People in Udine* by Luigi Pignat, for example, manages to document the poor as a class only because the people in the image are faceless; they give their back to us.[16] Were the poor to stare at the musing viewer, as they do in Walker Evans's photographs, for instance, they might break away from an enforced abstract identity, become something else, and perilously instigate the spectator's imitative desire of what they have. Such is the power of pictures. In Vincenzo Balocchi's *Passersby*, a busy city crowd followed by shadows walks by a poster of 'Il Duce'.[17] The geometrical quality of the composition is meant to evoke the rhythm of the city but only leaves the viewer oppressed by a claustrophobic dejection that is absent from Berenice Abbott's renowned 'Tempo of the City' series, which Sontag appreciated, where even the anonymity of an urban crowd wearing identical clothes transmits something uplifting.[18] Similarly oppressive is the atmosphere in *State Examinations in Milan.*[19] The serial arrangement in space of the bodies of the examined projects less the image of the diligent and contented community and more a social world in agony, paralysed by the obsession with a punishing sameness. It is difficult to look at these pictures and mourn the past, unless one wishes to orientalise Italy. But that is not what Sontag had in mind. The instinct of the critical theorist in her – the mind thinking against itself – would probably not allow it. The photographs she writes about illustrate key themes of modernity, yet reach the viewer with dread.

The mix of modernity and dread may be said to reach a climax with *The Family, Luzzara*, by American photographer Paul Strand.[20] It was taken in 1953, less than a decade after the Second World War. The narrative of loss and pain, which viewers learn from commentaries on the image, is disjointed from the phantom of a stifling patriarchalism which the image exhibits like a trophy. Here is the narrative as told by Anne M. Leyden in a relatively recent catalogue of Strand photographs. In her short commentary, Leyden frames the portrait as a specific example of collective sorrow linked to the experience of the war, 'still very tangible for most townspeople, all of whom had been affected in some way' (78). She explains:

> In this portrait of the Lusetti family, Anna Spagiari Lusetti is surrounded by four of her sons: Bruno, Guerrino, Afro, and Remo. Her story is one of personal loss and hardship. Married at eighteen, she bore fifteen children, four of whom died young. Her husband, after enduring years of politically motivated beatings, died on Christmas Eve in 1933, and all but one of her sons fought in the war. At the time of this photograph, the mother and five of her offspring were living together in the small house, barely surviving on the little money they made from working the land. Strand deliberately arranged the composition, placing the sons around their mother, who stands erect in the doorway, her strong features visible in their faces. (Leyden 78)

The patriarchal world of Strand's image meets the viewer as a spectral space of genderless mothers at one with their sons. The photographer himself seems surprised to have found such a world; the careful arrangement comments on a certain anthropological intent to document something 'primitive' that has been lost. The hard surface is inhospitable to the intellect: it promises to strip the mind bare, arrest it before language and symbolic acts, especially interpretation. With the grace of the erudite commentator, Sontag glosses over the spectral force of the surface. She rather proceeds to integrate Strand's (and similar images in the volume) to the vanished world of Pier Paolo Pasolini's *Uccellacci & Uccellini*.[21]

In the passage already quoted above, at the essay's close, Sontag distances a potential source of dread ('the depth possessed by these images') which causes the mind to fail. In the space of aesthetic absorption, a harmony-breaking force repels; distanced, it is 'thinned out' and hardens in material marks, which, barely recognisable, have become illegible. Depth is declared 'meaningless' while the abstract composition of the illegible marks in the distance indicates the beholder in flight from interpretation. The marks are not signs; they do not beckon back, inviting the reader into the play of unlimited semiosis which Sontag calls sauntering ('that is not meant to be sauntered through'). While they can still evoke the possibility of semiotic enchantment ('To be seen as an image'), the material marks seem to remain inscrutable, a symbolic hostility blocking their legibility. The flight from interpretation announced in the earlier essays has, with time, developed into the question of the aesthetic encounter, of the technique of the encounter.

The scene of the event

The photography Sontag fed on must have encouraged the movement of the mind in the act of understanding as a play of intimacy and distance. Images such as those of Henri Cartier-Bresson, which document Europe devastated after the Second World War, with their stark atmosphere, with their damaged humanity, with their ruins, form the objective correlative of Sontag's primary scene – the scene of insight, of the intellectual event. Knowledge is associated less with cosy and bookish interiors and more with impoverished sites of material life. She simulates the scene at the beginning of *Under the Sign of Saturn*, her sustained meditation on the philosophical and critical tradition from which she hailed:

> I am writing this in a tiny room in Paris, sitting on a wicker chair at a typing table in front of a window which looks onto a garden; at my back is a cot and a night table; on the floor and under the table are manuscripts, notebooks, and two or three paperback books. That I have been living and working for more than a year in such small bare quarters, though not at the beginning planned or thought out, undoubtedly answers some need to strip down, to close off for a while, to make a new start with as little as possible to fall back on. ('On Paul Goodman' 3)

The small bare shelter, the cot, the paucity of objects and possessions ('as little as possible') – every detail, on the first page of her fourth collection of essays, combined with the epigraph from Beckett's *Endgame*,[22] informs us that the possibility of thinking and productivity depends on a scene of subtraction rather than plenty and accumulation.

In the anthology of photographs entitled *The Europeans* (1955), Cartier-Bresson invites the viewer to detect something beyond the visible ravages:

> Countries, like men, do not all have the same age, nor the same degree of prosperity. Their level of maturity varies according to each domain. Sometimes, too, in spite of profound changes, you come upon traits you would have thought vanished long ago – as one recognizes a young girl from a portrait of her grandmother, long since passed away. (Intro. n.p.)

In a play of distance and proximity, the ruins of history may regress in the backdrop, pushing to the foreground our perception of a previously neglected connection between past and present, another order of somatic continuity that sears the symbolic shell of language and understanding and, in the fashion of Benjamin's mimetic cognition, appears only in flashes (Benjamin 'On the Mimetic Faculty'). Historical time is altered by the upsurge of another transgenerational time, glimpsed in the visual apprehension of our bond to our ancestors. Like Bresson, Sontag envisions another semiotic plane of disseminated, dispersed meanings, where the nauseating waves of destructive repetition on an epic scale abide and dread passes into a form of knowledge.

'Body-thinking'[23]

The dialectic of proximity and distance presides over the possibility of a more ample critical theory which, however, seems inseparable from the image of thinking as a clash against a raw nakedness. This is Sontag's way of dealing with the question of the copy, with the world encased in 'a spectral and mortuary cosmos' of reproduced images.[24]

In the essay on camp, in an initial enthusiastic encounter with Benjamin's idea of the destruction of the aura, Sontag had celebrated the copy. In 'The Aesthetics of Silence' (1967), a key essay in her second collection, her concern with repetition and the copy becomes more pronounced. She goes on to speculate explicitly about how art can afford a way out of the ennui of total reproduction. She speaks of the artist's 'enslavement to history' and of the 'already done' (15). The writer and the artists she writes about are mutually locked in the claustrophobic order of total reproduction:

> Modern art thus transmits in full the alienation produced by historical consciousness. Whatever the artist does is in (usually conscious) alignment with something else already done, producing a compulsion to be continually checking his situation, his own stance against those of his predecessors and contemporaries. (15)

The contemporary experimental art she examines, however, seems to meets the beholder with other possibilities. At the centre of the essay towers the stare of contemporary art, also called 'silent' art: 'Traditional art invites a look. Art that is silent engenders a stare' (16). The stare beyond the look holds the promise 'for the continuing or exploring of thought' (19).

Reviewing the landscape of total reproduction, Sontag now seeks to affirm the possibility of the new. Despite the enslavement to history and the inhibition of the 'already done', time might be arrested, and mental activity propelled forward, towards 'interminable, unanswered questions' (17). She phrases the clash of faculties – the senses and the intellect, seeing and thinking – with John Cage: 'No one can hear an idea once he starts really listening' (16). Thus phrased, the clash is justified; it can be pursued and renewed each time because it secures the sweet deferral of the thinker's union with a thought that continues.

Although 'The Aesthetics of Silence' was written under the spell of Jasper Johns, of his mysteriousness, his intelligence, his difficult art rife with questions and hospitable to mental acts, to describe the alternative route to total reproduction Sontag has recourse to John Keats. The passage might be worth quoting in full:

> But the opaqueness of silence can be conceived more positively, as free from anxiety. For Keats, the silence of the Grecian urn is a locus of spiritual nourishment: 'unheard' melodies endure, whereas those that pipe to 'the sensual ear' decay. Silence is equated with arresting time ('slow time'). One can stare endlessly at the Grecian urn. Eternity, in the argument of Keats' poem, is the only interesting stimulus to thought and also the sole occasion for coming to the end of mental activity, which means interminable, unanswered questions ('Thou, silent form, dost tease us out of thought/ As doth eternity'), in order to arrive at a final equation of ideas ('Beauty is truth, truth beauty') which is both absolutely vacuous and completely full. (17)

The silence of contemporary art, like the silence of Keats' urn, is baffling because it is full of the power of the work of art to arrest time, to alter the order of history, and prepare the possibility of a 'thought beyond thought', which, as Sontag specifies, may manifest as no thought at all, like the banality of Keats' equation, or as the 'emblem of new, "difficult" thinking' (17).

Chapter 2

Aesthetic Experience and Critical Theory

Aesthetic experience

The new role for the critic beyond solitary exegesis implies a transition from criticism to the notion of critical theory: 'The great task which remains to critical theory is to examine in detail the formal function of subject-matter' ('On Style' 20). As we have seen, one of the reasons why Sontag took her stand 'against interpretation' was its standard treatment of the works of art as 'statements' (21). Against this long-established trend, she contends: 'A work of art encountered as a work of art is an experience, not a statement or an answer to a question. Art is not only about something; it is something. A work of art is a thing *in* the world, not just a text or a commentary *on* the world' (21). In emphasising the idea of art as an encounter, she places herself in the tradition of Adorno while making the effort to revisit his notion of aesthetic experience to overcome the limits of the contemplative state it implies. While Adorno did not exclude the production of reflection from this contemplative state, he discouraged the passage to discursive meaning when he predicted that meaning drawn from the aesthetic encounter would be an 'abomination of the useful' (qtd. in Jauss 19).

Hans Robert Jauss's critique of Adorno, with specific reference to his posthumously published *Ästhetische Theorie* (1970), is particularly useful for understanding better what lies behind Sontag's position against interpretation. Adorno assumes an initial distance between subject and object. Aesthetic experience first of all creates distance between the observer and the object. The distance makes possible a state of absorption in which the recipient 'forgets himself and disappears in the work' (qtd. in Jauss 20), but this experience (also called perplexity or shock), as Jauss points out, does not lead to discursive production. The recipient is 'incapable of crossing the line from contemplative acceptance to dialogic interaction' (Jauss 20).

The solitary subject in Adorno remains trapped in a state of 'disinterested contemplation' (qtd. in Jauss 18). While, as a thinking subject, he or she rises to the purity of reflection, he or she, and this is the core of Jauss's critique, does not cross to the communicative efficacy of the aesthetic experience because of Adorno's 'therapy of negativity against the seductions of the culture industry' (21). Adorno admonishes that 'artistic experience is autonomous only where it rids itself of taste and its pleasures' (qtd. in Jauss 21). Jauss rejects Adorno's 'aesthetic purism' (21) and, contrary to Adorno, argues that pleasure, 'that attitude of enjoyment which art creates and makes possible', is, in fact, 'the aesthetic experience par excellence' (21). For Jauss, pleasure should become once again 'the object of theoretical reflection where renewed meaning is to be given to the aesthetic practice of a productive, receptive, and communicative attitude for our time' (21). For Adorno, in the crossing from contemplation to communication, the mind adapts to the useful and becomes a commodity among others: 'what is called meaning today participates in this abomination', he writes (qtd. in Jauss 19). Sontag's problem is somewhat similar to the problem of Jauss in his critique of Adorno, that is to say, that Adorno's interpreter, 'incapable of crossing the line from contemplative acceptance to dialogic interaction', is denied 'the active share in the formation and reformation of meaning' (Jauss 20).[1]

Responding to Adorno, Jauss asserts that 'aesthetic experience turns into symbolic or communicative action' (19). For Jauss, aesthetic experience has a social function that cannot be accounted for by Adorno's theory of negativity (18). He values what for Adorno was a source of embarrassment, the receiver's primary identifications (admiration, laughing and crying with the hero) and, while Adorno and also Gadamer dismissed them, gives them renewed attention in the conviction that they make for 'that attitude of enjoyment which art creates and makes possible' (21).[2] His affirmative notion of aesthetic experience enables Jauss to focus on a question also deeply felt by Sontag, that is to say, how 'aesthetic experience turns into symbolic or communicative action' (19). Rather than throw away the notion of art, Jauss urges a theory of aesthetic experience adapted to the present, based, in other words, on a 'questioning of the classical achievements of aesthesis which characterizes the present situation of aesthetic experience' (61). Jauss refers to Benjamin and to the unfulfilled hopes that he 'wished to derive some forty years ago from the abolition of autonomous art' (62). While the destruction of the aura did bring a 'sense for the universal equality of things,' writes Jauss, 'a new sensory and simultaneously communicative experience which did not continually have to maintain itself against the constraints of adaptation to the world of consumption did not come into existence' (62). Like Jauss, Sontag was particularly sensitive to Benjamin's unfulfilled hopes. She, too, in her journals, noted them, using the same words as Jauss. In particular, she questioned Benjamin's hopes for technological reproduction and contended that his notion of technological reproduction was 'misleading':

> Technological reproduction not simply
> an 'era,' as Benjamin says. That's
> misleading. It has its history – rather, is inserted into history. Its
> artifacts become 'historical,' not merely contemporary.[3]

She criticises Benjamin's idea that technological reproduction 'made everything into an eternal present – a Hegelian end-of-history'. Echoing Jauss, she muses: 'Another four decades of living in this/ "era" has disproved this.'[4]

Jauss's claim[5] that the communicative function is part and parcel of aesthetic experience has the merit of posing the problem of the transition from encounter to interpretation: how does a reader become an interpreter? When, in *Against Interpretation*, Sontag declared that, instead of 'a hermeneutics of art we need an erotics of art', she was steadying herself between the critical theory of Adorno and Benjamin, in the effort to overcome Adorno's prohibition of beauty and reclaim, beyond the concern with consumption, the freedom of an expanded sensory experience conducive to a renewed critical speech based on the capacity to see more, hear more, feel more.

The potential of aesthesis, one of the three fundamental categories of aesthetic experience as discussed by Jauss, is helpful to understand Sontag's view of aesthetic experience:[6]

> In the contemplative act which renews perception, the viewer may understand what he has perceived as a communication about the world of the other or adopt through an aesthetic judgment a norm of action. But aesthesis can also pass over into poiesis. The observer may consider an aesthetic object to be incomplete, abandon his contemplative attitude, and become a creator of the work by completing the concretization of its form and significance. And finally, aesthetic experience can be included in the process of the aesthetic creation of identity if the reader accompanies his receptive activity by reflection on his own development. (Jauss 36)

Sontag's admiration is a way of completing the work contemplated. We have discussed the importance of the beholder in her early critical work. In her later work, she kept insisting on the stance of the observer, who sees herself only as a voracious reader, as an amateur who begins again each time ('Singleness'). This emphasis on the beholder and reader is a way of foregrounding the problem of the transit from aesthesis to poiesis, which Jauss mentions above. Sontag's 'beginner' remarks on the active stance of her observer, on the ongoing labour to complete the concretisation of the aesthetic object's form and significance. Sontag is continuously alert to the potential of the work of art to produce criticism. But while she agreed with Jauss on the capacity of aesthetic experience to free the viewer 'from and for something' (Jauss 35), she also resisted any systematic description of the transition from contemplation to critical speech. Rather, she preferred to pose the potential of the work of art to produce criticism as a problem; she allowed it to stand as a problem. From within the tradition of critical theory, she made the effort to reimagine a connection between aesthetic experience and reflection. She was especially concerned with how aesthetic experience might afford the opportunity for reflection of a different kind that breaks away from traditional conceptual knowledge.

Like Jauss, Sontag resisted the 'muteness' of Adorno's interpreter who derogates all communicative functions because the critical speech that can arise from the work of art risks being an adaptation to the useful. Moreover, she was interested in reflection that moves beyond the merely interesting gesture of perceiving, reading or understanding.[7] As early as 1956 she notes in her journals:

> the texture of a
> forgotten mode of
> thought.[8]

Intellectually restless, dissatisfied with philosophy as a system, Sontag would abandon it on a quest towards what her mentor Kenneth Burke calls 'body-thinking'.[9] Certainly, her aesthetic theory is not as systematic as Jauss's; she shows little interest in conceptualising pleasure. But neither is the pleasure of the text she champions – her 'erotics of art' – a form of anarchic bliss. Her emphasis on pleasure depends on the quest for a different thought:

> I am not saying that a work of art creates a world which is entirely self-referring . . . But their distinctive feature is that *they give rise not to conceptual knowledge* (which is the distinctive feature of discursive or scientific knowledge – e.g., philosophy, sociology, psychology, history)

> *but to something like an excitation, a phenomenon of commitment, judgment in a state of thralldom or captivation.* Which is to say that the knowledge we gain through art is an experience of the form or *style of knowing something*, rather than a knowledge of something . . . in itself. ('On Style' 22; my emphasis)

In the above passage, Sontag identifies the understudied phase of aesthetic experience associated with absorption. In absorption, one loses oneself, one becomes other than oneself (Benson). Sontag refers to absorption as 'excitation' and 'thralldom or captivation'. On the first page of his study of the absorbed self, Ciarán Benson offers examples of such a state from major modernist poets, such as Stevens, Eliot and Yeats. Here is Stevens, from 'The House Was Quiet and the World Was Calm':

> The house was quiet and the world was calm.
> The reader became the book: and summer night
> Was like the conscious being of the book.[10]

These lines illustrate well what Sontag termed thralldom or captivation: the whisper of life from something inert, the merging and fusion out of which a 'conscious being' emerges. The state of thralldom, Sontag contends, holds the potential for 'judgment', suggesting a space of cathartic, transformational and intellectual possibilities for the self, much like an opportunity for a symbolic adjustment in the social family. Her use of the word 'judgment' (in the phrase 'judgment in a state of thralldom or captivation') indicates that she is talking about the repositioning of the subject of language and thought, as if the self needed to be connected to the symbolic realm with a fuller sense of citizenship in it (a 'style of knowing something'). For Sontag, unlike Kant, the beautiful is not a judgement dictated by a quality that exceeds both usefulness and self-interest (the form of the object is delightful because it could be enjoyed by anyone); rather, it is recognisable because it acts on the individual self. If aesthetic experience is, as Dewey said, a 'rhythm of surrender and reflection' (qtd. in Benson 12), then the surrender part, which Sontag stretches to thralldom and captivation, is an ally of self-realisation. The beholder's consciousness of the world's effect on him or her is intensified, while at the same time he or she becomes appreciative of his or her possibilities of acting in the world. In thralldom and captivation one senses a coherence, an organisation, an integration that ordinary experiences lack. The problem has always been the role of intellect in this kind of aesthetic absorption. With Dewey, Sontag thinks that the intellect has a key function which should not be diminished or overshadowed by the emphasis put on the pleasurable aspects of aesthetic experience. No longer something that is objectively enjoyable, the beautiful is close to an alternative conceptual knowledge that, in a state of thralldom, seems within our reach. Like Jauss, Sontag wishes to rehabilitate the intellectual possibilities of pleasure, but her real topic is thinking, and the ways in which new thoughts can become available for our perception.

Adorno's melancholy science

Sontag places a special emphasis on style, which is a sign of the influence of Adorno. Sontag inherited one of the central themes in the critical theory of Adorno, that is, the relation of philosophy to writing. She encountered Adorno (together with the other Frankfurt School thinker Walter Benjamin and the Marxist György Lukács) in the earlier part of the 1960s, as she was tracking a different sensibility. In the summer of 1964 she tried to describe it: 'there's no syntax for sensibility – hence it's ignored'.[11] What she liked about the 'typical Frankfurt thinking' was its interest, reminiscent of Nietzsche, in the invisible boundaries of domination, its special attention to any simulation of freedom.[12] Adorno was the first modern philosopher to turn so radically to different intellectual disciplines, always remaining especially attentive to the bond of interlocution between philosophy and literature. Although she never realised her project of an essay solely devoted to Adorno, her notebooks and her library are proof to a long-term commitment to his work.[13] Her library contained a number of books by Adorno, most of which have annotated sections. She owned two editions of *Prisms*, a copy of the 1967 edition, translated by Samuel and Shierry Weber, probably bought during one of her trips to London (the price is given in pounds), and a copy of the 1981 edition. In 1973 she bought a copy of *Negative Dialectics*, which in the inside cover is signed 'Susan Sontag, NYC, Sept. 6, 1973.' She owned the 1973 English edition of *Philosophy of Modern Music* published by the Seabury Press, and the 1974 NLB edition of *Minima Moralia*, also bought in London.[14] Adorno continued to remain one of her 'points de re-père' with regard to the question of philosophical style.[15]

In his effort to capture what in reality is more than can be reduced to a static structure or category, Adorno inaugurated the modern question of writing. He argued that the exposition or expression of thought is not an exterior surface but something essential. A linear sequence of concepts does not suffice to communicate reality. If thought is to try and give voice to what eludes conceptuality, its relation to language cannot be simply instrumental. For Adorno, 'knowledge and expression mutually call to each other; both are necessarily separate but converge in the same truth' (Petrucciani 130).[16] Thought should liberate its expressive and mimetic moment through all the resources of language. This does not mean that it should become poetry; it simply means that, as Stefano Petrucciani argues, Adorno's philosophy does not accept acritically idealism's division between the concept, associated with the capacity to convey truth, and the mimetic or expressive dimension of art, supposedly devoid of cognitive or critical function (130).

Among the Adorno volumes that Sontag owned, *Minima Moralia* is the most heavily underlined. From the recurrence of the markings it is possible to conclude that she shared Adorno's main point of cultural critique: standardisation and the danger of the erasure of individual experience. For Adorno such a danger radically redefines thinking: its task is no longer the construction of the subject but the necessity to face the negative, that is to say, the particular, the subjective and what is likely to remain in obscurity. However, in turning the gaze to the immanent content of the material and to the private sphere of experience, philosophy becomes a 'melancholy science', as he says on the opening page of the Dedication (*Minima Moralia* 15). As it directs itself towards the obscure zones, thinking breaks into fragments; it becomes aphoristic. Given her own preference for aphoristic writing (Sayres, 'Susan Sontag' 596), the notion of a fragmentary philosophical practice, never complete and definitive, which finds itself always approaching a zone of evanescence constitutes a powerful tie to the critical theory of Adorno. Besides having effects on her own style, this tie may have bearings on her interest in photography. In relation to her own thinking, photography may be seen, to borrow a phrase that Rosalind Krauss used for Rauschenberg's art, as a 'materialized image' of Adorno's idea of mental activity. Influenced by Hegel, Adorno defined the power of the mind as '*looking* the negative in the face' (Hegel qtd. in *Minima Moralia* 16; my emphasis).

The underlined parts of *Minima Moralia* confirm Sontag's special interest in Adorno's problem of philosophical style. The problem of style proceeds from the philosopher's will not to overlook matter. In the 'Dedication' she underlines: 'If today the subject is vanishing, aphorisms take upon themselves the duty "to consider the evanescent itself as essential"' (16).[17] While his fragments remonstrate against 'the system's claim to totality', their negativity, their melancholy science, is necessary to refuse to look over matter. The choice has consequences. The mind seems to have no props; it seems to grasp no knowledge, but rather feels itself as light and of no consequence, drifting towards the evanescent. In the words that Adorno quotes from Hegel, the life of the mind 'only attains its truth when discovering itself in absolute desolation' (16). Sontag's markings suggest that she sympathised with Adorno's experiment with an open philosophy that investigates what remains unsaid even in other fields and disciplines. If philosophy must be written 'from the standpoint of the subjective' (*Minima Moralia* 18), what is the style in which it should be written? The aphoristic style, of which *Minima Moralia* is an example, seems inevitable. It consists in fragments that never 'pretend [. . .] to be complete or definitive', and, precisely for this reason, become an appropriate form 'to furnish models for a future exertion of thought' (18).

In early September 1976 (at the same time that she was reading Jauss), she glued into her notebook three fragments from *Minima Moralia*, all under the heading 'on writing'.[18] The three fragments are 'Memento' (fragment 51), from the beginning of Part II, the part that comprises pieces dated 1945; 'Second Harvest' (fragment 72), still in Part II; and 'Sacrificial Lamb' (fragment 135), from Part III, the part dated 1946–47. As the dates indicate, Adorno's fragments form a writing dictated by the ruins of the war. They issue from the damaged life, embattled and committed, against an overwhelming historical scenario. Part II bears an epigraph from F. H. Bradley: 'Where everything is bad it must be good to know the worst.' It would appear that Sontag photocopied the fragments from her own annotated copy of *Minima Moralia* and glued to the pages of her notebook the copies containing the parts that she had already underlined. It is worth pausing for a moment to consider this reading procedure. If only in the privacy and restricted existence of her notebooks, Sontag shows herself holding the reproduction of Adorno's broken writing close to her. The material montage is enough to raise the question of how technological reproduction affects reflection. The question is, in fact, indirectly 'phrased' by her markings. If the markings in a book we read mean some sort of special connection with what the text at that point says, Sontag's markings reveal that she was particularly receptive to a core motif in Adorno's thought, that is, the relation of philosophy to language: the underlined parts concern the relation of the concept to its expression.

On the one hand, Sontag's method of reading Adorno – based on selecting, technologically reproducing, cutting and gluing the fragments – indicates an adherence to his position. His book is a bit like

Wallace Stevens's 'extremest book' which the reader presses close to her. On the other hand, her reading technique, close to artistic montage, suggests the recontextualisation of the beloved book in the present of her own reflection, focused on experimental art and visual forms of expression. In both cases, the private and affective use of Adorno suggests that his problem, that of the relation of philosophy to language, had been her problem all along. Like Adorno, Sontag questioned the divide between metaphor and concept. In 1961 she had made the following note in her journal: 'a metaphor is the spasm – the little orgasm – of a thought; and it consummates it – so one doesn't have to go on with the endless horizontal explication'.[19] Sontag's reader relation to Adorno but also, as we shall see, to Benjamin is a good example of what Boris Groys calls 'diasporic copy' (Groys 104). The phrase refers to the potential of the copy to produce something new especially through recontextualisation. With the material collage of Adorno's fragments, it is as if Sontag were holding the copy of his 'thought' in the secrecy of her working notebooks. In her reading procedure, she exposes herself to his work over time, until his ideas become submerged in the stream of her thinking and, when she finally happens on them, they feel like a moment of recognition: the other gives credibility to her insight. More than a decade later, Adorno's remark on the linearity of concepts sounds like a familiar return to Sontag's own dissatisfaction with endless horizontal explication.

For Adorno 'conceptual thinking and categorizing are instrumental; they reduce and, in a certain sense, falsify the hypercomplexity of reality, schematizing it for the end of manipulation and domination' (Petrucciani 129). Philosophy would like to withdraw from this falsification and get to 'things in themselves' without reducing them to a ready-made form for the aim of self-preservation. At the same time, philosophy also realises the impossibility of this need because thinking is based on structures and categories, and it is only through structures and categories that any object can be thought (Petrucciani 129). In the attempt to say what cannot be said, the philosopher seems destined to the work of Sisyphus. On the one hand, the necessary task of philosophy is to transcend the labelling and mutilating work of the concept and get to the a-conceptual; on the other hand, the task only proves the naivety by which philosophy is affected (Petrucciani 129). Like Adorno, Sontag would like to get to things themselves without reducing them to ready-made forms. Like Adorno, she wants to reject a use of concepts that reduces the complexity of reality and is functional to manipulation and domination.

The other two fragments she glues into her notebook insist on style, especially on the individual element in creative and intellectual acts. In fragment 135, 'Sacrificial Lamb', Adorno writes and Sontag underlines: 'the writer need have no fear of committing something inadequate to paper'.[20] It amounts to an invitation, to which Sontag could not be insensitive, to abandon oneself to the expressive or mimetic power of language. The overall topic of the fragment is the 'difficulty . . . of making every theoretical utterance' and Adorno condemns the procedure of making one's formulations innocuous first by producing them in the form of a 'memorandum', then by reducing them to 'work on something already existing' (*Minima Moralia* 212). In fragment 72, 'Second Harvest', Adorno writes and Sontag underlines: 'Talent is perhaps nothing other than sublimated rage.'[21] These markings suggest that she shared Adorno's defence of an individual style of thinking. From Adorno she seems to have inherited a critical view of style which considers it not just as a formal fixture but as the symptom of what a society propounds and wants us to think about. Adorno would go to extremes in his uncompromising denunciation of the 'liquidation of the individual' in mass society. Sontag did not agree with his extreme position, but she valued it. Selected, photocopied, cut and glued to the blank working space of the notebook, Adorno's thoughts are not simply an annotation to go back to. Preserved jealously, inside the pre-written space of reflection in its finished public form, in the rawness of the in-progress journal form, the glued copies of his thoughts become a visual montage and, like art, invite an absorption that may be generous with a different kind of reflection.

Adorno's pieces together, in the notebook, also make for a piece of Adorno. Reproduced, they form a found object from Sontag's everyday existence. The Adorno-object stands out in a live practice of the writing-thinking continuum. Had Sontag written Adorno's words by hand, this kind of duplication might have stressed primarily her bond of admiration, perhaps a certain amorous contemplation of his thought; it would have strangely tamed the contact with his mind. Instead, the montage of photocopied textual fragments, whose content emphasises the relation of writing to philosophy, gives us a greater, livelier sense of the extent to which Sontag shares Adorno's story of the intellectual as the transformation of the philosopher into a kind of Bartleby reduced to performing 'impartial, responsible work' (*Minima Moralia* 33). The rise of Bartleby results in the waning of thinking as an autoaffective relation. If Adorno's thinker was expropriated of his relation to thought, Sontag represents herself to the world by holding thought close to her, precisely when she repeats the copy (Adorno). In the very materiality of the montage in the journals, hence in the incomplete, unwritten essay on Adorno, the copy becomes diasporic, that is to say, rife with the potential of new thought.

A brief history of philosophy

In her second collection of essays, *Styles of Radical Will* (1969), a piece on the Romanian-born philosopher Emil Cioran (1911–95) offers the opportunity to discuss the transformation of modern philosophy. As she reviews for her readers those changes which led to the emergence of the broken discourse or aphoristic style of the philosophers she admired, we may grasp the consequences of those changes on Sontag's work. While the explicit theme is Cioran, the implicit subject is her affiliation to the tradition of critical theory and the problem that Adorno had bequeathed her: the relation of philosophy to writing. In the earlier essay on Lévi-Strauss, 'The Anthropologist as Hero', she had spoken about the effect of modernism and the avant-gardes on critical thought in terms of a 'psychological revolution' (75). The revolution had put an end to the traditional exceptionalism of philosophy, and consigned us to a present where any claim for truth is fatally undermined ('Thinking Against Oneself' 74).

Describing the same exceptionalism that Sontag outlines in her essay on Cioran, Boris Groys writes: 'philosophy can be characterized as production, distribution and consumption of discourses that generate an effect of universal self-evidence, or a "truth-effect"' (viii). Not only are philosophical texts, unlike scientific texts, assumed to depend on a self-evidence that is independent of any external factor, but philosophy's exceptionalism demands that the philosopher be capable of a 'secular form of *metanoia*', a discipline in transcending 'the relationship to his or her own cultural identity and life situation' (Groys ix). It is these traditional requirements that have come to appear as a 'laughable' pretension (x). Sontag had come to the same conclusion and denounced the 'childishness' of philosophy's traditional quest for truth ('Thinking Against Oneself' 77). Cioran enabled her to engage a modernity in which philosophy has 'dwindled into an outmoded fantasy of the mind, part of the provincialism of the spirit, the childhood of man' (77).

In the moving opening paragraphs of '"Thinking Against Oneself": Reflections on Cioran', Sontag depicts the quicksands of cultural relativism. Historicised, meaning rises and falls. Any claim to self-evident truths becomes anachronistic.[22] In this opening, we are made to feel all the force of Sontag's definitive awakening from the dream of the philosopher's desire to be united with wisdom, *sophia*. 'Philosophy lives,' writes Groys, 'from the impossibility of ever satisfying its yearning for truth – the impossibility of a definitive union with *sophia*' (92–3). Sontag describes a state of perplexity and desolation which confirms the impossibility and augments the yearning. Philosophers have transformed themselves into so many 'precocious archeologists of [. . .] ruins-in-the-making' ('Thinking Against Oneself' 75). Although she never mentions the word deconstruction, she is reckoning with the deconstructive turn of the mind, the apocalyptic 'destiny of every profound idea to be quickly checkmated by another idea, which it itself has implicitly generated' (79).

Sontag's short history of philosophy begins with philosophy's traditional authority, which rested on 'abstract atemporal discourse' – 'the non-concrete "universals" or stable forms that underpin the mutable world' (76). It continues with the French revolution, when history replaced nature as a 'decisive framework for human experience' (76) and traditional ahistorical categories became 'hollowed out', and ends with Hegel and his effort to establish the eternal once more by turning philosophy into the philosophy of history. After Hegel, we find ourselves stranded on the shores of the present, when the quest for truth, 'once so glamorous and inevitable a gesture of consciousness', lies exposed 'in all its pathos and childishness' (77).

In the Cioran essay philosophy's convictions prove to be untenable. Its words can no longer be heard or understood by a human will 'bent on manipulating and modifying nature' (77). Even when it takes on concrete ethical and political questions, philosophy lags behind the accelerating historical change, further alienating its addressees. Philosophical discourse is either 'undernourished', a metaphor which reveals that philosophy is an obstacle to the present in its restless desire to thrive, or 'emptied of meaning', like an utterly private discourse, as when we think we are writing for a community but we are not; its traditionally 'abstract' procedures no longer 'address themselves to anything' (77).

Two kinds of responses are possible to this loss of meaning: the first is the replacement of philosophical systems by the descriptive sciences of man (Marx, Freud, anthropology, etc., which Sontag calls 'ideologies'); the second is a 'modern post-philosophic tradition of philosophizing' (78). It consists in a new kind of philosophising: 'personal (even autobiographical), aphoristic, lyrical, anti-systematic' (78).[23] Sontag's modern post-philosophic tradition describes what

Boris Groys, decades after her, calls antiphilosophy, a philosophy which, marked by reproduction and by the experience of avant-garde art, has taken flight and migrated elsewhere. Its traditional forms 'have been broken' and the question arises of the genres and forms in which philosophy has taken shelter (78). Which new lodgings does it occupy at its own risk? The question, therefore, arises of the event of thinking, that is, of the capacity to recognise the form in which thinking expresses itself.

Compellingly, Sontag depicts philosophy as it retreats into the distance and, by doing so, can manifest itself only in the question of a possible contact. By itself, philosophy does not communicate; it cannot reach and touch her addressees, but it can encounter us as something incomplete, illegible even, through the metamorphosis into other forms. The starting point for this modern post-philosophic tradition of philosophising is therefore the awareness of philosophy's incompleteness: it has either become an incomplete discourse – the aphorism, the note or jotting – or migrated to other forms. It is an interior writing latent in discursive forms: 'the parable, the poem, the philosophical tale, the critical exegesis' (78). Sontag includes criticism in the list, but uses the term 'critical exegesis'. Critical exegesis, of course, works by giving one's full attention to the object of inquiry. The term, therefore, emphasises the devotion, the fidelity of the reader to the object of understanding. It foregrounds the ineluctable intimacy between absorption and production (writing) while also reminding us of the function of the object of inquiry to prevent reflection from becoming too much of an interior writing illegible to others. In the colloquy of critical exegesis, the object of inquiry is the other that functions as reference and company, protecting us from the risk, always inherent in discourse, of being swept away in a sea of words, of not being understood, of ending up like lonely Ariadnes. Absorption, losing oneself in the object, is a way that philosophy has of being latent, of being illegible but also of becoming legible.

As Sontag intends it, the aphoristic style withstands the apocalyptic trajectory of the speculative mind, 'which moves outward only to be checked and broken off by the complexity of its own stance' (79). The broken unity of the aphoristic writing – Sontag talks of Cioran's mistrust of the book and references his essay 'Style at Risk' – becomes a new means of certification for philosophy, its conceptual tool: 'the passion of the thinker' (79). By this standard, philosophy can be recognised in its nomadic meandering as the philosophical attitude. In her journals, where she writes that her thinking is reduced to 'passionateness',[24] and in her self-portrait as a displaced American who wants 'to move the world' ('The Idea of Europe' 286), the philosophical attitude occupies her and defines her. Philosophy, she concludes, becomes a personal task; thinking an extreme act – 'confessional, exorcist' ('Thinking Against Oneself' 79). In the essay on Cioran, she returns to that 'certain kind of *difficult* thinking' (79) which she had envisioned in 'The Aesthetics of Silence' through her reference to Keats ('Aesthetics of Silence' 17). No longer cogitation, philosophy devours itself in repeated acts of 'self-cannibalism' ('Thinking Against Oneself' 80) as the philosopher longs to get to the end of thought 'to recover grace and innocence' (80), and becomes concerned, as she did, 'with the reduction or circumspection of thought to thinking about thinking' (80).

The already done

In Sontag's overview, philosophy, like art, confronts the question of reproduction head on. Like art-making, thinking has to reckon with repetition; in fact, it is now conceived as the re-presentation of the already done. She asks: 'why does a subtle, powerful mind consent to say what has, for the most part, already been said? In order to make his ideas genuinely his own?' ('Thinking Against Oneself' 81). The philosopher appropriates ideas whose value has already been recognised, and, by consenting to say what has been said, through a gesture that externalises those ideas even further, comes to be as if in closer proximity to them, just as a contemporary artist does when he or she works after another artist from the past.[25] Thinking, like art, develops as the recontextualisation of the already done, but, as Sontag's question suggests, it may not stop at appropriation (in order to make another's ideas of value our own). She further asks: 'Because, while they were true when originally set down, they have since become *more* true?' (81). The gesture of recontextualisation holds a valued idea/work to the spectators' or readers' attention; it retrieves the already done as if from the ghostly distance to which time has banished it, and brings it into the light of palpable reality. The relief brought on by a more rarefied sense of ghostliness causes the already done to open to the plane of the diasporic copy, that is to say, to a generous repetition that produces the new. In 'The Aesthetics of Silence' Sontag had imagined the diasporic plane as 'wholly ahistorical' and a compensation for the artist's 'ignominious enslavement to history' (15).

The emphasis on writing should not be underestimated. The already thought presents itself as something 'originally set down', that is to say, written down. It is therefore conjoined with the question of the passage from thinking to writing. In the externalisation of something that has been already thought, it is the cryptic quality of the writing that makes it possible for thought to go on without feeling like a replica. Cioran exemplifies modern philosophy's struggle (after Nietzsche) to transit to writing. His writing is even more cryptic, denser with allusions – a writing that 'must tighten the screws' ('Thinking Against Oneself' 81). It does not aim at persuading but asks to be 'recognized' without help (81). It addresses its receiver in a style of implosion, with a personal inflection, in the manner of a radical withdrawal from argument and persuasion.

For Sontag, the Cioran essay is a feast. She is poised between Adorno and modernism. Philosophy has vanished into the distance only to become a personal address: like a message in a bottle, it will be legible only to its destined reader. The philosopher's new 'kind of difficult thinking' (79) approaches us like a difficult modernist text. Soon enough, Cioran, with his 'ambivalence toward his own vocation', his 'intellectual impasses', swept by ideas immediately followed by their own dissipation, begins to resemble T. S. Eliot's Prufrock. The lyricism of his 'closed universe', made of 'nuance, irony and refinement', recalls closely enough Eliot's modernist hero (82).[26]

'Nothing is more fragile than subtlety' (82), Sontag writes, and the essay on Cioran comments on the fragility of her own quest for subtlety. The solitude of the writer and the sacrifice of mundane happiness, the oscillation between mind and world, intellect and body, the 'paradoxical experience' of the thinker who longs to be free but, as a public intellectual, must also win an audience (83) – all these topics touched her personally, as becomes clear to anyone who reads her published work *face-en-face* with her journals and notebooks. The histrionics of Cioran, however, solicit her fondness and identification as much as her impatience. On the one hand, he recalls Nietzsche's 'dramaturgical' model of the philosopher, which she favoured: the philosopher as dandy and artist, as a performer who thinks with his whole body, who flatters, seduces, attacks and mocks his audience.[27] On the other hand, she dislikes Cioran's theatricality. While describing him as a spiritual atheist who envies the mystics but searches for the 'residue of intemporality under the ego's vibrations' (87), she betrays an aversion for the artificial ecstasies likely to be produced by hermeneutical skills, something of which she would later accuse Benjamin.[28] As she makes her way through Cioran, we hear disappointment at missed 'fruitful exaltation', her longing for ideas of 'transport'[29] and her yearning for an unattainable grace.

Towards the dream: Artaud

In an interview with Derek Attridge, Jacques Derrida talked of his dream of 'literature', by which he meant an uninterrupted labour of writing without genres. Since the early years of his education, he recounts, literature came with

> a movement of nostalgic, mournful lyricism to reserve, perhaps encode, in short to render both accessible and inaccessible. And deep down this is still my most naive desire. I don't dream of either a literary work, or a philosophical work, but that everything that occurs, happens to me or fails to, should be as it were sealed (placed in reserve, hidden so as to be kept, and this in its very signature, really like a signature, in the very form of the seal, with all the paradoxes that traverse the structure of a seal). (Attridge 35)

For Derrida, philosophy is close to literature and, by extension, to criticism. He dreams of writing everything, of writing a long, infinite notebook that would make a gift of the newest thought to the world; an infinite notebook without the finitude of the book or the labour of forms, in whose flux truth would be told and lost, legible and illegible – 'in the very form of the seal', he says. Like Sontag, the French philosopher was seduced by modernism. Sontag admired Pound for his 'impatience' with 'the zeal of interpreters' ('Against Interpretation' 10), but one thinks also of Stein and the centrality of notebooks in her mythology. Readers of *The Autobiography of Alice B. Toklas* are made to bear witness to the unpublished writing contained in the notebooks piled on the Renaissance table of Stein's atelier (Stein 8).

In the generation after Adorno the intertwining of philosophy and literature seems to have been a given. Like Derrida's, Sontag's education assumed a productive dialogue between philosophy and literature. The 'Selected Readings' for her college courses at Chicago were a compilation of literary and philosophical texts (McQuade 272). Moreover, at Chicago, where she arrived in 1949, she learned to thrive intellectually through a comparative, 'ahistorical' method which relied on the decontextualisation of ideas and valued above all 'a constant dialogue of texts' (McQuade 273). Her best professors there – Joseph Schwab, Richard McKeon, Leo Strauss, Kenneth

Burke, who was the author of *The Philosophy of Literary Forms* and became her mentor – encouraged the movement of ideas across disciplinary and historical boundaries.

For both Derrida and Sontag, 'writer' is a good metaphor for the philosopher in post-philosophic times, who must reckon with hesitations of genre and style. Despite the common propensity to walk the boundary of the disciplines, however, Sontag's dream is different from Derrida's. For Derrida, philosophy and literature seem to merge almost oneirically. He evidently yearns for a type of writing that might read like an avant-garde text. From this perspective, he is animated by the same dream that Sontag detects in Cioran's performance. By contrast, Sontag's turn towards criticism is motivated by what we might call a poetics of proximity.[30] She is concerned with a critical thought that neither becomes art nor manipulates the work of art to assert its own vitality, but remains near art. Nowhere is the simultaneous vitality and danger of such a proximity illustrated as eloquently as in her encounter with Antonin Artaud.

Sontag had been reading about Artaud as early as 1961.[31] Four years later, in 1965, reviewing her 'intellectual formation', he opens the list of her French influences: 'Artaud, Barthes, Cioran, Sartre'.[32] In the early 1960s Artaud was avidly read by critics and theorists. He constituted a reference point for the New York avant-garde, especially for the performing artists of The Living Theater.[33] Sontag was at the centre of an appropriation which flowed both in an artistic practice direction and in a theoretical direction. Her active interest in preserving and disseminating the legacy of Artaud culminated with the edited volume *Antonin Artaud: Selected Writings* (1976), the only editing labour in Sontag's career. Her introductory essay to the volume first appeared, in somewhat different form, in *The New Yorker* (19 May 1973), when Sontag was already engaging the work of Benjamin and photography.[34] In July 1973, around the time of the Artaud essay, she included her work on Artaud in the ongoing rough draft of the table of contents of her third book of essays, which would develop as two books: the originally planned essay 'The Art of Photography' would become her book on photography, while only one of the essays listed, 'On Paul Goodman', and the Artaud piece made their way into *Under the Sign of Saturn*.[35] The draft of the table of contents is interesting because it shows that Artaud belongs in a constellation of philosophers like Adorno and Hannah Arendt whom Sontag clearly wished to write about. With Nietzsche, Adorno, Benjamin, Barthes and the New York School, Artaud is up there among her primary reference points, those 'great intransigent arguments' and 'those extremes' in relation to which she recognised herself as an intellectual.[36]

Her special interest in Artaud, much like her interest in Benjamin, though in a different way, can illuminate Sontag's active role in the flow and circulation of those ideas that will be later known under the label of 'theory'. In 1977, after completing her book on photography and at the time of her edited volume on Artaud, she is finally able to assess her own contribution to the movement of theory. She realises that the theorists around her have walked parallel paths. Considering the specific case of Deleuze and Guattari, she notes that they have 'caught up' with her argument: she sees their schizoanalysis as a reprise of her 'against interpretation'.[37] What must have enhanced her self-awareness as an agent in the new critical movement was the fact that Artaud happened to be one of the points of intersection of her work with that of French philosopher Jacques Derrida.

In her own copy of Derrida's 'Force et Signification (I)', a review of Jean Rousset's *Forme et signification. Essais sur les structures littéraires de Corneille à Claudel*, published in *Critique* no. 193 (1963), and included, with the title 'Force and Signification', in *Writing and Difference* (1978), she marks in pencil note 17. It is a note on Antonin Artaud which gives Blanchot as the source of the quotation from Artaud.[38] The quotation reads thus:

> I made my debut in literature by writing books in order to say that I could write nothing at all. My thoughts, when I had something to say or write, were that which was furthest from me. I never had any ideas, and two short books, each seventy pages long, are about this profound, inveterate, endemic absence of any idea. These books are l'Ombelic des limbes, and Le Pèse-nerfs. ('Force' 8)

Derrida relies on Artaud to present the modernist revolution as a form of blank writing: modernists like Proust, T. S. Eliot and Virginia Woolf, he contends, had a profound consciousness that the situation of literature is emptiness (8). Modernist writing hinges on pure absence: the work has 'a blind origin in darkness (8). As a result, the literary act amounts to the 'creation of a universe to be added on a universe', a universe 'which articulates only that which is in excess of everything, the essential nothing on whose basis everything can appear and be produced within language' (8). When Derrida writes that '[o]nly *pure absence* . . . can *inspire*, in other words, can *work*, and then make one work' (8), he is ostensibly echoing Blanchot but, in fact, referring to Artaud, the emblem of a modernist literature whose 'first and proper content' is the same pure absence on which the philosopher will build his deconstructive ethics in defence of the priority of all possible meanings (8). Artaud helps Derrida identify the philosopher's problem in the post-philosophic scenario that Sontag had described so compellingly in her Cioran essay: first of all something called 'speech', then, the fear of speech. By becoming breath, Derrida writes, 'speech restricts meaning – and our responsibility for it' (9). Artaud's work encouraged serious consideration of what Derrida calls the 'anguish' and the 'responsibility of *angustia*': 'the necessarily restricted passageway of speech against which all possible meanings push each other, preventing each other's emergence' (9), paving the way for his grammatology. Assisted by Artaud, Derrida begins his search for the vitality of the written word and of critical reflection. In his essay on Artaud, 'The Theater of Cruelty and the Closure of Representation', Derrida focuses on the 'tragedy of repetition' and begins to mount his critique of representation and of the systematic suppression of 'that which has no meaning, no presence, no legibility' (247).

Artaud sought the indefinite. With him, pure absence enters the horizon of thought. Like Derrida, Sontag registers the event, but this does not lead her to any systematic critique of the Western logos. She is absorbed more by Artaud's capacity to expand, weaken and erase the boundaries between genres and styles of writing, a capacity that flowed directly from the radical convergence, in the figure of Artaud, of the writer and the philosopher. Sontag's Artaud *is* the philosopher in the post-philosophic world. At first, he adheres to Nietzsche's model of the dramaturgical philosopher, who uses language unmediated by physical presence, an experimentalist who 'mixed voices of incantation and discursive explanation' (Sontag, 'Artaud' xxv). Soon, however, it becomes clear that, even more than Nietzsche, Artaud confirms Sontag in her early choice to abandon academic philosophy in pursuit of an alternative thought, convinced that art was the real site of thinking. Sontag's Artaud has 'an alternative relation to the mind' (xxxv); he 'denies that there is any difference between art and thought' (xxxv). In his anguished experiments she recognises her own search for a different thought. 'To incarnate thought' is Artaud's aim (xxxiii), and this appealed to Sontag, who conceived the life of the mind as a living thought-writing without genre. In her essay on Artaud, which might be read as a follow-up to the essay on Cioran, we witness the demise of the philosopher and his metamorphosis into the practitioner of the 'total art form' (xxix), a practitioner in which Sontag herself – philosopher, novelist, playwright, critic, theater director, film maker and even actress – found a model.[39]

The Artaud that Sontag presents is, like Derrida's, against interpretation. But, unlike Derrida, Sontag refrains from relying on Artaud for the critique of key concepts. From the theoretical point of view, therefore, the encounter results in failure. In his presence, theory seems to recoil from its potential as public expression to some intimate fold of thought. The retreat, which, Sontag specifies, can be appreciated only by those who actually read through Artaud rather than merely referring to his ideas (lix), enhances the sense of a precarious, unshaped philosophical-critical reflection in a world of silence and epigrams.

The influence of Artaud runs deep; it will resurface in Sontag's second book on photography, *Regarding the Pain of Others* (2003). There, having worked through the legacy of Benjamin, she returns to Artaud in ways that further her dialogue with Derrida and his notion of meaning. To the French philosopher's jubilant rejection of hermeneutic meaning ('Signature Event Context'), she contrasts a version of the hermeneutic act which echoes Artaud's dissenting notion of spectacle. 'Artaud's criterion of spectacle is sensory violence, not sensory enchantment', she had written in her essay on the French poet-philosopher ('Artaud' xxxii). Thirty years later, in *Regarding the Pain of Others*, she picks up the thread of her discussion of the 'cognitive function' of violence ('Artaud' xxxv) to propose that harrowing photographs do not make us understand: 'they haunt us' (*Regarding* 89).[40] What, in fact, haunts us is the hermeneutic depth that deconstruction had disposed of. The almost otherworldly vulnerability of victims in harrowing photographs addresses itself *to* thought with the question of an unbridgeable distance between victim and executioner, viewed and viewer. The spacing of power inherent in photographs of horror is inseparable from the act of understanding. The latter, as inherited from critical theory, is invested in annihilating the distance of power. Cutting off the signifier from its hermeneutic depth (as Derrida had done) might be a solution, Sontag suggests, but the annihilation of hermeneutic depth may imply a critical gesture bent precisely on the closure of the gap between observer and observed. Photographs of violence forecast that understanding happens when the two trade places, therefore, only with the closure of the space of metaphor and of all symbolic space. Such a concern recurs time and again in the entire work of Susan Sontag, a thinker whose primary scene remains a harsh landscape hostile to symbolisation.

Chapter 3

The Public Intellectual

The voyeuristic crowd

Sontag's rise as a public intellectual in the 1960s is so legendary that anyone writing about her is compelled to revisit the story. This chapter will consider the consequences of the loss of philosophy, discussed in the previous chapter, on Sontag's performance of the public intellectual. Philosophy's metamorphosis into an incomplete critical discourse that resists the 'spectral and mortuary cosmos' of total reproduction[1] both enhanced and questioned her public image. Progressively, she realised that the public intellectual is pinned to a scene of utterance that produces assenting crowds, and therefore is thrown into question. The second part of this chapter concentrates on Sontag's visual iconography, on how it set her at odds with rising feminism and theories of language, and created the popular if limiting image of the melancholy modernist. The chapter concludes with a discussion of the ultimate consequences of this popular image, to raise the question of the mutual dependence of Sontag and modernism as objects of study.

The figure of the artist presented in 'The Aesthetics of Silence' essentially continues to draw on the unassimilated energies of modernism. Sontag's artist believes in the supremacy of form and struggles to free himself or herself from a 'servile bondage to the world' (6). We have seen that the ruling concern of 'The Aesthetics of Silence' is the production of the new. As philosophy dwindles, Sontag turns to contemporary art to muse a 'thought beyond thought' (17). But the essay is important for its additional emphasis on the artist's relation with the audience, which is one of open challenge and even hostility.

In 'The Aesthetics of Silence', Sontag writes that silence is 'a highly social gesture' (6) because it manifests itself in hostility towards the audience and the rejection of an assenting crowd:

> The characteristic aim of modern art, to be unacceptable to its audience, inversely states the unacceptability to the artist of the very presence of an audience – audience in the modern sense, an assembly of voyeuristic spectators. (8)

Her survey of modernism-inspired contemporary art, in fact, takes stock of the impasse of modernism. Despite its prolonged temporality, modernism results in a dulled mode of reception that leaves the audience untouched. She foregrounds the impotence of artistic production and reception to make communities out of crowds. The spectators that she surveys, far from being guided by a common purpose, are left to their destiny of voyeuristic crowds:

> And none of the aggressions committed intentionally or inadvertently by modern artists has succeeded in either abolishing the audience or transforming it into something else, a community engaged in a common activity. They cannot. As long as art is understood and valued as an 'absolute' activity, it will be a separate, elitist one. Elites presuppose masses. So far as the best art defines itself by essentially 'priestly' aims, it presupposes and confirms the existence of a relatively passive, never fully initiated, voyeuristic laity that is regularly convoked to watch, listen, read, or hear – and then sent away. (8)

Voyeuristic crowds are unthinking crowds. They are convoked to a kind of reception (watch, listen, read or hear) which does not promise any productive transformation: neither catharsis (the reassessment of one's place in a community) nor poiesis (production that comes from reception, either in the form of other artefacts or self-transformation). Both experiences are replaced by a void: ' – and then sent away'.

As the public intellectual, Sontag cannot just be sent away. In 'The Aesthetics of Silence' the question of modernist iconoclasm finally impacts on the public intellectual: the artistic gesture is shown in all its power, not only as an object of inquiry, but as a force that shapes the very contours of the thinker and of art-related critical reflection. The essay on Cioran and 'The Aesthetics of Silence' were written in the same year, 1967. In the first, philosophy dwindles, breaks, migrates, leaving the thinker impoverished, a nomadic writer wandering the labyrinth of possible forms. In the second, the philosopher reappears in the person of Sontag, who, as the heir of Cioran's philosophical tradition, becomes someone 'using (her) mind in public' ('Thinking Against Oneself' 83), facing the problem of committing to a 'voyeuristic laity'.

By the time of 'The Aesthetics of Silence' Sontag had quickly settled into the image of the acclaimed intellectual, but the question of the audience informs us that she was already struggling with reservations about that identity. A rift emerges between the needs of the thinker and the commitment of the public intellectual to having an audience. Speaking of Johns, Rauschenberg, Cage and the other New York artists enables Sontag to dwell on aggressive artistic gestures that impact on the observers differently because they prompt the thinker to question a scene of utterance in which a speaking subject binds people into an assenting crowd. As a subject of language, is the public intellectual necessarily involved in rites of assent? Must Sontag, as someone using her mind in public, inevitably use words to bind listeners in a monolithic assembly? The question of the audience as an 'assembly of voyeuristic spectators' obviously does not only apply to the struggle of the contemporary artist but personally concerned Sontag as a rising New York public intellectual.

Legend

Legend has it that at the age of fifteen, while still in high school, Sontag was at a newsstand in Hollywood and for the first time looked at the literary magazine *Partisan Review*: 'I started to read "Art and Fortune" by Lionel Trilling; and I just began to tremble with excitement, and from then on, my dream was to grow up, move to New York, and write for *Partisan Review*' (qtd. in Copeland 191).[2]

When she arrived in New York in January 1959, 'a querulous staleness affect[ed]' the milieu of New York public intellectuals (Lopate 48). These were essayists like Irving Howe, Irving Kristol, Norman Podhoretz and Nathan Glazer, who had all written for *Partisan Review*, *Commentary*, *New Leader* and *Dissent* mainly on historical political events like the Cold War, the Rosenberg case, and Sacco and Vanzetti (Lopate 48). Their preoccupations revolved around one political issue: the debate over communism. By the time Sontag did publish in *Partisan Review*, in 1963, she was already aware of the limits of politics. In the first article she contributed to the 1963 summer issue, 'Is The Reader Necessary', she positioned herself against the grain of the New York intellectual elite. The essay previews many of the ideas presented in its revised version, 'Nathalie Sarraute and the Novel', included in *Against Interpretation*.[3] Taking her cue from the New French Novel's rejection of realism, Sontag aligned herself with a new type of criticism which moved beyond the 'passion to understand':

> I whole-heartedly sympathize with what she objected to in the old-fashioned novel: *Vanity Fair* and *Buddenbrooks*, when I reread them recently, however marvellous they still seemed, also made me wince. I could not stand the omnipotent author showing me that's how life is, making me compassionate and tearful; with his obstreperous irony, his confidential air of perfectly knowing his characters and leading me, the reader, to feel I knew them too. I no longer trust novels which fully satisfy my passion to understand. ('Nathalie Sarraute' 106)

The cinema now does much better what realism once did. It can, in fact, provide the occasion for the kind of criticism with a more ample breadth that she had glimpsed in the 'theory' of Lévi-Strauss. Her preference for the cinema over the calligraphic precision of the novel suggests a post-Saussurean view of language that values less its naming and descriptive functions and more its potential to connect us to 'a substratum of hidden thoughts and feelings' ('Nathalie Sarraute' 106). In her first collection of essays, film enabled her to access the deconstructive turn of the mind, which she would discuss in the Cioran essay. She grasps the onset of the poststructuralist and deconstructive mode in the films of Godard. When she points to his irony and to the erosion of rhetoric, when she says that each of his films 'is a provisional network of emotional and intellectual impasses' ('Godard' 183), she is describing, without using labels, the apocalyptic trajectory along which an idea rises to be immediately bracketed by another idea which it has generated. Like her colleague Jacques Derrida, she moves away from hermeneutic meaning. In her case, what she moves towards is less a systematic theory of the signifier and more something like the mystery of the aesthetic presence of signs.

In the passage I have quoted from 'Nathalie Sarraute and the Novel', Sontag uses the first-person pronoun to signal the shift towards a subterranean symbolic world, but the string of verbs – I sympathise; I could not stand; I no longer trust – indicates that her different critical stance is still in the making: it is affective rather than epistemic. Nevertheless, the essay is proof that, while Sontag may have inherited the figure of the public intellectual as a spokesperson for a cause, she was occupied with the question of a desirable disarticulation of thinking from ideology. In this sense she belonged to a new generation.

Mary McCarthy described the climate of that time as one dominated by 'the desire [of a new generation of intellectuals] to make a sensation' (qtd. in Brightman 491). In such a climate, her elders were likely to see Sontag as opportunistic or even rapacious (a trait that she later transferred to photography). When *Against Interpretation* came out in January 1966, her 'polemical intention' was assumed to be the sign of a wilful self-fashioning against the patriarchal models available. So, for example, in his indispensable reconstruction of the New York intellectuals, Mark Krupnick opposes Sontag's celebration of surfaces to Lionel Trilling's 'quest for deep places' (65). But there are more similarities than differences with Trilling. We have seen that in her essay on Sarraute, Sontag inherits rather than repudiates her elder's preoccupation with 'the deep places of the imagination'.[4]

A member of the *Partisan Review* circle, but also editor of *Commentary* and professor at Columbia University, Trilling, unlike most people in his circle, defined 'the vocation of the public intellectual in broader cultural terms' (Krupnick 61), steering attention away from doctrine and towards 'sentiments'.[5] Trilling's assertion of an identity in between literature and culture, on the one hand, and politics, on the other, together with his emphasis on sentiments, proved decisive for Sontag's version of the intellectual in the first phase of her career. Like Trilling, she became suspicious of the political process – involving organisation, rationalisation, bureaucratisation (Krupnick 63) – and came to favour the stance of the observer. She chose, therefore, a more theoretical criticism interested in the undercurrents of public language and keyed to, as she put it in the Sarraute essay, 'a substratum of hidden thoughts and feelings' (106).[6]

Getting beyond the surface markings

If in 'The Aesthetics of Silence' the notion of the public intellectual as spokesperson and guardian is on the wane, it finally breaks down in 'Trip to Hanoi' (1968), the last essay in her second collection, *Styles of Radical Will*. Sontag's effort to reimagine the public intellectual can be heard in the fall of ideology from its power to ensnare reality, in the inability to cross over to a post-ideological space of thought.

The essay was meant to canonise Sontag as an *intellectuel engagé*, on the model of the intellectuals she had celebrated in *Against Interpretation*, where Simone Weil, Jean Paul Sartre and Cesare Pavese had admirably exemplified the thinker open to the world. But 'Trip to Hanoi' marks a crisis. It registers the disconnect between thinking and ideology in a definitive way. The author meets her readers with only 'a disoriented sensibility for an instrument' (209); she comes forward much like the disoriented beholder whom we have encountered in earlier chapters of this book.

The disorientation is palpable in the aphoristic style. The essay has the form that Sontag favoured: a series of notes and fragments in which she shows herself in the process of resisting formal mastery. It is essays like 'Trip to Hanoi' that must have prompted Cary Nelson to credit Sontag for not assimilating the other, for surrounding the object with silence ('Soliciting' 720). In 'Trip to Hanoi', she presents herself as a writer without a language. Obviously, she *has* English, but the basic mastery of the mother tongue is endangered as she crosses over to the unknown zone represented by Vietnamese culture. She finds that she is placed in the position of the child; she regresses to 'baby language', caught in a web of social relations that are spawned by the nightmare of simplification, of people and worlds reduced to surfaces. She insists on the loss of mastery with phrases like 'flattening out of language' and 'inadequacy of language' (216). The simplified world into which she is thrown conjures the limits of a political and moral framework. It undermines the traditional image of the public intellectual as the articulate spokesperson of the many. In the face of this public silence, her private notebook must do what critical speech cannot: 'My problem was that I [. . .] was unable to make the full intellectual and emotional connections that my political and moral solidarity with Vietnam implied' (212). She can understand Vietnam only 'at a distance' (211), that is to say, as a mental object created by the progressive anti-war politics within a national Cold War American culture. Once in Vietnam, that object proves hostile to modes of understanding other than the moral and the political. She experiences a loss of insight; she can see only marks on a surface: 'I can't get beyond the surface markings' (213). Once again, language dies; it hardens in illegible material signs, the arcane reminder of a hermeneutic meaning out of the beholder's reach. The atmosphere of the essay is the same as that which she would court twenty years later in 'One Hundred Years of Italian Photography' (1987): her reader is treated to the same disorientation, the same retreat of language and symbolic props.

The intellectual failure at the centre of the Vietnam essay only foregrounds more strikingly Sontag's illumination: 'I think, I really understand – for the first time – the difference between history and psychology. It is the world of psychology that I miss. (What I meant yesterday by the "adult" world)' (219). She was already drifting towards a mode of critical thinking that moved beyond the hardened dichotomies – Vietnamese vs. American, us vs. them – imposed by the political language of her time, and by the violence of the Cold War culture of which she was a glamorous product. The distance between interpreter and beholder in the earlier work now redoubles as the gap between public intellectual and thinker. The linguistic inadequacy leaves her oscillating between two possible scenes of utterance that are labelled 'history' and 'psychology'. What is in crisis in 'Trip to Hanoi' is precisely the public intellectual as the guardian of the social and literary ideas of a national culture, as a speaking subject whose representative words constitute the public in a choreographic ensemble of spectators bound in a monody of consenting voyeurs.

Siding with the contemporary artist, Sontag had questioned this scene of utterance in 'The Aesthetics of Silence', but, at that time, she had also occupied it in the first person. Among the images that document Sontag's public role there is a photograph taken by Diana Davies, preserved in the Sophia Smith Collection at Smith College. It captures Sontag reading at an anti-Vietnam War event organized by the 'Angry Arts in New York' in 1967. It is a still of Sontag, standing up, in the presence of an audience around her.[7] The photographer not only took the picture but also labelled the folders that contain it. A copy can be found in the same folder with images of Angela Davis, Jill Johnston, Andrea Dworkin, Jean Genet – activists, public speakers, writers. The original is included in the 'Women and Peace' folder. The double location reflects a double perception of Sontag by her contemporaries. She is poised between the activist and the writer, the public speaker and the thinker; she is seen as someone striving for an accord between thought and action. Of course, there had never been for her a clear-cut division between the roles. But her connection to the New York context seems to have made the division both meaningful and problematic to her, as shown by the crisis in 'Trip to Hanoi'. With this photograph in mind, let me try and better explain Sontag's redrawing of the public intellectual with the help of the work of Edward Said and Julia Kristeva.

The public intellectual

Perhaps more than anyone else, Edward Said has passionately defended the notion of the public intellectual against the widespread acknowledgement of its decline. Many would argue that the public intellectual has vanished, dislodged first by the cultural critic and the theorist, and more recently by the citizens of the Internet, invisibly decentred in every corner of the globe.[8] Said defends the public intellectual as a heroic figure, a fantastically independent being 'set apart, someone able to speak the truth to power, a crusty, eloquent, fantastically courageous and angry individual for whom no worldly power is too big and imposing to be criticized and pointedly taken to task' (Said qtd. in Makdisi 22). Even the most devoted Said scholar might wonder whether this creature still exists. In the end, they concur with the general thesis on the disappearance of the intellectual. Saare Makdisi singles out Sontag to mark the beginning of the decline: 'Susan Sontag's death may have marked the end of an era' (Makdisi 32). Sontag herself marked the decline with the death of Walter Benjamin, who took his life in 1940. She called him 'the last intellectual'.[9] What stands out in Said's argument is the term 'intellectual' as the cogent figure of a special relation to language. He rightly points out that the phrase 'public intellectual' is redundant: 'There is no such thing as a private intellectual, since the moment you set down words and then publish them you have entered the public world' (Said, *Representations* 12; see also Said, 'Public Role'). When Said therefore speaks of the intellectual as someone who 'visibly represents' the speaking subject in our culture, he is presenting the intellectual first and foremost as the public effigy of the intersubjective I/you structural situation of language. Even when we speak privately, we speak to an audience. Speech – written speech is no exception – is public from the beginning, Said reminds us. The intellectual projects the dialogic property of language out into the world and amplifies it. This would seem to account for his or her heroism. But as a speaking subject, he or she is also positioned within a scene of utterance. And here problems arise.

As noble as he or she may appear, Said's intellectual must take his or her place in a choreographic ensemble in which the function of representative speech (to and for others) is to bind people into crowds, possibly assenting crowds. The photograph of Sontag that can be found in the archive at Smith College immortalises its subject exactly in this position. The camera captures a moment at the reading event when Sontag, taking a pause from reading, book and glasses in her hands, appears to be in a dialogue with the audience, perhaps taking questions.[10] She appears to be thinking and speaking at the same time, her gaze turned towards some spectator we cannot see in the frame. She is surrounded by listeners whose gaze converges on her. Some are sitting on chairs, others are crouching on the floor.

She is standing and stares into the distance, somewhere outside the frame. The arrangement underscores her position as a public intellectual in Said's terms: she is someone who 'visibly represents a standpoint' and 'who makes articulate representations to [and for] his or her public despite all sorts of barriers' (Said, *Representations* 12). This scene was coming under attack in Sontag's work.[11] If we look well, the seeds of conflict are already in the photograph.

Sontag's reassuring presence contradicts the title of the event – 'Angry Arts'. She is captured in the act of thought and dialogue. She is not shouting slogans, but is stilled in a moment of effortless speech and thought, less an effigy of violent history and more an icon of the pleasure of belief. But this choreographic ensemble of viewers bonded in the act of spectatorship around one speaking to and for them would collapse a year later in the Vietnam essay. There, Sontag was moving towards a different understanding of the role of the public intellectual, one closer to what Julia Kristeva terms the 'dissident function' ('New Type' 294).

Unlike Said, Kristeva places the intellectual within a scene of utterance that is no longer heroic. She defines the intellectual as an independent individual who wishes to rise above 'the mire of common sense and identity' (298). Rather than emphasise the 'vocation for the art of representing', Kristeva defends the 'dissident function' (294). In the wake of political extremism and/or fanaticism, the dissident function is an 'analytical position', a critical capacity aimed at the symbolic substratum of national culture, at the folds of common sense (Kristeva, 'New Type' 298). As the Latin etymology of dissident suggests (akin to the verb *dissĭdĕo*: *dis* + *sedeo*), Kristeva's intellectual is someone who *sits separately*, apart from the majority in the public assembly. The dissident intellectual takes his or her place on the other side of a cohesive, organised group, at the margins of the noise of public speech, the figure of a silent observer absorbed in the task of dissolving and undoing. Before him or her lies a path that he or she may or may not wish to choose because it is fraught with dangers. Kristeva's intellectual conjures a theoretical tradition that would comprise Walter Benjamin, Georges Bataille and Jacques Derrida, for which the invention of concepts *is* a form of dissent, for which '[t]rue dissidence is thought' (299).

Like Kristeva's intellectual, Sontag was faced with the choice of the critical path. She strove to be the observer who stands on the side of a shared national language and culture. Like Kristeva, she came to believe that 'true dissidence is thought' and longed to decode the symbolic substratum of national culture. Not in the beginning, certainly.

She evolved into this kind of intellectual. By now, however, we begin to hear in her published work the sense of a conflict that might accompany the practice of the 'mind as passion'.[12] Yet, as we shall see in the next chapter, it is only by encountering Sontag in her archive that we can begin to really grasp the dissonance in her persona. Only in the archive is the dissonance elevated to epic motif, shedding new light not only on Sontag but on the poststructuralist culture around her, and perhaps enabling us to cast a different gaze on it.

Anachronism

One of the most widely reproduced images of Sontag is a 1975 photographic portrait by Peter Hujar. It was used to advertise 'On Photography. A Tribute to Susan Sontag', the exhibition held at the Metropolitan Museum of New York in 2006, the year in which I began to work on this book.[13] It shows her absorbed, enraptured, somewhere where we are not. In this photograph she incarnates the mind in pursuit of a 'thought beyond thought' ('Aesthetics of Silence' 17). The reclining pose, the threadbare, bookless interior, the reverie – all recall the Wittgenstein maxim she recalled in her essay on silence: 'Everything that can be thought at all can be thought clearly. Everything that can be said at all can be said clearly. But not everything that can be thought can be said' (18). A reviewer of the MET exhibition describes the subject of Hujar's portrait as 'looking spent and entranced', associating her pose with the experimentalist amateur who courts danger in a region of the mind 'where it all blows up' (Cotter). Hujar's Sontag belongs among those images of women who do not offer themselves to the viewer in the self-designating pose of the speaking subject; rather, like Donizetti's Adina, they seduce because of the capacity for abandon to a state of absorption (see Bollmann). Placing the stress on mortality – on the flesh to which consciousness is harnessed – her absorption suggests the mind's yearning for a knowledge beyond discourse.

Put back into its historical moment, Sontag's silence contrasts with the more epic scenario around her, one dominated by political protest. In the late 1960s and throughout the 1970s, as a woman intellectual, Sontag compared unfavourably with her feminist colleagues. Blossoming feminism reminded everyone how important the birth of a speaking subject was at that historical juncture. Looking at the archive it is possible to reconstruct that climate when language was not simply a theoretical turn but held the promise of social change.

A representative photograph by Diana Davies, *Women's Liberation March in New York City, in 1972*, meets the eye with a choreographic ensemble of women moving and speaking.[14] Like hundreds of similar images, it remarks eloquently on the emergence of that fundamentally dynamic sense of linguistic subjectivity which, at the time, was best theorised by Emile Benveniste.[15] The photograph of the women's march seems to amplify the linguistic *and* corporeal achievement of a unique, embodied person designating herself as 'I', who comes forward in a spatial vista to be kinaesthetically apprehended by another. Documents of feminist expression like the Davies photograph appropriated for women a basic kinship with language and made it available to the mind as an existential pose, as a balancing of the self.[16] In *Women's Liberation March in New York City, in 1972*, urban space is presented as the site of a contagious speaking position that relocates the spectators as potential linguistic subjects rising from the torpor of the mind and poised on the threshold of speech. Although she had crossed paths with feminism more than once, by and large Sontag remained suspicious of the simplifications of feminist discourse.[17] Despite her earlier political activism, Sontag did not seem to fit completely the model of the leftist intellectual, but neither could she be defined as a feminist intellectual. Both models were predicated on the passionate, representative individual in Said's sense and, while she did speak up to power, her anti-rhetorical strain meant that she could not convincingly play the available roles. Instead, she struck the public imagination through images like Hujar's, where everything conjures to associate her with a secular ascesis in which the thinker is unmoored from the world and transcends self-interest.

By contrast, feminist intellectuals contemporary to Sontag appear as a direct emanation of the new faith in language. Photography consigns them to us as activists and public speakers who impress on the spectators the urgency of the spoken word. From the iconographic point of view, it is especially useful to compare the image of Sontag to that of Gloria Steinem, perhaps the foremost feminist intellectual at the time of Hujar's portrait.

Steinem and Sontag belonged to the same generation. Born only a year apart, they shared a childhood in the American provinces and a 'passion to be published'.[18] They also shared a desire for travelling and for observing other cultures.[19] But here the similarities end. Unlike Steinem, the feminist activist and public speaker, Sontag wished to transcend – not remark on – origins, gender, material constraints and the role they play in our public image. A review of the photographs of

Steinem in the Gloria Steinem Papers housed at Smith College reveals that they celebrate the public intellectual while speaking in public, at women's solidarity rallies. In this type of setting, the podium, the microphone, the banners, the crowds, the cameras become the defining props of a scene of utterance where speech dramatically departs from a slow gouging out of meaning.[20] In striking contrast, Hujar's photographic portrait of Sontag displays its subject in an interior, in the absorptive pose of a mind roaming freely. While Hujar's Sontag evokes the silent decoding of signs, Steinem seems to inscribe them in public space. It might be argued that both women represent the dissident function of the intellectual, as described by Julia Kristeva: both 'produce [the] right to speak and behave in an individual way in our culture' ('New Type' 294). However, the production of this right is informed by different concerns.

In the Steinem Papers in the Sophia Smith Collection there is a picture labelled *Gloria Steinem at the Podium* (1970), taken by Lynn Spence.[21] It shows Steinem in full-length profile, as if the camera were curious about her as a woman who takes on language publicly, and wished to remark on that. In the process, the apparatus construes speech as a rebellious act. Recognisable signs of Steinem's femininity are put on display: the print dress, the mass of hair, the slingbacks. Her image, a collage of traditionally feminine traits and the public arena of speech, emphasises the achievement of linguistic subjectivity as a rebellion against norms. It politically codes the gendered speaking subject as heroic. By contrast, Sontag's legendary black uniform prevents the disclosure of the gender-collage. In the Hujar's portrait, mind and body are united. Her black uniform is about this flawless suture; she seems one with Adorno's aesthetics of negativity. Steinem confidently offers herself up for scrutiny, from head to *mezzo busto* to the mundane revelation of her full presence. Looking at her images, we get a range of movement; we follow the progress of the woman towards the podium.[22] In Sontag's case, the range is more restricted. Her image seems more claustrophobic.[23] Symbolically sutured to critical theory, she is the private side of feminism's political subject. While, in the external world, public intellectuals speak out of belief, she appears as a witness to the interior side of belief.

Unlike Steinem in the Spence photograph, Sontag does not want to be scrutinised as a heroic woman; she prefers to be an image, a desire which she lists among other contrasting desires in 'Fragments of an Aesthetic of Melancholy':[24] 'to reduce the world to matter, something one can inscribe oneself on, sink into, be saturated with . . . to become image; artefact; art; form . . .' (6). We can actually see the force of such contradictory desires at work in the most popular portraits of her feminist colleagues. The photographed subject's intellectual desire to inscribe herself on the world – sink into a cause, into an idea, be saturated with a belief – inevitably converges with the desire to become image, artefact, form. When looked at from Sontag's 'secular form of *metanoia*' (Groys ix), portraits like Steinem's come to illustrate the vertiginous conflation of being and seeming. They insist on the fact that being relentlessly freezes into seeming.

Take, for example, another historical feminist icon of the time, Kate Millett. In a photograph of 1971 by Diana Davies, *Kate Millett, writer, artist, feminist activist*,[25] the public intellectual appears first and foremost as an empathising listener. Millett stares directly at the viewer; she returns the gaze of the spectators in earnestness, in a silence filled with the promise of words, though at the moment of the shot she is not using language. She is looking, not speaking, holding her head with her hands, her lips closed. She invites us to fill the distance with speech, and this, somehow, saves the photograph from becoming the cold evidence of the past. Indeed, the silent image of the feminist intellectual is not silent at all; it presents knowledge that holds in itself the sunny promise of breaking into action. But the contact sheet of the photographic session awakens us to the fact that this thinking woman on the verge of speech is also the achievement of a pose,[26] and so is the expression of earnestness in the final negative chosen for print and publication, with the legend: 'Kate Millett, writer, artist, feminist, activist.' Sontag was very much aware of a conflict of desires – inscribing oneself on the world *and* becoming image, being a public intellectual *and* thinking – which could be more easily elided in the public career of her contemporaries.[27]

The silent muse

Dryade
Schläft sie?

Najade
Nein! Sie weinet!

Dryade
Weinet im Schlafe.
Horch! Sie stöhnet.

(Dryad.
Sleepeth she?

Naiad.
No, she weepeth!

Dryad.
Weepeth sleeping! Hear her moaning!)

Richard Strauss, *Ariadne auf Naxos*, libretto
by Hugo von Hoffmanstahl

Our comparative iconographic reading shows that Sontag resembles less a feminist subject and more a modernist object. In contrast to the clamour of feminism, her silence bespeaks her intimacy with a critical thought given to perennial unmasking. The density of Hujar's composition, which is rich with diverse allusions, the timeless atmosphere of the image, its focus on the union of the mental event with the fragility of life, on thinking as a *lento franamento* in the words of Eugenio Montale ('Mediterraneo'), a slow fall or a falling apart, all remove the model further into the distance. Everything conjures to link the image of Sontag to other representations of the melancholy of thought. She is like a silent statue, like De Chirico's silent statue. *La Statue silencieuse* (1913) is the first in a series of paintings on the theme of knowledge or, rather, of a knowing that is inseparable from enigma and melancholy.[28] It was inspired by a sculpture of Ariadne that De Chirico had seen in the Vatican Museums. In mythology, Ariadne, daughter of the Cretan king Minos, betrayed her father by helping the Athenian hero Theseus to kill her brother the Minotaur and escape. She is the one who knows the secrets of negotiating the Labyrinth, and Theseus employs her skills to escape, takes her with him, but abandons her on the island of Naxos to desolation and solitude until Dionysus takes her as his companion.[29] De Chirico places the mythical emblem of the interpreter in the foreground of the modern cityscape, where she towers against its clean architectural lines. But the new Ariadne has shed her sleep of sorrow for the metaphysical silence of an enigmatic knowlege that fits no existing discourse.[30]

De Chirico's Ariadne not only differs from the myth but also from revisitations contemporary to him. In Hugo von Hoffmastahl's libretto for Richard Strauss's *Ariadne auf Naxos*, produced in 1912, a year before the silent statue, Ariadne remains essentially a woman pining for love. By contrast, De Chirico's Ariadne stands for the labyrinth of meaning but also the lassitude and nostalgia of infinite meaning.[31] In a subsequent image of the silent statue (1914), the title becomes 'Melancholy' (*Melanconia*).[32] Not only does it clarify the association of knowledge and melancholia, it also stresses the iconographic connection with Dürer's *Melancholia I*, one of the most influential images of thought.[33] As De Chirico's Ariadne quotes Dürer's Melancholia – the head of the statue resting on her hand – the mythical interpreter becomes the thinker paralysed by thought.

Sontag had encountered Dürer's image in Benjamin's *Trauerspiel* book, where Benjamin resorts to Panofsky to describe baroque interpretation, the vicissitude of thought from power to non-meaning, from elation to dejection and detachment from the external world.[34] Moreover, Sontag had read Panofsky, who had shown that, as a representation of 'vita speculativa', Dürer's figure is more akin to a generous, therefore productive, melancholia than to a subjective morbidity.[35] To understand the title of Dürer's engraving Panofsky refers to the ancient doctrine of the 'four humours'. He explains that in Dürer, the word melancholia does not carry its generic meaning – mental depression, lack of cheerfulness and so on – but has a different history. In the theory of the 'four humours', melancholy 'was supposed to be coessential with the earth and to be dry and cold; it was related to the rough Boreas, to autumn, evening, and age about sixty' (Panofsky, *Albrecht Dürer* vol. 1, 157). Appealing to this theory, Dürer departs from the iconography of his time, which associated melancholy with *otium* (inactivity), and instead offers the figure of a woman who is 'super-awake': 'her fixed stare is one of intent though fruitless searching. She is inactive not because she is too lazy to work but because work has become meaningless to her; her energy is paralyzed not by sleep but by thought' (Panofsky, *Albrecht Dürer* vol. 1, 160).

Even before she read Panofsky in 1979, Sontag was interested in the difference between a bad and a good melancholia. In a journal entry for 1976 she transcribes a passage from Helen Waddel's translation of *Vitae patrum*, *The Desert Farthers*: 'ακησία, accidie, tedium or perturbation of the heart – akin to dejection – especially felt by wondering monks and solitaries'. The passage continues: 'when this besieges the unhappy mind, it begets aversion from the place, boredom with one's cell, and scorn and contempt for one's brethren . . . also towards any work that may be done within the enclosure of our own lair, we become listless and inert'.[36] Acedia, however, suggests a lower kind of melancholia, a more subjective mood of morbidity that endangers the monks' devotion to 'vita contemplativa'. It refers to an unproductive state of abandon, a negative inertia similar to the kind of solitary exegesis that Sontag rejected. Instead Dürer's Melancholia is 'super-awake', intent on a search, though that search may temporarily fail; 'her energy is paralyzed', that is overwhelmed, 'by thought' (Panofsky, *Albrecht Dürer* vol. 1, 160).[37]

At the end of the 1970s, while working at her essay on Benjamin, Sontag retraced her career in terms of Panofsky's idea of Melancholia in a journal entry beginning: 'My first novel is a portrait/ of Melancholy, I discover –/ re-reading Panofsky's essay/ 'Symbolism and Dürer's Melancholia I.'[38] Benjamin had elevated Dürer's figure to the muse of modern illumination. He had redrawn philosophical life as the broken discourse symbolised by the broken instruments lying at the feet of the seated woman in Dürer's engraving. Thinking was now inseparable from the silent catastrophe, which he called depersonalisation, when the world appears as distant, life transforms into a heap of fragments, and truth, enclosed in itself, emanates only from symbolic concepts which, in their turn, irradiate other meanings at a felicitous rendezvous that he called the 'now of knowability'.[39] As she worked on Benjamin, Sontag identified with the figure; in other words, she came to realise her belonging in a tradition where, from Dürer to De Chirico and Benjamin, Melancholia had been a favoured iconographic site of the speculative life, at important historical junctures when the mind had rejected the past, and, under the sign of Saturn, had affirmed the freedom of intellectual yearning.[40]

The Sontag who shows up at the rendezvous arranged by Benjamin with Panofsky's Dürer in the *Trauerspiel* book is the same author of the brief history of philosophy at the start of the Cioran essay, where philosophy metamorphoses into a broken discourse, and she is the same author of 'The Aesthetics of Silence', where contemporary art supplements the fragility of philosophy with a *melancholia generosa* which motivates the intellect to create.

After the modernist object

In a pioneering study, Sohnya Sayres presents Sontag as an 'elegiac modernist', as the heir of '"nolition" – an inability to wish or want anything', a form of negativity that refers to the artist's lack of will (*Elegiac Modernist* 53). Failing the artist's will, 'the challenge moves to the reader, to the artist inside the critic', and Sontag appears as an earnest artist-critic 'challenged to investigate Nietzsche's thought that art is . . . a way of nourishing with its graces our capacity for willing' (53). This narrative crucially highlights Sontag's fidelity to modernism, but it also suggests her ambivalent attitude towards it. While she harbours modernism's 'apocalyptic sense of negation' (55), she must also defend herself from it. Sayres writes: 'She is always buttressing the citadels of modernism to keep them from leaking into the present, spilling out their creeds into our lives' (55). Sontag's particular kind of modernist fidelity, which makes her essentially a prisoner of the 'desire to negate' and of an 'excessive self-consciousness' (55), is destined to shroud her persona in melancholia. Interestingly, this critical understanding of Sontag seems mimetic of the image that Sontag herself encouraged. We have already referred to the self-portrait embedded in 'The Idea of Europe'; here is a longer quote from that passage:

> If I must describe what Europe means to me as an American, I would start with liberation. Liberation from what passes in America for a culture. The diversity, seriousness, fastidiousness, density of European culture constitute an Archimedean point from which I can, mentally, move the world. I cannot do that from America, from what American culture gives me, as a collection of standards, a legacy. Hence Europe is essential to me, more essential than America, although all my sojourns in Europe do not make me an expatriate. (286)

Sontag presents herself as a struggling American thinker whose very identity is pinned to a European depth ('density') that she must conquer, after the great example of Henry James or T. S. Eliot. In a confessional mode, she reveals that European density, a version of the modernist darkness through which she has been understood, is indeed her 'prescription for intelligence' (Sayres, *Elegiac Modernist* 55); it translates into qualities and attitudes – the 'power to be critical, intelligent, angry, difficult' (106) – that otherwise she may not have. She goes so far as to expose her fear of not being capable of mental acts without it, giving herself to the audience as someone who fears the loss of her capacity to think, who fears she will be robbed of her mind if that prop were to be taken away from her. As we read the self-portrait, we are led to ask: what or who can rob us of our mind? Under what conditions? There may be, in fact, a touch of the performative in Sontag's self-fashioning here. She would probably say 'dramaturgical'. She prods; she provokes. What would happen to this thinker who depends so much on a certain European morbidity if 'Europe' were to be taken away from her? Would she be left naked, stripped of a mind finally revealed to be only a patchwork of ideas from the past, indeed a patchwork of emotional fidelities and longings? What would she be – what is she – without her melancholy uniform?

Hujar's portrait may not refute our image of Sontag as an elegiac modernist; it may even play it up. It exhausts its possibilities until the model in the portrait becomes one with the modernism that she is supposed to incorporate melancholically. Featuring on the poster of the MET exhibition devoted to her, Sontag's image is joined, to form a continuous plane, to the other visual objects in the exhibit rooms. These objects are the forms created by the abstracting eye of the modernist photographers she celebrated (Stieglitz, Weston, Strand) as the true heirs of the Eliot–Stein–Pound tradition. With its rich texture of allusions, Hujar's photographic portrait begins to transform Sontag's image into a free-floating signifier. It begins to inscribe her on to the surface of the world precisely as image, artefact, form, in a broad iconographic spectrum in which the modernist object and the critical theorist incorporate each other. Thus it happens that, through her conflicting desires – the 'desire to compete with one's own image, to become image; artifact; art; form' ('Fragments' 6) – she can take up her place in the theoretical tradition (mainly through Benjamin), as if only when we exhaust the meanings of Sontag as modernist object do we get to raise the question of Sontag the thinker and theorist.

We might wonder: Now that modernism has overcome its own melancholy darkness, the very thing that Sontag sheltered in herself, now that it has transformed into something as expansive as a planetary sensibility, how has Sontag changed? Conversely, how might Sontag, as an object of renewed interest, change modernism?

Chapter 4

Modernism and Theory

The intimate link

In the last section of Chapter 3 I suggested that Sontag and modernism are two interconnected intellectual objects. From the perspective of her visual persona, melancholia transfigures Sontag into a beautiful modernist ruin. This chapter explores the connection from the vantage point of the archive. We shall see how, in the archive, Sontag's fidelity to modernism becomes, in fact, her relation to theory, and she re-emerges as a mind among the theorists. The chapter illuminates the understudied role and place of Sontag in the critical movement called 'theory'.

In her early essays Sontag had raised the question of a more ample criticism beyond the isolated exegesis of individual texts and authors. Against this kind of interpretation, she had pointed to the task of 'critical theory' ('On Style' 20) to examine the unexamined formal function of subject matter, and to the 'theory' of thinkers like Lévi-Strauss, who had dissolved established meanings to create a map of functions and relations. Her sympathy for the critical theory of Adorno naturally led her to explore the untapped potential of material reality, to hold the previously unseen and neglected as worthy objects of inquiry. In this earlier work, theory means rearranging the cultural landscape so that she might feel at ease in it. 'I create the world,' she writes in her notebooks from that time.[1]

In the previous chapter we saw that becoming a public intellectual by no means meant the absence of contradictions and conflicting forces. Sontag's public image appeased the conflicts and struggles by projecting a 'silent statue', freezing her in time. But the struggles are there, and, depending on how one approaches Sontag, in her archive it is possible to find sadness or bliss. So far, most accounts that have drawn on her papers have incorporated that sense of struggle in her personal narrative to offer an intimate account of her life. The aim of this study, of this chapter in particular, is different. It wishes to include that sense of struggle in a broader context.

Sontag's mentor Kenneth Burke called her a 'reporter' of modernity.[2] By modernity she meant exactly what other illustrious reporters before her had meant: the waning of perception. The objects of the world stand before us and we know about them, but 'we do not see them, hence we cannot say anything specific about' them, wrote Russian formalist Victor Shlovsky (21). Sontag shares a common view according to which modernism refers to the set of aesthetic practices the sum of which makes up for an 'adversarial sensibility' (Kennedy 75) that reacts to this state of silence and sensorial death either by acting it out or by countering it. 'We must learn to see more, to hear more, to feel more,' she said as early as 1964 ('Against Interpretation').[3] However, because it exists within 'modernity's rapid dynamic of change' (Friedman, 'Planetarity' 475), modernism has no fixed boundaries. It rolls before the critical eye like a procession of works or schools derived from adversarial gestures, and becomes a question of how to be open to change: 'Every great work of art (school?) violates, smashes, disregards some principle of taste one holds dear. How to keep open for that?'[4]

'How to keep open for that?' From Sontag's point of view, what we call theory arose in response to this question. Like Hungarian critic Peter Szondi, she called theory *écriture* and saw its great practitioners, like Roland Barthes, as the heirs of Mallarmé. They formed yet another school in the modernist procession, and transferred aesthetic modernism to interpretation to make the latter new: no longer solitary observation but 'a moment of life breaking through' (Schleiermacher qtd. in Szondi 114).

In the early 1970s Peter Szondi was perhaps the first to glimpse a connection between modernism and the new emerging critical movement. In a passing remark of his *Introduction to Literary Hermeneutics*, Szondi mentions 'a new theory of literature issuing from Mallarmé, which is founded on the central concept of *écriture* and has its major spokesmen in Roland Barthes, Gérard Genette, but especially in Jacques Derrida' (159). The name of Mallarmé here is a signpost for the avant-garde text. Szondi implicitly harks back to Renato Poggioli's pioneering study *Theory of the Avant-Garde*, where the name of Mallarmé serves to evoke precisely the modernist text. Poggioli quotes from a letter of Valéry:

> I said sometimes to Mallarmé: There are some who blame you, and some who despise you. It has become an easy thing for the reporters to amuse the people at your expense, while your friends shake their heads . . . But do you not know, do you not feel, that there is, in every city of France,

> a youth who would let himself be cut into pieces for your verses and for you? You are his pride, his craft, his vice. He cuts himself off from everyone by his love of, faith in, your work, hard to find, to understand and to defend. (qtd. in Poggioli 91)

Poggioli's avant-garde is, in fact, what scholars now understand as the modernist revolution. Many would concur that the modernist revolution consists in the radical repositioning of the reader/beholder in an existential, subjectively meaningful relation of complicity with the aesthetic object. A text can no longer be reduced to modes of understanding that 'locate [it] at a historical and social nexus'; modernist texts insist on something that 'is irreducible to history and to society' (Ayers 13).[5]

In light of Poggioli's use of Mallarmé, Szondi's own return to (Valéry's) Mallarmé suggests, more vividly than one could tell at first, an imaginative continuity between artistic modernism and the new theory, conjuring a felicitous migration of avant-garde energies from art to criticism. Szondi casts his gaze on his contemporary scene in its evolution from the New Criticism to formalism, structuralism and deconstruction,[6] and finds that the new theory, with its definitive rejection of solitary exegesis, continues in fact the ideas of German philosopher Friedrich Schleiermacher (1768–1834), the first to defend the act of understanding as 'the welling up of a vital moment' (as an act in an environment of other acts, and therefore in relation with other acts). Schleiermacher's vital moment is therefore behind theory, the focal point of discussion today, writes Szondi, even though 'Schleiermacher's name is not mentioned' (Szondi 159). The implicit point is that the Mallarmists of the present, the critical avant-garde, come from a certain hope in the past. 'Hoffnung im Vergangenen' is also the title of an essay by Szondi on Walter Benjamin which can be found, written in pencil, in Sontag's own copy of Benjamin's *Reflections*.

Szondi was the first to raise the question of an intimate tie between modernism *and* theory. Ultimately, it is the question of the distance and proximity of artistic and critical gestures. Susan Sontag's archive is one of the best places for the study of this intimacy. I first visited the archive before I came into contact (at the Modernist Association Conference in Buffalo in 2011) with colleagues working on the link. For this reason, perhaps, the impression, in Sontag's archive, of being reintroduced to modernism through its proximity with theory was so extraordinary. Since then, Sontag has been for me more than an author: she has offered an opportunity for a fresh outlook on modernism.

Weak theory

The striking feature of Sontag's journals is that modernism and theory seem to happen at the same time. Her journals are a feast of booklists; some of them arrange in visual proximity titles that we would associate with modernism and titles that we would associate with theory. Jacques Derrida's *Margins of Philosophy* coexists with Van Gogh's *Letters*, Gramsci and Kafka with Michel Foucault's *Birth of the Clinic* (Fig. 1).[7] She reads Walter Benjamin at the same time that she engages with the ideas of Roland Barthes and Lacan.[8] The same notebook that contains her notes on Derrida's lecture version of 'Restitutions of Truth in Pointure' also contains a reference to T. S. Eliot: 'Criticism is as inevitable as breathing (Eliot)' (Figs 2 and 3).[9]

BOOKS

1. ed. Francis Steegmuller, Flaubert in Egypt (Atlantic, Little-Brown)
2. Black Elk Speaks
3. Gaudier-Brzeska, Letters
4. Van Gogh, Letters
5. Robertson, Chaucer (Princeton UP)
6. Bauhaus book (MIT)
7. Makers of Modern Lit: Kafka essays
8. Gramsci, Letters
9. Amphigorey
10. Korsch (NLR)
11. Mann, Last Essays
12. Derrida, Marges (Editions de Minuit)
13. Grandville – 2 vols. – German ed.

NLR 75, 77, 78

14. Leo Steinberg, Other Criteria (O.U.P., 1972)
15. Kafka, Letters to Felice (Schocken)
16. Pessoa – Swallow Press
17. Foucault, Birth of the Clinic (Pantheon)
18. André Kertesz, 60 Years of Photography (Grossman, 1972) – \$19.95
19. Plates from Encyclopedie (Dover)

1. Susan Sontag Papers, Booklist, c. 1973. Box 126, Folder 10.

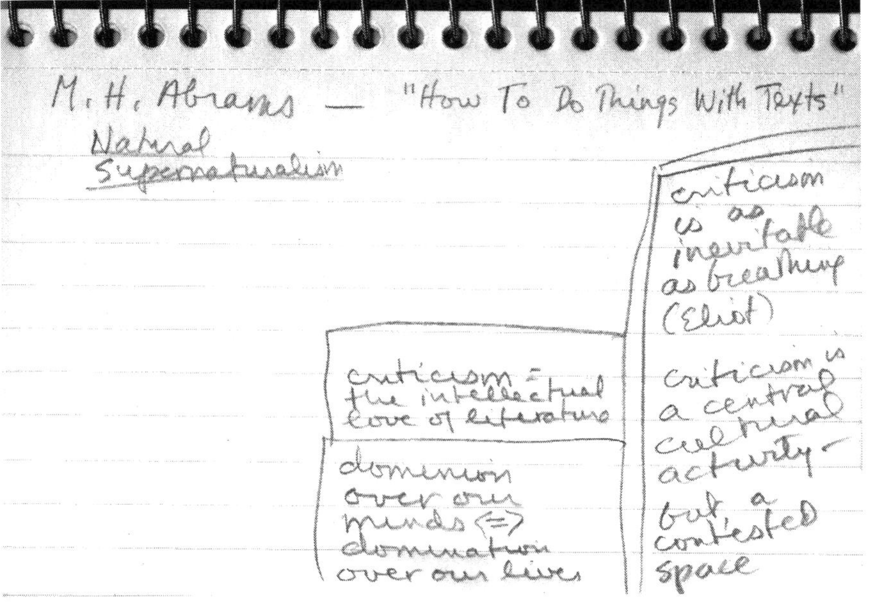

2. Susan Sontag Papers, Notebook (the 'Derrida Notebook'), 1977, page. Box 134, Folder 10.

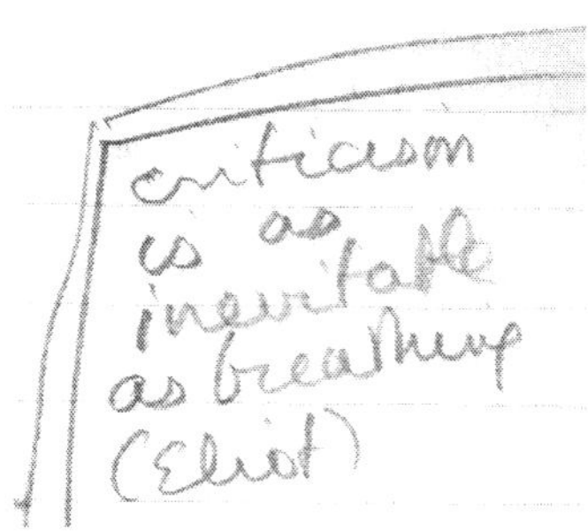

3. Susan Sontag Papers, Notebook (the 'Derrida Notebook'), 1977, detail (T. S. Eliot fragment). Box 134, Folder 10.

The spatial proximity of the titles positions Sontag at the heady intersection of two movements, at the confluence of a migration and transference of ideas from one movement to the other. The first impression is strong and indelible. Modernism and theory meet us as mutually sustaining forces. The archive lodges itself in the mind as the impression of such a mutuality; it entrusts modernism to the reader in a relation that redraws its distance from theory (if there ever was any), linking the two in a co-emergent mutuality. In Sontag's archive, modernism and theory form a simultaneous order, and the materiality of her notes is the vector which can orient us in this new archival order.

What about the proximity of these titles, these names? What is this material proximity? Certainly, it is a form of inscription, but of what kind? It cannot be said to be a documentary trace, if by documentary trace we understand the documents physically housed in the archive. When the archive is understood as a physical place, it may be said to contain documents that are historical materials. These, in a sense, remain inert until they are woven in discursive intersubjectivity; they are 'external marks' strictly pertaining to the archive as a social institution (Ricoeur 427). At the stage of my research when I opened the boxes of Collection 612 (Susan Sontag Papers) in the Charles E. Young Research Library at UCLA, I found the external marks. These are the materials that, because they have been assembled and made available to others, can also be controlled by a higher authority; there are boxes I cannot open, documents I cannot read.[10] But the documentary trace is no simple or autonomous notion. As Paul Ricoeur explains, it is part of a rich dialectic of clue and testimony, out of which different types of traces arise.[11] In Ricoeur's classification of traces, it is the third kind that most closely interests me. He calls it the 'psychical trace': 'it consists in the passive persistence of first impressions: an event has struck us, touched us, affected us, and the affective mark remains in our mind' (427). Ricoeur notes that it is also 'the most problematic trace' and 'the most significant' (427), specifying that the key experience of the psychical trace is that of recognition (416). The psychical trace is the type of 'documentary' trace that is unlinked to the authority of the archive as a social institution, and to the authority of its guardians to keep the researcher outside the archive. Its question arises in the encounter of the individual researcher with the archived memory, and it is therefore steeped in the intersubjective interaction of two minds – the author in the archive and his or her reader. For this reason, it bears the potential for a production of knowledge that would be better called knowing because it does not thrive under the gaze of another (the guardian of the archive, etc.) and escapes equally the modality of embattled knowledge, produced to resist something, and that of 'hysterical' knowledge, produced to say what we think a subject who we imagine we know would want us to say.

Although it is impressed on a material external mark (her journals), the proximity of the titles in certain Sontag lists is not in itself a material external mark. In other words, it is not a testimony that can be used as documentary evidence. Like the psychical trace, the proximity is a form of inscription, but inscription with an amplitude; it is more like a clue, and, as such, a tenuous, uncertified testimony of the simultaneous order that modernism and theory form once we begin to work on and with Sontag. Like Ricoeur's psychical trace, the proximity of Sontag's titles endures beyond forgetting; it takes on the 'primordial attribute of affections to survive, to persist, to remain, to endure, while keeping the mark of absence and of distance' (Ricoeur 427).

Sontag's journals are a testimony (a preserved documentary trace) of her persisting engagement with the most influential contemporary theorists. The list includes Michel Foucault, whose notion of power roughly corresponds to Sontag's aesthetics of fascism;[12] Gilles Deleuze and Felix Guattari, whose schizoanalysis she saw as a new wave of her 'against interpretation';[13] Fredric Jameson, whom she read with an eye to the reparative idea that art 'allow[s] us to be reborn to the world in its existential freshness and horror';[14] and, of course, Jacques Derrida, who also corresponded with her. In one of the two letters in the archive, probably written when he was reading the manuscript of *Against Interpretation* (it is dated 1965, a year before the publication of the book), Derrida responds to her work with enthusiasm and recognises himself in her project. The French philosopher addresses himself to her as someone who moves about in the same enigmatic 'zone-Concept', that of mimesis or representation. He closes the letter by affirming their philosophical neighbourliness. He, too, Derrida informs her, is working 'against interpretation', only he calls it 'grammatology': 'I will send you today my last two articles in Critique, against interpretation. This I call of Grammatology.'[15]

In the rawness of the journal form, Sontag's engagement of theory, her dialogue with it, spawns a universe that parallels not only her own published writing but also the published work of contemporary theorists, especially those she references in her notes. A 'weak theory' seems to unfold at the same time that Sontag works through the idea of modernism.

Notes on modernism

Summarising the vicissitudes of the concept of modernism, Vivian Liska dates its decline to the early 1980s. By that time, the avant-garde energy of the major modernist works had been domesticated and for some critics they had even become 'synonymous of authority, hierarchy, patriarchy, phallogocentrism, and so on'. Modernism, Liska continues, became conservative, formalist, elitist:

> It is only with the 'ethical turn' taken by deconstruction, in its interaction with cultural studies, that poststructuralist strategies of reading, which project their own premises onto modernist texts, would be taken into the service of detecting and rescuing the subversive thrust of such texts. This turn coincided with the next move in the story, a large-scale defense of modernism against postmodernists' accusations of its ethical and ideological emptiness and irresponsibility. This response is still largely with us today. The values that postmodernist or cultural critics had found lacking in modernism – openness, mobility, social awareness, opposition to the established order, proximity to popular culture, and participation in a multicultural decentering of a hegemonic West, to name only a few of the features deemed to distinguish postmodernism from its predecessor – were read back into modernism. (Liska 80–1)

Liska's reconstruction of the concept outlines the salvaging of modernism in the present. She notices that the semantic openness, mobility and social awareness that once were found to be lacking in modernism have been read back into modernism. New chronologies are interrupted, new temporalities emerge, in a 'broadening of modernism made to matter in the present' (Liska 80).

The archive's simultaneous order speaks to these altered temporalities in the silence of notebooks, journals and papers. Perhaps it is significant that, at the onset of the 1980s, when modernism was in decline, Sontag decided to put herself under the sign of Walter Benjamin. The title of her fourth collection of essays, *Under the Sign of Saturn*, is a quote from Benjamin, a modernist whose influence continues to shape critical thought in the present. The core of the collection brings together great modernists like Artaud, Benjamin and Canetti. Certainly, while the last two may be more properly classified as late modernists, their work is premised on the earlier modernist and avant-gardist revolution. The essays in this collection have commonly been seen as portraits, a fact that makes them even more interesting for our discussion of Sontag's altered temporalities. Since the essays are portraits of intellectuals she admired, they somehow also function like banners behind which she 'hid' at times when modernism was coming under attack. At the time of modernism's decline, Sontag was altering temporalities and 'broadening' the concept in the silence of the journals. When they came out, the portraits of *Under the Sign of Saturn* were public markers of the confusion of tongues of modernism and theory which had been taking place, unseen, in her thinking.

Sontag registers the decline of modernism as early as 1974. The occasion was her attendance at a seminar on modernism at the Humanities Conference organised by the Rockefeller Foundation.[16] On that occasion she explicitly begins to reassess modernism (Fig. 4). At the conference, the dominant idea seemed to be the association of modernism with the notion of a high-culture elite. The participants in a roundtable (among them Lionel Trilling, Richard Poirier and Stephen Marcus) were asked to debate whether modernism was dead, and decide whether a cultural elite was a thing of the past. Sontag's notes on the roundtable suggest that she found this to be a restricted view. In response to presentations by Marcus and Trilling, who expanded on the opposition between modernist high culture and the counterculture of consumption, she noted: 'modernism wished to seem a more radical break with (high?) culture than it was (wished to be) intractable, adversary'.[17] At the top of one of her pages, she wrote down, as if it were a motto, Trilling's phrase about a 'modernism in the streets'.[18] The phrase encapsulated the Rockefeller event, its leitmotif of the high/low divide. The common consensus was that modernism had passed into popular culture and the passage had been attended by the decline of intellectual guardians (especially academics), whose ideas 'have been coopted, become "fashionable"'.[19] The notes Sontag took show her interest in defining modernism: 'Modernism picks up butt-ends of popular culture + combines with high culture (Exemplary text: The Wasteland).'[20] But the academic event also offered an opportunity for self-examination. While the speakers expounded on the diffusion of modernism among the young in the 1960s, Sontag realised that 'what I was responding to

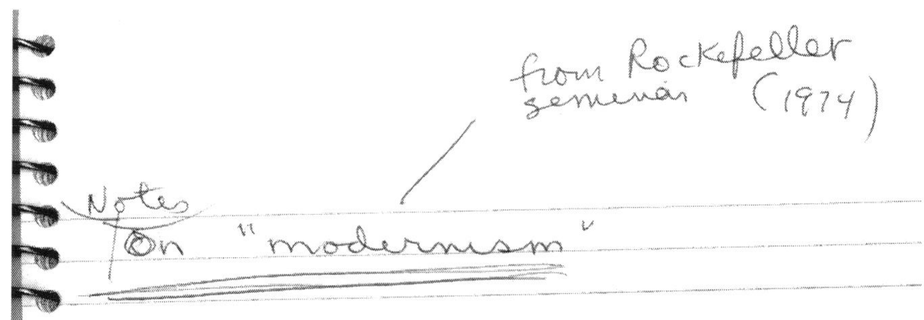

4. Susan Sontag Papers, Journals, 1974, detail ('Notes on modernism' fragment). Box 127, Folder 9.

was the infusion of modernism in popular culture'.[21] She had clearly associated modernism with adversary taste, but as the guardianship of ideas by a few was thrown into question that view of modernism lost meaning. She began to see herself as part of a historical moment, as the product of a narrative which made sense only insofar as it accounted for her investment in an adversary sensibility.

Sontag began to detach herself from the dominant narrative that linked modernism to the question of the intellectual, that is to say, to the necessity of an elite that explicates a difficult sensibility to the masses. A comment with her initials next to it reads 'modernism is elitist/ ARTIST AS SHAMAN, EXCEPTION – makes exemplary voyage/ Implies that not everybody/ will do it'.[22] Yet she is reluctant to let go of the notion of an intellectual capital to be guarded by a coterie of a few. She senses the dangers and the void beyond that step. She reaches a discouraging point in her notes when she fears that ideas will lose their seduction once they are brought to the masses: 'Some ideas only bearable when they are the property of a responsible élite.'[23] She does not seem interested in holding fast to an elitist modernism; she is concerned that modernism's generalised invitation to make judgements of taste, a consequence of its 'didactic cultivation of perception' (*On Photography* 93), might bespeak an alliance not only with consumer culture but also with 'ideas and yearnings that were made explicit in fascism'.[24]

Sontag's reading lists after the Rockefeller event suggest a new curiosity about modernism, even a wish to rediscover its aesthetic through the less 'priestly' figure of Apollinaire, now preferred to Mallarmé, or through Schwitters' 'Merz', or through the connection of the historical avant-garde to media art.[25] She contemplates modernism as if from a distance, as an object of inquiry. The inquiry is part of an intellectual transformation which yields her essays on photography, written between 1973 and 1977 for the *New York Review of Books*. In the corner of one of her journal pages in 1973 she jotted a quote from a Bob Dylan song: 'Busy being born'.[26] She studies Adorno, planning the ever-deferred essay on him, but wonders whether he is 'a cultural reactionary', and attempts to emancipate herself from his legacy by reading Hans Robert Jauss.[27] She engages with the work of Michel Foucault, whose notion of 'aimer le pouvoir' somehow parallels her critique of fascism, and the work of Jacques Derrida.[28] The rediscovery of modernism is simultaneous with the exposure to the new theory.[29]

As modernism becomes an object of critical inquiry,[30] Sontag also begins to see her impasse more clearly. She has reservations about the dominant view of modernism based on the high/low cultural divide, but cannot completely reject it without questioning radically her own role as a public intellectual:

> I am an adversary writer,/ a polemical writer. I/ write to support what is/ attacked, to attack what is/ acclaimed. But thereby I/ put myself in an emotionally/ uncomfortable position./ I don't, secretly, hope to/ convince, and can't help/ being dismayed when my/ minority taste (ideas)/ becomes majority taste (ideas):/ then I want to attack/ again. I can't help but/ be in an adversary relation/ to my own work.[31]

The essays on photography register the impasse, but are also the place to start from if we wish to understand her reassessment of modernism.

Photography as modernist poetry

Sontag's third collection of essays, *On Photography*, is composed of six essays and 'A Brief Anthology of Quotations' dedicated to Walter Benjamin. The fourth essay, 'The Heroism of Vision', first came out in 1974 and is the most straightforward account of high modernism in Sontag's published work.[32] Photography serves to explicate modernist aesthetics. She expands on the modernist technique of the 'abstracting eye' between the two world wars through Edward Weston's brilliant close-ups of objects and natural forms like *Cabbage Leaf* (1931) or *Green Pepper*, one in a series of photographs on the same subject taken between 1929 and 1930. Weston transforms a banal cabbage leaf until the viewer can no longer recognise the photographed object with any certainty: it 'looks like a fall of gathered cloth' (*On Photography* 92). For this reason Sontag calls modernism the 'beauty treatment', which was the original title of 'The Heroism of Vision' when it first appeared in the *New York Times Review of Books*.

Like early modernist poetry, photography is not interested in the reproduction of reality but in a more genuine form of realism grounded in the intensity of perception. The beauty treatment discussed by Sontag corresponds to the centrality of the image for early modernists like Pound and Eliot. For these poets, the importance of the image is 'designed to convey the intensity of the poet's experience to the reader with the greatest immediacy possible' (Beasley 41).

Sontag reads photography through the physicality of the object celebrated by these precursors.

Like modernist poetry, photography charges ordinary objects – real, substantial, material – with the extraordinary task of re-making the world. Like William Carlos Williams's wheelbarrow, Weston's cabbages, artichokes and peppers exude a commitment to concreteness that defamiliarises the everyday so that it can be experienced anew. In Sontag's account, Weston, like Strand, exemplifies a certain 'didactic cultivation of perception, independent of notions about what is worth perceiving, which animates all modernist movements in the arts' (*On Photography* 93). Like literary modernism, his photography bends to an unprecedented degree the experimental autonomy of the medium – in this case, not the poet's voice but the camera eye. Like the poet, the photographer is capable of an unprecedented faith in subjective expression. The latter, especially, accounts for the photographer's affinity with high modernists for whom art should not imitate but create.

Compared to his nudes, especially the popular image of his wife, Charis Wilson, Weston's green pepper becomes 'voluptuous in a way that his female nudes rarely are' (Sontag, *On Photography* 98). While the sensuality of the female nude is diminished – the woman's flesh rendered opaque by focus, normal lighting and cropped extremities – the sensuality of everyday objects is heightened: the pepper meets the eye with the 'erotic suggestiveness' of its polished or oiled skin, with its 'seeming palpability' (98). Sontag pushes for the spectatorial identification of photography and poetic modernism.

Since Apollinaire, Eliot, Pound and William Carlos Williams, she continues, modernist poetry, which has increasingly defined itself as concerned with the visual' (96), has espoused the ethos of photography, which 'school[s] us' in 'intensive seeing' (she borrows the phrase from Moholy-Nagy) (95):

> Poetry's commitment to concreteness and to the autonomy of the poem's language parallels photography's commitment to pure seeing. Both imply discontinuity, disarticulated forms and compensatory unity: wrenching things from their context (to see them in a fresh way), bringing things together elliptically, according to the imperious but often arbitrary demands of subjectivity. (96)

Weston's photography is heroic in the sense that the modernist avant-garde was: it illustrates an aesthetic of revelation. Battling against conformist sensibilities, its visual shock therapy made the old ideals crash on all sides, and brought about the 'revaluation of life' (97).

Sontag's claim is that American photography is heroic because it can preserve and continue the radical spirit of early literary modernism. In fact, Sontag's narrative of photography incorporates modernism in ways that reveal the limits of a concept on which she nevertheless must rely. One of the limits is indicated by the adjective she uses when she speaks of a 'didactic cultivation of perception'. As a mirror of the modernist avant-garde, photography also reflects its cyclical logic of life and death, of novelty and cliché. Before such a cycle, the beholder feels undermined, reduced of necessity to a nostalgic intellectual historian forced to observe – inert and powerless – the procession of experimental schools that slowly become of common domain:

> The avant-garde vision of Strand in the twenties, of Weston in the late twenties and early thirties, was quickly assimilated. Their rigorous close-up studies of plants, shells, leaves, time-withered trees, kelp, driftwood, eroded rocks, pelicans' wings, gnarled cypress roots, and gnarled workers' hands have become clichés of a merely photographic way of seeing. What it once took a very intelligent eye to see, anyone can see now. (99–100)

Photography helps Sontag overview the theoretical problem of modernism: while it invests in the aesthetic re-evaluation of life, it also ties this re-evaluation to an elite intelligence. Modernism subsists on a cultural gap which is a structure of opposition but also of belatedness (elite/masses). The figure of the intellectual as a mediator between the two is tied to the reproduction of this structure.[33]

The subjective expression typical of modernism is redoubled in the photographic image. Weston's camera eye frees the authority of individual perception to the extent that it drifts towards a utopian ecological humanism, the vision of an infinity of forms that echo and repeat each other exactly like the nude and the pepper, the cabbage and the drapery. The vista vanquishes equally the work of the critic, because the forms are unquantifiable, and the work of the philosopher, for whom art might be a receptacle of discourse. Literary and artistic schools become waves of destruction. Aiming the periscope of photography on modernism, Sontag finds herself in a landscape of historical *disjecta* dominated by the authority of individual perception, in the same climate that she had described in her essay on Cioran. Yet she also looks for something different: 'We need a new idea. It will probably be a primitive one (Will we be able to recognize it?).'[34]

'True modernism'

The pieces that make up *On Photography* are not homogeneous. The montage is the product of Sontag's traversal of the idea of modernism, and it is possible to perceive a change in the idea, especially in the chapter entitled 'Melancholy Objects'.[35]

In 'The Heroism of Vision', photography's incorporation of modernist poetry's search for the new had run up against an apocalyptic vista. In that essay, the modernist celebration of the autonomy of art had actually resulted in a ceaseless procession of self-destructive movements. Against this nihilistic backdrop, Abbott's photographs of New York, which Sontag discusses in 'Melancholy Objects', are not simply a geographical relocation, from Europe to America, of the 'ceaseless replacement of the new', but mark an important transition in Sontag's thinking. In 'Melancholy Objects', her thinking is fast. She touches on more than explains, but, clearly, Abbott's photographs not only confirm that modernism is an idea in movement but also encourage her to see modernism as one of her own 'means of transport'.[36] Abbott's images mark a shift from an 'archaeological view of modernism',[37] which fosters dichotomies, gaps and belatedness, to another, expanded view of modernism, which facilitates a larger discourse on the fragility of being.[38] It is possible to hear a transition from the emphasis on aesthetic surfaces to the question of the transmission of being, raised with some urgency by a transhistorical and transgenerational human landscape.

Sontag frames her brief but memorable discussion of Abbott's images with the association of photography and loss: 'The effectiveness of photography's statement of loss depends on its steadily enlarging the familiar iconography of mystery, mortality, transience' (*On Photography* 67). By the time she mentions Abbott, her images can aptly illustrate the capacity of the photographer not so much to record the past as to invent it (67). Ostensibly taken to denounce 'ten years of the chronic self-destruct quality of American experience' from 1929 to 1939, Abbott's images of New York actually perform a much subtler transformative work, enabling Sontag to name a bond with the past which persists even in the age of the loss of the aura. Within a context of loss, she manages to enumerate 'objects that have a patina, old furniture, grandparents' pots and pans – the used things, warm with generations of human touch, that Rilke celebrated in *The Duino Elegies* as being essential to a human landscape' (68). The persistence of the bond can avert 'solitude, sadness, ugliness, melancholia' (73). She begins to excavate an affective depth inside the notion of modernism that was not there before.

Berenice Abbott had learned photography in Man Ray's darkroom in 1924 and was a disciple of the great Atget. During her eight years in Paris she met and photographed some of the most prominent modernist writers, artists and performers, and their patrons. But she was also a modernist artist in her own right, and, upon her return, transferred this to her images of New York. *Changing New York*, the series of photographs funded by the Works Progress Administration from 1935 to 1939, reflected Abbott's intention of 'remaining true to [the city's] essential fact, its hurrying tempo, its congested streets, the past jostling the present' ('Changing' 24). Many of her images of the city's 'state of flux' court the plasticity of modernist abstractions (Abbott qtd. in Yochelson 13).[39] Some of her images of Midtown uncannily meet the eye like a faraway lyrical echo of a luscious Klimt painting drained of colour. This is true especially of the shots taken from an upper terrace of the 46-storey Nelson Tower from which Abbott photographed the canyon created by new skyscrapers in the heart of the garment district.[40] Many of her images play up the visual pleasure afforded in architecture by repetition and seriality. The spectacular *Tempo of the City II, Fifth Avenue and 42nd Street* evokes the strange exciting mix of movement and compressed space. These documentary photographs echo modernist formalism and layer New York in the present with the experimental and adventurous past. But Abbott also photographed other less glamorous sites, so that her images of the truth or essential fact of New York is far from unitary. *Roast Corn Man, Orchard and Hester Streets*[41] or *Bread Store, 259 Bleecker Street*[42] cannot be read in terms of the formal drive of the other images. They seem to 'look' at us, even when their subjects avert their gaze. While these images do not literally show 'used things', apart from the glaringly worn clothes and shoes of the roast corn vendor, they are layered with memory in a way that other photographs documenting the tempo of the city are not; they seem covered with the patina of time. There is something that makes the spectator vulnerable. The gaze of the woman standing behind the glass window of her bakery, almost an evanescent silhouette staring at the photographer then and at us now, or the absorbed expression of the corn vendor going about his business in his worn clothes stop the viewer in her tracks, discouraging the ambiguous gaze invented by modernist abstractions, 'both intense and cool, solicitous and detached' (Sontag, *On Photography* 99).

But in Sontag's discussion, Abbott represents connection not discontinuity with the earlier avant-gardes. She had moved from immortalising modernist genius to photographing the vulnerability of being. In a journal entry later in life (1984), Abbott writes: 'I am not interested in people's little quirks which have been pasted [?] upon them by society-products of luck-of chance of genes and health conditions.'[43] Her idea of photography had transformed into a new 'abstracting eye', one that severs the individual from luck, chance, fate, from history, in an absolute portrait which ultimately questions 'the fate of man'. In her journals, the photographer wonders, gently, without forcing the point: 'Aims of mankind diverted by brain filled garbage – is that the fate of man? One half bullies and oppresses the other half because it doesn't have as much muscle – ridicules it – oppresses it – misjudges it.'[44]

The American photographer's visual quest for 'humanity, its meaning, all its thoughts, emotions, characteristics' (Abbott qtd. in Van Haaften 12) counters the 'abbreviation of history' of surrealist montage (Sontag, *On Photography* 73), but does not demand the rejection of aesthetic modernism. Photography remains the heir of Surrealism, addicted to the inventory of incongruous details – 'trash, eyesores, rejects, peeling surfaces, odd stuff, kitsch' (78) – but Sontag mentally rearranges the incongruous inventory into a continuum of past and present. In this landscape strewn with traces of the living, the primacy of abstraction is displaced by the question of a bond of 'tender regard' (71). With fast and wide strokes of the mind, Sontag glimpses a 'true modernism' that makes 'brilliant objects out of refuse' (68), a 'strewn plenitude' (68–9) that converges with photography's 'inventory of mortality' (70). After excavating an unprecedented affective depth inside the notion of modernism, photography re-emerges as the iconology of a new modernism whose affinity with an enfeebled notion of Being broadens it but also dissolves it until it becomes an atmosphere, a mood. It is comparable to a cosmic condition of nomadism and precariousness, marked by the fleetingness of any sense of belonging and community: 'people and things which a moment later have already disbanded, changed, continued along the course of their independent destinies' (70).

Abstraction/rigidification

After her work on photography, Sontag looks at modernist abstractions with a different eye. She no longer sees hieratic surfaces that demand an 'erotics of art' but senses a more complex play of movement and rigidification. In a journal entry for 1979 occasioned by Mondrian's painting, Sontag writes:

> What is not talked about: the
> small pathological impulse(s)
> behind many of the dogmas
> of modernism (modernist
> aesthetics). For example:
> the fascination with grids
> and repression, rigidification.
> Mondrian.[45]

In this entry she attempts to clarify the modernist depth which in 'Melancholy Objects', the third essay of *On Photography*, could only manifest in the flash of an eye, as the fleeting impression of a broken cognition. The depth is indicated by the phrase 'small pathological impulse(s)' which evokes a substantial conceptuality, an understudied modernism (what is not talked about) behind the 'archeological' or dominant view of modernism which she had reviewed in 'The Heroism of Vision'. There, the 'abstracting eye' had revealed and celebrated the everydayness of the objects around us; now, abstraction turns into repression. She begins to probe modernism as a cultural field of paradoxes.[46] Mondrian's grids are exemplary because they prefigure a particular structure which she would also call 'metaphysical landscape'.[47] She experiments with the phrase, which refers to things as diverse as Benjamin's writing,[48] winter Venice[49] and De Chirico's empty cities,[50] but essentially suggests a structure of illumination and repression whose effect is an accelerating sense of proximity to something live, vital and unthought.

To be sure, there is more than one way of reading Sontag's unsystematic modernism. She may be looking at modernist abstractions through Adorno's notion of 'immanent regression' and seeing them as the correlate of the 'rigidification of bourgeois society in an impenetrable nature' (Adorno qtd. in Petrucciani 78). The grids would then emanate the same tension between modernity and archaism that underpins Adorno's thought, and might be seen in terms of the terror implied in that thought. They might be seen as the traces of the neutralisation of a menace or threat at the heart of the dialectic of modernity and regression. But Sontag was struggling to overcome Adorno, and the space that her mind excavates in aesthetic modernism enables her to question the trajectory of modernism-related critical thought: should the post-philosophic thought she had outlined in the Cioran essay in fact be anchored in Adorno's constellation of terror? That is to say, should critical thought necessarily be invested in a modality of incorporation and melancholia? Conversely, the space that her mind excavates in modernist abstractions might be indebted to memories of Plato. The word 'pathological' contains the Greek work πάθος, pathos, 'feeling, suffering', and names the element of agitation, excitement and passion that Plato renders with the disorderly kinesis of the Receptacle in *Timaeus*. The movement of the Receptacle is a kind of pathos, and modernist abstractions recall the harmony-breaking movement of Plato's Receptacle: they offer themselves to the eye as the shelter of a formless receptivity which approximates Plato's idea of Space/Χωρα, the empty void filled with aboriginal motions associated to the principle of random motion that is psyche.

At Harvard, as a student of Raphael Demos on the course on Plato that he offered in the autumn of 1955, Sontag had become fascinated with Plato's psyche as a propulsive and irreducible principle of activity and change, as an 'element of sheer creativity'.[51] Psyche, she writes in her graduate notes, is 'change, motion, activity, spontaneity, self-initiating, source of change and activity in other things' (Fig. 5).[52] She had learned to conceive of psyche as a non-directed and essentially non-moral, non-relational drive, associated neither with Eros, love of goodness and beauty, nor with mind (*nous*), apprehension and cognitive recognition; rather, it was a neutral principle coinciding with freedom.[53] Seen through the colouring of Plato's primordial kinesis, modernist abstractions do transform into a 'metaphysical landscape', a phrase in which the meaning of metaphysical is closer to the event than to noumena or ideas only accessible through the mind rather than perception.

As a student of philosophy, Sontag had studied metaphysics, but the study of things in themselves had actually aroused an interest in processes and events. She had been especially attracted to Plato's notion of psyche because she had come to associate it with being as becoming. Her reading of Plato seems to have been inflected by Heraclitus and modern philosophy alike. Philosopher Alfred North Whitehead was the first to ask the question of the event and proposed that everything is an event; even a seemingly solid and permanent object, like a monument, is an event, or a multiplicity of events, because it is never the same but always caught in a process of active happening. One could argue that Whitehead's conception of processes and events was foreshadowed in Heraclitus' conception of becoming – something that Plato seems to have wanted to constrain.

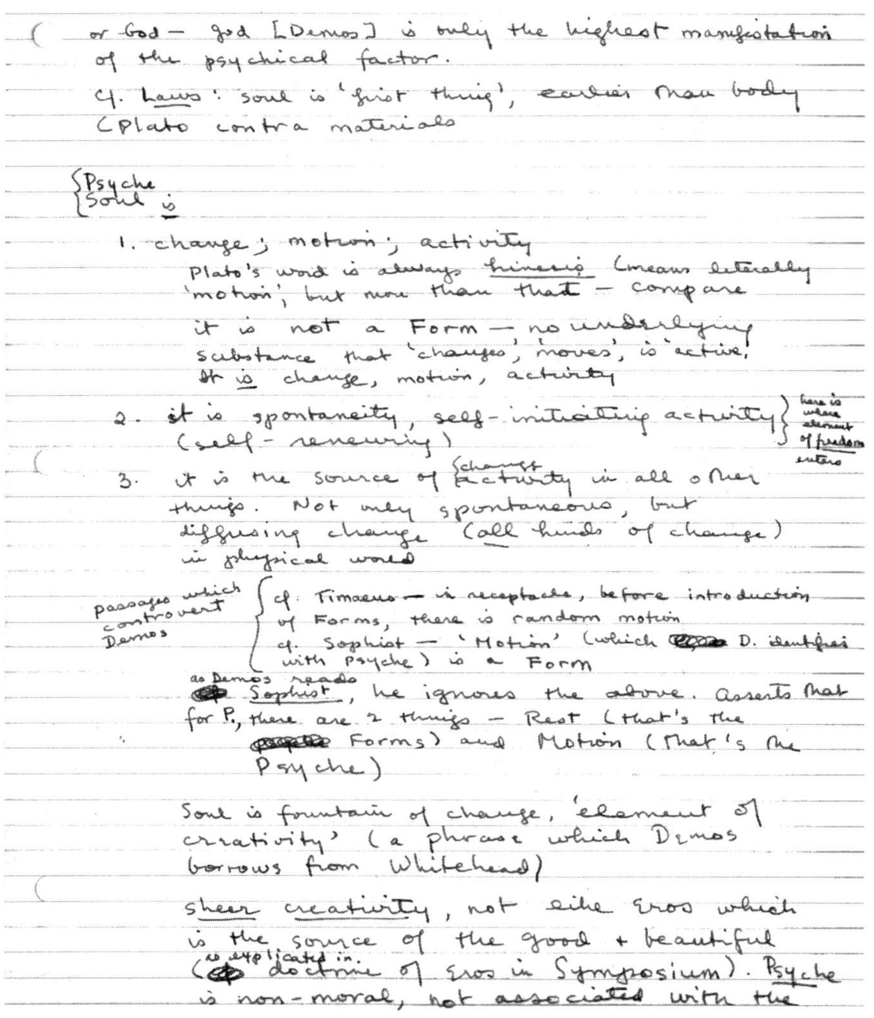

or God – god [Demos] is only the highest manifestation of the psychical factor.
cf. Laws: soul is 'first thing', earlier than body
(Plato contra materials

{Psyche
{Soul is

1. change; motion; activity
Plato's word is always kinesis (means literally 'motion', but more than that – compare
it is not a Form – no underlying substance that 'changes', 'moves', is 'active'.
It is change, motion, activity

2. it is spontaneity, self-initiating activity (self-renewing) } here is where element of freedom enters

3. it is the source of change/activity in all other things. Not only spontaneous, but diffusing change (all kinds of change) in physical world

passages which controvert Demos { cf. Timaeus – in receptacle, before introduction of Forms, there is random motion
cf. Sophist – 'Motion' (which D. identifies with psyche) is a Form

as Demos reads Sophist, he ignores the above. Asserts that for P., there are 2 things – Rest (that's the Forms) and Motion (that's the Psyche)

Soul is fountain of change, 'element of creativity' (a phrase which Demos borrows from Whitehead)

sheer creativity, not like Eros which is the source of the good + beautiful (as explicated in doctrine of Eros in Symposium). Psyche is non-moral, not associated with the

5. Susan Sontag Papers, graduate notes on Plato, autumn 1955. Box 149, Folder 5.

In any case, North's question – What is an 'event'? – without quotes, occupies the centre of an otherwise blank page that can be found among the papers documenting the metaphysics course that Sontag took between 1954 and 1956.[54] The question suggests that, from the very beginning, during her academic formation, even as she studied metaphysics, Sontag was interested in *becoming* as the deepest dimension of Being. The study of metaphysics raised the question of the difference between substance and event: 'We say substances "exist" but events "happen"'.[55] She might be studying Plato's ontology, but she was interested in the notion of event. Her interest would persist and possibly intensify throughout her career. There is evidence that she kept track of the work of Gilles Deleuze, one of the most prominent contemporary thinkers of the event.

Certainly Sontag, the Adorno follower, might have grasped modernist structures as a transposition or an incorporation of his dialectical model; in their democratising didacticism, those structures might have appeared to withstand the spectral return of archaic, disruptive forces. But seen through Plato's notion of psyche, which Sontag understood as a principle of freedom, modernist grids seem to house a principle of insuppressible motion and suggest a modernism that exceeds the standard narrative. Modernist grids appear to shelter the promise of something about to happen; they remind her, like the *vaporetto* on the waters of Venice, that only ideas of transport concern her.[56] Aesthetic modernism and thinking (the movement of ideas) are united in one and the same continuum.

In the entry from 1979 Mondrian is not a random choice. It was Mondrian who spoke insistently of harmony – 'the perfect harmony' – in the same paradoxical way as Plato: his perfect harmony is actually harmony-breaking and closely recalls the primordial kinesis of Plato's psyche. In the statement 'Abstract Art [Non-subjective Art]' (October 1941), he writes that abstract art 'aims to represent reality in its closest approximation. It endeavors to express the dynamic movement of life in equilibrium solely by means of lines, planes, volumes and pure color, seeking to avoid the creation of all limiting particular forms which evoke particular feelings' (Mondrian 333). In order to convey movement and not repress it, a new beauty is created based on harmony. 'When we speak of "harmony," we do not mean anything like traditional harmony. Everything that for us springs from the new spirit – and is therefore of the future – appears rather as *disharmony* to conservative feeling, even though it is pure equilibrium' (200). Elsewhere in Mondrian's writings, the notion of a harmony-breaking harmony evokes the psychoanalytic notion of the unconscious. In 'Down with Traditional Harmony!' (1924) he equates traditional harmony to the conscious and individual and confutes it as an 'illusion' of harmony. By contrast, abstraction in art is an expression of the 'pure unity' that is integral to the unconscious ego (191). The harmony-breaking harmony of Mondrian's grids moves beyond the monadic self and towards unconscious cultural undercurrents that elude subjective sensibility.[57] Similarly, Sontag speaks of the depth of pathological impulses in modernist abstractions in her attempt to rid modernism of its conceptual past so that the notion might liberate new intellectual potential. In the process, she seems closer to theories of abstract art which, like Kandinsky's, saw it 'primarily in spiritual terms, as an attempt to discovery a reality behind surface appearances' (McLeod 205).[58]

Pound's famous phrase 'Make it New', writes Peter Nicholls, means that 'two different times are grafted together, each somehow "supplementing" the other' (Nicholls 179). In Sontag's assessment of modernism in the age of its decline, Plato's *chora* and Mondrian's harmony seem 'grafted together'; they somehow 'supplement' each other, to suggest a dynamic conceptuality.

As the structures of aesthetic modernism make themselves available to Sontag in the shape of a primordial motility that eludes language and concept, the connection with Julia Kristeva cannot be avoided. Kristeva was the first to theorise modernism as a topology of Plato's *chora*. In *Revolution in Poetic Language*, published in French in 1974, Kristeva drew on the *Timaeus* to supplement a history-bound theory of meaning with a more dynamic level of sense that escapes ready formulation. She grasps this other level of meaning in terms of Plato's aboriginal motility: it 'precedes evidence, verisimilitude, spatiality and temporality' (Kristeva, *Revolution* 26). Using a more lyrical expression than Sontag's 'pathological impulse(s)', Kristeva sees in modernist abstractions a 'song beneath the text' (28). Sontag's harmony-breaking depth, in Kristeva, translates as a doubly articulated 'rhythmic space' which will become the celebrated interplay of the symbolic, or the level of comprehensible meaning, and the semiotic, a more conceptually elusive level. In Kristeva's hands, artistic modernism becomes the powerful support for an act of the mind that, in open antagonism with the philosophical tradition, refuses the idea that thought is the history of the subject present to himself (215–16).[59]

Kristeva takes from modernism a conceptual energy that delivers where philosophy fails. Like Kristeva, Sontag grasped the great theoretical potential of aesthetic modernism; unlike Kristeva, however, she had given her allegiance to the aphoristic mode of the post-philosophic present, and took her place in the strewn plenitude of broken discourse. Kristeva's published theory helps reveal Sontag's theory *in nuce*, in the rawness of the journal form. There, rather than drawing conceptuality from modernism, Sontag seems to abide by a certain 'modernist resistance to concepts as such' (Bell 10). From the vantage point of her archive, because of the intimate link with modernism, theory becomes a question of style. In Sontag's case, the style of theory is decided precisely by the modernist enterprise as she saw it emblematised by Pound's flight from the 'rough grip of interpretation'

('Against Interpretation' 10); it is decided by the consuming need for 'a new idea',[60] by the yearning for 'the situation of thinking'.[61]

From this perspective, modernism is Sontag's 'archive'. According to Foucault, the analysis of the archive 'involves a privileged region: at once close to us, and different from our present existence'; he calls it 'the border of time': it 'surrounds' our present, 'overhangs it' and 'indicates it in its otherness' (Foucault 130). It is, Foucault writes, 'that which, outside ourselves, delimits us' (130). Modernism is to Sontag that 'border of time' around her actuality. The high and late modernists were the border of time outside her and delimited her. She thought with them; she could not imagine herself as a thinker without them. Because of her admiration, she could experience history as 'the difference of times' (Foucault 131), she could feel the break and the rupture, she could experience the tender bond of belonging ('the infusion of modernism in popular culture').[62] She could also experience herself as 'the difference of masks' (Foucault 131), that is to say, as a mask of those who had come before her, and, as such, an adversarial intellectual. As this masked I, she appears to us as the *durée* of modernism.

'The situation of thinking'

'Why do we read a writer's journal?' Sontag asked in an early essay on the Italian writer Cesare Pavese. 'Because it illuminates his books?' she continues. 'Often it does not. More likely because of the rawness of the journal form . . . Here we read the writer in the first person; we encounter the ego behind the masks of ego in an author's work' ('The Artist as Exemplary Sufferer' 41). The first person I encountered in Sontag's journals was someone trained in philosophy. It is common knowledge that she did her graduate work in philosophy. In 1957 she earned a master's degree from Harvard and was awarded a fellowship at St Anne's College, Oxford, where she studied the linguistic philosophers A. J. Ayer, Paul Grice and J. L. Austin. She dutifully summed up Austin's lectures in *How to Do Things with Words*, including his theory of performative statements, but without becoming enamoured of the new credo that, as she put it in her journals, 'we can only think what we can say'.[63] The archive amplifies the importance of her philosophical training to the extent that at a certain point I began to wonder whether I could write about Sontag (Fig. 6). The archive enhances the transformation of philosophy into a broken discourse, and her notebooks and journals become a marvellous record of her efforts to adjust. As I have already said in the introduction to this book, encountered in the archive Sontag gives the impression of having

HUMANITIES 5 SPRING TERM 1955-56

Suggested Term Paper Topics

- 1. The Method of Doubt and Scepticism: Descartes and Hume
2. Doubt and Faith: Descartes and Kierkegaard
- 3. The Rationale for Revolution: Locke and Marx
4. Labor and Property: Locke and Marx
5. The Social Contract in Plato and Locke
6. Reason and the Moral Law: Locke and Hegel
7. Hume's Religious Views
8. Kant and Utilitarianism
9. The Realm of the Ethical: Kierkegaard and Kant
10. Locke and Hegel on the State of Nature
11. The Hero: Hegel and Kierkegaard
12. The Individual and the State: Hegel and Mill
13. The Lessons of History: Hegel and Marx
- 14. The Tragic Hero: Aristotle and Kierkegaard
- 15. The Reasons for Religious Belief: Marx and Freud
16. Kierkegaard: Mount Moriah and the Plain of Aulis
17. Ethics and the Individual: Hegel and Kant
- 18. Freud on the Self and Society
- 19. The Tyranny of the Majority: Mill and Locke
- 20. The Existentialism of Kierkegaard and Sartre
- 21. The Role of Religion: Freud and Santayana
22. The Method of Pragmatism: Peirce, James and Dewey
23. Philosophy and History: Croce and Hegel
24. Moore and Carnap: What is Philosophy?
25. Empirical Ethics: Carnap and Kant

Other topics can be chosen only with the section leader's consent.

Term papers are due in the sections on April 26, 27 and 28.

Supplementary Reading List

Readings in White: The Age of Analysis, will be as follows: pp. 13-64; pp. 116-243.

6. Susan Sontag Papers, graduate work, 'Suggested Term Papers Topics' list, spring term 1955–56, Humanities 5, Harvard. Box 149, Folder 7.

departed from philosophy, but without turning her back on it; she appears to have taken it elsewhere. The simultaneous order formed by modernism and theory in her archive gives us another Sontag. Neither the nostalgic modernist nor the aggressive self-made icon, she inscribes herself in an 'endless, open' philosophical project that, exactly like desire, 'resists its complete fulfillment (Groys 92). She can be seen leaning towards what she calls 'the situation of thinking', advancing, moving slowly, in a progressive sliding motion that resembles a graceful fall.

Paris, summer 1976. Sontag wonders about Plato's metaphor of the cave (Fig. 7):

> . . . But here the metaphor isn't just. Having an idea is more like going into a cave than it is like emerging from one, more like a (voluntary) confinement than a standing in open, undefined space. (Ideas define; confine). More like a going down than a going up.[64]

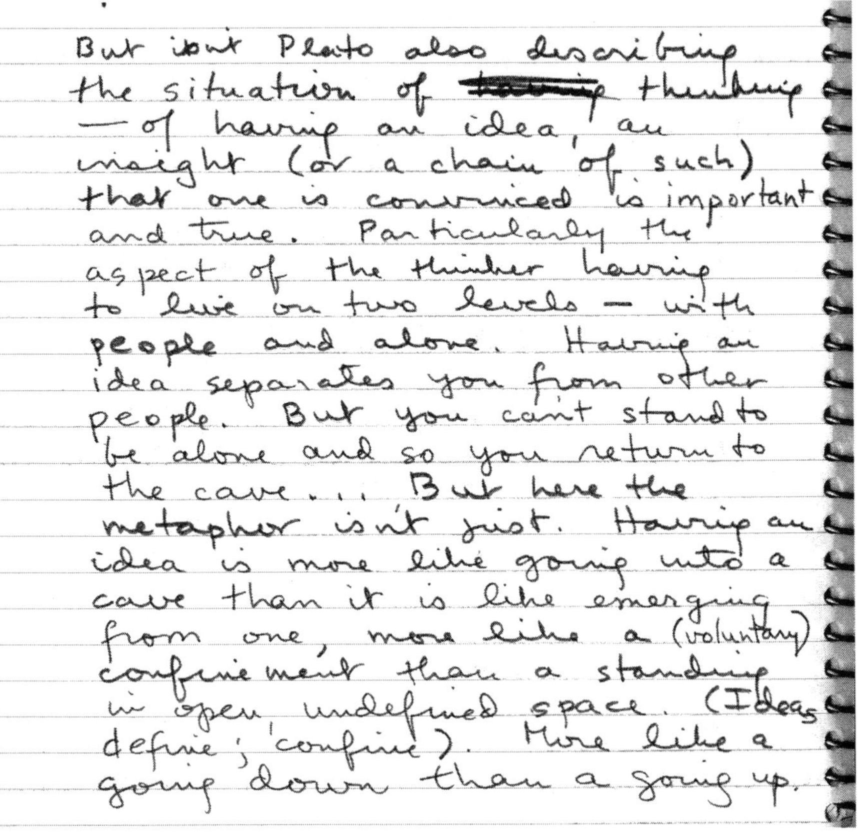

But isn't Plato also describing
the situation of ~~having~~ thinking
— of having an idea, an
insight (or a chain of such)
that one is convinced is important
and true. Particularly the
aspect of the thinker having
to live on two levels — with
people and alone. Having an
idea separates you from other
people. But you can't stand to
be alone and so you return to
the cave . . . But here the
metaphor isn't just. Having an
idea is more like going into a
cave than it is like emerging
from one, more like a (voluntary)
confinement than a standing
in open undefined space. (Ideas
define; confine). More like a
going down than a going up.

7. Susan Sontag Papers, Notebook, 1976, detail ('Plato's cave' fragment). Box 128, Folder 1.

In March 1977 she longs to write philosophy:

> I want to write an essay like
> a fist. I want to write an essay
> where the date (year) it's written
> isn't important. Philosophical, not historical; not culture-criticism.[65]

She longs to transcend history, personal and cultural identity.

In May 1980 the descent of the Plato entry of the summer of 1976 progresses; the slow, sliding motion towards the situation of thinking refines into a substance-less something, a passionate vacillation, a state of vulnerability (Fig. 8):

> If there is a unifying theme of
> my work it is naive. The theme
> of moral seriousness, of
> passionateness. A mood, a tone.[66]

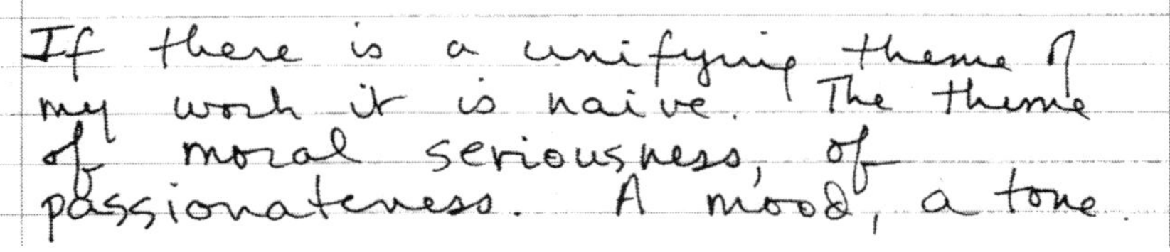

If there is a unifying theme of
my work it is naive. The theme
of moral seriousness, of
passionateness. A mood, a tone.

8. Susan Sontag Papers, Notebook, 9 May 1980, detail ('passionateness' fragment). Box 128, Folder 8.

She is in flight from thinking reduced to a demagogic activity. In the same entry she writes (Fig. 9):

> I must give up writing essays
> because that inevitably becomes
> a demagogic activity. I seem
> to be the bearer of certainties
> that I <u>don't</u> possess – am not
> near to possessing.[67]

I must give up writing essays
because that inevitably becomes
a demagogic activity. I seem
to be the bearer of certainties
that I <u>don't</u> possess — am not
near to possessing.

9. Susan Sontag Papers, Notebook, 9 May 1980, detail ('possessing' fragment). Box 128, Folder 8.

Donald Richie, a legendary associate of the Japan Society in New York, with whom Sontag had come into contact while curating film series there, writes in a journal entry:

> Thinking back over New York – Jonathan [Rauch], Chester [Biscardi], Tom [Wolfe]. They live in an element I do not. This is the current of contemporary thought, and they swim – mostly against it – and grow sleek. I have no intellectual climate at all. (267)

Suspicious of labels, Sontag may have swum against contemporary thought, theory especially, but that did not mean that she always felt self-assured about having an 'intellectual environment'.

In her journals, especially as she traverses the notion of modernism and this becomes conjoined with contemporary thought, Sontag appears as someone yearning for truth in the profane world of non-belief which she had inherited simultaneously from critical theory and the displaced Jewish intellectuals and from the modernist artists, all of whom were, as she put it, her 'amphetamine'.[68] She inherited an opaque world, impenetrable to the thinker, to whom illegibility thus becomes as important as the capacity to understand. In her journals, more than once she is halted, stopped in her tracks. In particular, her reassessment of modernism, as she reads theory and takes notes, intensifies her longing for the new idea, which presents itself in the hazy contours of an unattainable grace on the other side of the noetic grasp.

Chapter 5

Iconologies

I think often how close we were, but we should have been closer.

Paul Thek to Sontag, 2 March 1970, from Luxor

The same 'zone-Concept'

Certain New York School artists played a decisive role in Sontag's acceptance of the post-philosophic metamorphosis of philosophy into a formally heterogeneous discourse. They helped her embrace the precariousness of a cultural expanse, symbolised by the city environment, where the philosopher is one with the archetype of the solitary artist lost in the crowd, where thinking and writing are experienced as a pressure coming from the outside: 'I write what I can: that is, what's given to me and what seems worth writing, by me' ('Singleness' 259)

Paul Thek (1933–88) was the first decisive influence in this transition. Sontag met him not long after leaving graduate school, in 1959, and they were close until about 1965, when she started to gravitate more towards Jasper Johns. What went on between Thek and Sontag has all the nature of a collaboration.[1] For a while they were a struggling pair, and formed a 'school' of two, united by a meditation on the work of art in the age of technological reproduction. Thek's daring search for meaning encouraged Sontag to veer towards a more experimental position (the thinker as writer). The proximity to the artist and his practice kindled her desire to make a new contribution to criticism, to redraw its relation with art. *Against Interpretation* is dedicated to Paul Thek. The dedication reads 'for Paul Thek' – 'for' rather than 'to'. Rather than addressing herself to the artist, the author is making him a gift of her essays: they are a homage, thus not necessarily to be read by him but to be had and kept. The implication is that the essays have somehow come into existence thanks to him. The gift places Sontag's project, 'against interpretation', on the side of Thek's practice.

The slogan championed a view of meaning freed from all restrictions that bears similarities with Jacques Derrida's decentring or dissemination of meaning, while her emphasis on surfaces may even suggest the alternative spatio-temporal plane of *différance*, in which there is no point of origin for the understanding of meaning. When Derrida read the manuscript of *Against Interpretation*, he responded enthusiastically. He addresses himself to Sontag as a colleague working in the same 'zone-Concept' of mimesis – imitation or representation (Fig. 10).[2] In the same letter, he explicitly tells her that her work 'recalls my work' and, in closing, promises to send her evidence of the affinity: 'I will

10. Susan Sontag Papers, Letter from Jacques Derrida, 12 February 1965, detail (the 'zone-Concept' fragment). Box 84, Folder 43.

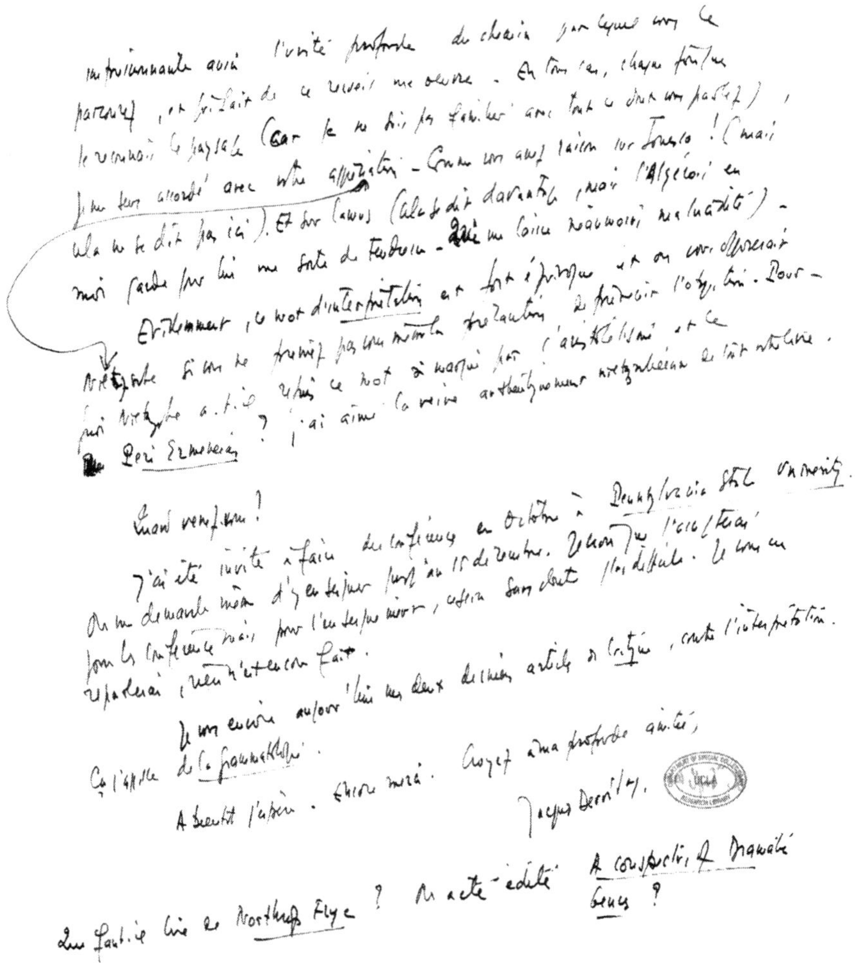

11. Susan Sontag Papers, Letter from Jacques Derrida, 12 February 1965, detail (the 'Grammatologie/Against Interpretation' fragment). Box 84, Folder 43.

send you today my last two articles in Critique, against interpretation. This I call of Grammatology' (Fig. 11).[3] Grammatology and 'against interpretation' seem to be linked in the same philosophical pursuit of a departure from long-held ideas about the work of art (mimesis). But the philosophical kinship noticed by Derrida only makes us more curious as to Sontag's decision to move away from philosophy and closer to art.

Like Cy Twombly and Robert Rauschenberg, Paul Thek was a young American artist who responded to technological reproduction with borrowings from Mediterranean culture. Unlike Twombly and

Rauschenberg, however, he felt a strong spiritual affinity for Italy. He was raised as a Catholic, originally named George Joseph, but, as an adult, changed his name to Paul, after the Apostle who had come to believe only through the Word without ever meeting Jesus personally. Those who knew Thek and worked closely with him remember his commitment to religious mysteries. The Italian baroque and the votive artefacts in Italian churches were primary influences on his artistic imagination (Wilson, 'Beatitudes' 116). It is perhaps the capacity of these religious objects to condense historical layers of human affect and faith which struck the artist most. He wanted an art that could project a reality parallel to external reality, a reality different from the order of history.[4] Much like votive objects or devotional paintings, Thek's images and objects were meant to be experienced 'as icons and as prophecies' (Wilson, 'Beatitudes' 116): they confronted the viewer with the mystery of meaning, that is to say, with meaning that challenges and eludes hermeneutical skills.[5]

The remains of meaning

Technological Reliquaries (1963–67) is an example of the allegorical art from the time when Thek and Sontag were close. It was begun at the end of 1963, after Thek's first stay in Italy. More often referred to as 'Meat Pieces', the work consists of 'hyper-realistic slabs of meat sculpted in wax and paint, encased in specially fabricated vitrines of Plexiglas, Formica, and chrome' (Sussman and Zelvansky 13). While Thek uses the slabs of meat, 'sometimes adorned with giant flies or poked through with tubes suggesting dire illness' (Sussman and Zelevanski 13), to take an ironic distance from his contemporaries, especially Warhol and his Brillo Boxes, or minimalism, which was dominated by the rhetoric of the modern in the choice of art materials, his objects also transport the viewer to another level of meaning. The iconoclastic theatricality of the object may inhibit the full manifestation of this other level of meaning, creating the distinct impression of an allegorical enclosure which materialised in the plexiglass vitrines. These objects are the technological reliquaries of something. A reliquary is a depository or receptacle for relics, usually holy remains. It comes from the Latin word for 'remains'. In a religious context, it indicates the container of something valuable, inestimable or incalculable. The word refers to objects of devotion. In the installation of *Technological Reliquaries*, personal objects lie about like old ruins still warm with the human touch.[6] They are a prime example of how the artist's fascination with the antique and the religious elements in Italian culture, recontextualised, lends objects a ritualistic presence that carries them beyond their status as history-bound, local and supremely critical signs, into a realm of art that does not suppress emotion and does not shun the fragility of human life. Thek's objects pursue a discourse on the body, which the artist himself described as 'frightening', 'unpleasant,' and 'real' (qtd. in Zelevansky 13).[7] They stage the destruction of the flesh: 'phantasms of the dismembered body anticipate its decomposition. A tragic quality is conveyed; it is as if the ecstasy of the flesh could be attained only at the cost of death' (Loock 7).

The aggressive objecthood of Thek's creations is driven by an allegorical incorporation of the past. Excavated, selected, drained of complexity, the past is made to speak in the object as a simplified sign. In this abridged way, it creates an aura around the object, which seems to hold warm meaning that defeats the cool gesture of critique in its effort to unmask the 'swanky' materiality of the present. Thek's brand of minimalism consists in a critical gesture, in a brushstroke of the mind that drastically denies historical distance to hold before the viewer icons of human affect, of the human capability for emotions that remain uncomputed, uncalculated. Faith is among them. The votive objects that inspire him are offerings, gifts for something obtained through grace because it was unpromised. In this sense, they are a unique testimony of the human capacity to entrust life to a power beyond history.

Sontag must have been struck by the talent of such an adversarial artist, not least because his art seemed to resonate with her musings. When she first met Thek, she may not have been reading Benjamin first hand, but she was aware of him and of his discovery of the destruction of the aura. She saw that Thek rejected this idea, that the artist responded to the 'spectral and mortuary cosmos' denounced by the early Frankfurt School irreverently and freely, with nothing less than the soul: 'Paul Thek believed in the soul' (Wilson, 'Beatitudes' 116).

Thek's interest in religious objects and in the Italian baroque was Sontag's first introduction to allegory before she encountered Benjamin's 'theory of melancholy' which assumed the mystery of meaning topographically congealed in ruins (Sontag, 'Under the Sign of Saturn' 111). The catalyst of Thek's allegory was the body: the body not as thematic trope and object of contemplation, but the body unknown, in its flight from knowledge:

> For me it was absolutely obvious. Inside the glittery, swanky cases – the 'modern art' materials that were all the rage at the time, Formica and glass and plastic – was something very unpleasant, very frightening, and looking absolutely real. It seemed to me that nobody noticed the fact

> that I was dealing with a frightening subject with absolute patience and control so that it became serene. Nobody noticed that I was working with the hottest subject known to man – the human body – and doing it in a totally controlled way which, I thought, was the required distancing . . . (qtd. in Zelevansky 13)

The body is the affective palimpsest of a historical order that is significantly altered and reshuffled by the auratic action of the mystery of the flesh, of human emotion and faith. The thing-ness of the body refocuses the 'preoccupation with the lost, timeless, identity-less reality of the flesh', but also 'translates the desire to be outside oneself' (Loock 6–7). The phenomenological concern with the body foregrounds the conjoining of materiality and transcendence, matter and spirit, profane and spiritual. The conjoining is so vertiginous that it makes Thek's art difficult to handle and receive, but it begins to give an idea of how the practice behind this art might have appealed to Sontag who, constantly wavering between body and mind, was on a quest for embodied thought.

In 1960, as she was immersed in a wide range of readings – Plato (*Meno* and *Protagoras*), Aristotle (*Nicomachean Ethics* and *Rhetoric*), Plotinus and Augustine, as well as Jung, Duns Scotus and Paul Tillich in preparation for her courses at Columbia and Sarah Lawrence[8] – her note 'I create the world' carries all the active power of the thinking subject who structures the world according to her own categories in order to dominate it.[9] Only a few months later, the Cartesian (or even Fichtean) mood gives way to utter powerlessness: 'I don't really exist (count).'[10] Mind and body, whose opposition redoubles in a series of other binaries (thinking subject and the world, internal and external, spirit and matter) persist in a relation of 'dissociation'.[11] In her first novel, *The Benefactor* (1962), which is a meditation on Descartes,[12] the two poles of extension (the essence of matter) and thinking (the essence of soul or mind) are personified by Frau Anders and Hippolyte. Frau Anders stands for the body and is completely outside, while Hippolyte stands for the mind and feels completely inside. Sontag seeks a balance of the two – 'how to be neither totally outside (as with Frau Anders) or inside (as with Hippolyte)' – but unsuccessfully.[13] In 1964, as her identities multiply – philosopher, critic, public intellectual or, simply, writer – a clear sign of her experimental intellectual life, she continues to waver even more acutely:

> death=being
> completely inside
> one's own head
> life=the world.[14]

Thek echoes her. In a letter sent from Fire Island in the summer of 1965, he describes his 'death schedule', by which he meant his daily work discipline: 'up at 7, work till 10, exercise till 11:30, beach + lunch till 3, work till 6, guitar till 9, dinner + bed + Norman O. Brown till sleep.'[15] We hear the conflict between labour and art, process and form. Daily discipline is necessary to art making (as it is to intellectual output) but it conflicts with the aim of making an art of immediacy (of thinking an embodied thought of experience). In fact, it may be '[a] how-to-do-it on killing immediacy'.[16] The artist's days are spent in a practice designed to 'bring home' a 'flying quality', an evanescence that always keeps hovering elsewhere:

> There are moments here with that perfection like walking in lemon groves in Sicily. A flying quality, the big clarity thing. But mostly the quiet + the rhythm (brilliant red + brilliant yellow hidden behind blues, or vice versa) are hovering somewhere else. My death-schedule is designed to bring them home.[17]

For Sontag, the wavering would become acute. Even as she went on publishing successful books, it inhibited her own self-image as an authentic thinker. In a notebook entry for 1978 she writes:

> To feel the pressures of consciousness,
> to be informed, to understand
> anything, one must be alone.
> Being with people, being alone –
> like breathing in and breathing
> out, systole and diastole. As
> long as I'm so afraid of being
> alone, I'll never be real.
> I'm in hiding from myself.[18]

Sontag's friendship with Thek and her knowledge of his art of perilous oscillation between 'spiritual and profane, lyrical and base' (Zelevansky 11) further enhanced her search for a less abstract thought.[19] She gets to the point of asking the question: 'What is a body?'[20] She considers how neglected the question has been in the history of thought: 'Knowing has to do with an embodied [embodied is underlined] consciousness (not just a consciousness) this is the great neglected issue in phenomenology (from Descartes + Kant through Husserl + Heidegger) – Sartre + Merleau-Ponty have begun to take it up.'[21]

'Neitzsche'

Thek practised Whitman's levelling sensualism. He lived in Whitman's poetry. In the summer of 1965 he wrote to Sontag from Fire Island: 'But the beach is a poetic place, no doubt about it. It all adds up to the touching of deep places, covering my legs with sand. The 29th bather in his 32nd year.'[22] The 29th bather is the position of the beholder who experiences the complexity and depth of the world as a sensuous surface and can therefore dissolve the distance between himself or herself and the world – above all the distance between self and others – in an aesthetic view of the world. The position, of course, is not unproblematic, but it is the position that Sontag celebrates in 'Against Interpretation' (1964). To advocate an art that expands our capacity to perceive, she famously asserts: 'In place of a hermeneutics we need an erotics of art' ('Against Interpretation' 14). The slogan voluptuously cuts off artefacts from hermeneutic depth; it pushes works of art back into a pre-iconological environment of pure forms, where they float like so many illegible but seductive marks. The voluptuous gesture of the mind appeases the interpreter's struggle for meaning, the labour and the anxiety, while it simultaneously reclaims for the artist one of the central values of modernism: the autonomy of art.[23] Twenty years later Thek painted her slogan and signed it with his name in memory of their collaboration.[24]

At a key moment of her intellectual life, as she left academic philosophy, Thek inducted Sontag in an American modernist mythology, showing her that Whitman's 'polysensual world', as she would write in *On Photography* (93), was a desirable alternative. She switched to the dictum 'You can't say more than you see' (*On Photography* 93). In their collaboration, she played the role of the charismatic professor, whose lectures the artist wished to attend and by whose knowledge he wished to be guided. Sontag enabled him to connect art to a world of ideas, on the threshold of which she presided like a Sybil or an oracle.

The painting *Susan Lecturing on Neitzsche* (1987) confirms the collaboration as it emerges in the correspondence.[25] In a letter written when they were no longer close, in the 1970s, the artist reminisces: 'I don't know who I was, a blind cave fish, etc., you brought me so much, I was in your spell, it was awful, a tonguetied boy, over reaching . . . by far.'[26] And, in the same letter: 'You really rearranged my head, where is it now? Dissolved, gone.' The spelling mistake in Nietzsche's name, however, offers further insight into the kind of exchange that went on between them. The playful manipulation of the philosopher's name suggests a more private knowing gravitating around it. Nietzsche was a point of reference for both Thek's search for immediacy and Sontag's quest for a livelier thought. The quest importantly included the effort to flee the anxiety of the spectral hands of the interpreter 'sifting and measuring the ashes' for some other kind of lively knowledge (Brooks 20). In *Thus Spoke Zarathustra*, Nietzsche's allusive prose pits Dionysus, mythical symbol of aesthetic bliss and loss of self, against Ariadne, the archetype of the interpreter:

> To you, bold searchers, researchers, and whoever put to terrible seas with cunning sails –
> to you, the riddle-drunk, the twilight-happy whose souls are lured by flutes to every maelstrom:
> – because you do not want to probe along a thread with cowardly hands; and because where you can *guess*, there you hate to *deduce* –
> to you alone I tell the riddle that I saw – the vision of the loneliest one. – (Nietzsche 124)

The struggle between the intuitive vitalism symbolised by Dionysian energy and the labour of excavation and deduction evoked by Ariadne strongly resonated with both Thek and Sontag, who were united in their wavering between mind and body, discipline and ecstasy, aesthetic bliss and consciousness, between the lure of melody and the 'labyrinthine abysses', on the one hand, and the 'death schedule(s)' of art making and writing, on the other. As a result of the conflict, they both leaned towards a processual practice of 'unfinishedness', which included experimentalism and playfulness (Falckenberg, 'Why?!' 64).

The spelling mistake in Nietzsche's name preserves jealously the restricted nature of the collaboration of the two riddle-drunk bold searchers. In his last letter to her, Thek recalls: 'Our search, as ever, for something . . . beyond.'[27] Sontag's 'lecturing' points in the direction of that collaboration, alluding to an interior, a 'school' of two, an impassioned, free conversation in which one 'takes' from the other. Apart from Nietzsche they shared Freud, Norman Brown, Simone Weil and Rilke, to whom Sontag would refer in *On Photography* in her attempt to conceptualise a broader modernism of 'touch' beyond the modernism of abstraction.[28] Their conversation spanned art history, modern and contemporary art, including Duchamp. If the list attests to the intellectual nurture she brought to him, their own private inflection of 'Neitzsche' also enables us to better consider the role of Paul Thek: not only a student under her spell, but a privileged addressee, a sympathetic audience who validated her own unorthodox position as a philosopher in the post-philosophic world of broken discourse in which Nietzsche's performative and aphoristic style was a possible model.

Diver

Kenneth Burke, Sontag's former professor and mentor, was fond of her but disapproved of her aphoristic turn: in a letter to her he spoke of 'your hit-and-run asseverations'.[29] One such asseveration in her groundbreaking essay 'Against Interpretation' concerns 'transparence': 'Transparence is the highest value in art – and criticism – today. Transparence means experiencing the luminousness of the thing in itself' (13). A term of aesthetic judgement, 'transparence' here also bears the trace of her collaboration with Thek. It names their joint search for meaning and, in the spirit of the dedication – 'for Paul Thek' – seals and protects that collaboration in her critical writing. In his letter from Fire Island, written in the summer of 1965, Thek speaks of the 'big clarity thing', and echoes the term which Sontag had used in the essay written the year before. Her language becomes enfolded in Thek's language, her criticism in his art practice, which relied on process, flux, transience 'to present moments of personal insight' (Wilson, 'Voices' 68) and illustrated her own dissemination and decentring of meaning.

Thek's main values are poignantly exemplified by *Untitled (Diver)* (1969–70).[30] Painted on the Italian island of Ponza, to which the artist retreated regularly over the years, it gives us a solitary diver whose plunge into the sea resembles a descent into the depth of meaning. The action connotes freedom, ecstasy and isolation. As it dives, the lean pink male body seems limp, as if it were falling unguided by any intention, alone, naked, without possessions, giving itself to the element. The detail of the limp body calls attention to the sea; it is at the same time sensuous and metaphysical.[31] *Diver* reflects Thek's suspension between matter and spirit; it is the image of the artist as 'exemplary sufferer' which Sontag celebrated in her essay on the Italian writer Cesare Pavese. There, perhaps in Thek's honour, she redefines modernist alienation as a transhistorical mood that reaches back to the Christian theologians Paul and Augustine.[32]

Like the voice of Rilke's first Duino Elegy, neither Thek nor Sontag felt completely at home in the interpreted world (*gedeudeten Welt*).

Transparence may be another name for what, in the summer of 1964, Sontag had called sensibility: 'there's no syntax for sensibility – hence, it's ignored'.[33] In any case, the term unites her to Thek in a shared aesthetic theory of freedom and lightness. Their collaboration raised the question of interpretation. Transparence, in fact, evokes the waning of difference between the work and its hermeneutic meaning. In response to Heidegger, whose work she may have started to read first hand only in 1960,[34] Sontag extols a 'thing' covered in luminousness which resists the mind's translation; it resists the manipulation of the work of art reduced to allegorical content. A correlative of Thek's 'flying moment', transparence alludes to the deferred 'rhythm' of immediacy, to a fullness of meaning forever delayed. Thus it rises above the arbitrariness of mere acts of 'intellectual disburdenment' to defend an aesthetic experience that resists the appropriation of art by thought, and consists in the sense of the work's incomplete crossing to conceptual knowledge. Sontag's luminous thing, unlike the dark cavities of Van Gogh's peasant boots in Heidegger's reading in 'The Origin of the Work of Art' (1930), does not lend itself to hermeneutic excavation.

Sontag's friendship with Thek resulted in the experience of an unprecedented contact of critical reflection and art making. From the distance of art, the philosophical thought she had left behind probably seemed even more frayed and dejected in its lame desire to be more realistic and embodied. The fall of Thek's diver parallels in so many ways Sontag's own descent into 'the situation of thinking'.[35] It reflects the thinker's progress towards lightness and evanescence which is the central motif of my study.

Derrida lecturing on 'Vincent' (deconstruction live)

In one of the boxes in Susan Sontag's archive, mixed with papers that probably date from the 1980s and the early 1990s, there is a folder containing a small spiral notebook full of notes on a talk by Jacques Derrida. The talk was given at Columbia University on 6 October 1977, and later became 'Restitutions of Truth in Pointure'.[36] Sontag took down the title as '(Le) Restitutions de la vérité en peinture' (Fig. 12). The lecture focused on the debate between the German philosopher Martin Heidegger and the American art critic Meyer Shapiro on the attribution of Van Gogh's famous pair of peasant boots. In 28 pages of notes, Sontag follows Derrida's sustained questioning of the pairness of the shoes: 'both H. + S. [Heidegger and

Schapiro] assume that these are a pair of shoes are they? Who says so? if they are not, that changes everything' (p. 3). The pairness of the shoes joins H [Heidegger] and S [Schapiro] in a similar enterprise of restitution: they both want to restore the shoes to those who wore them (p. 4). While Heidegger 'returns them to the peasant woman (+ fields)' (p. 4), Shapiro 'returns them to Van Gogh (+ city)' (p. 5). In both cases, interpretation of the work of art is inseparable from the work's politico-institutional history and from the affective investment of the interpreter. Schapiro wanted to dismantle Heidegger's 'artisanal pathos' because of its link to Nazi ideology. Moreover, the fact that it was his friend Kurt Goldstein who alerted Schapiro to Heidegger's essay had its role in Schapiro's battle for restitution. Like Schapiro, Goldstein was a Jewish refugee. He had to flee Nazi Germany in 1933, stopping in Amsterdam and Paris, before emigrating to New York and Columbia University in 1936.

Sontag takes down in detail the part of Derrida's argument in which he demonstrates that for both Heidegger and Schapiro, thinking and interpretation merge in 'a desire to appropriate w-o-a or thing itself' (p. 5). They both want to appropriate: 'i.e. – says D. – S's theory of truth no different from Heidegger both want to fill the shoes w/the feet' (p. 23). Separated by remarkable differences in background, Heidegger, whose name was taboo in Sontag's formation at Chicago because of his Nazi collaboration, and Schapiro are conjoined in Derrida's critique: both construe the cavities of Van Gogh's shoes as the receptacle of a discourse that they wish to possess. Both turn the work of art into a test of their philosophical and critical mastery.

During the talk Sontag sat near Meyer Schapiro.[37] Perhaps she felt compelled to side with him, but the attention with which she took notes suggests that the talk must have resonated with her own critique of the manipulation of the work of art by the thinking subject in possession of himself. Derrida's deft argument must have reminded her of their kinship as fellow thinkers who moved in the same 'zone-Concept'. After all, he relied on the same intellectual resources as she did, especially Artaud and Freud. When he wants to transcend the Heidegger–Schapiro opposition, it is to Artaud that the philosopher appeals: 'as Artaud said suppress phantoms in V.G. is another way of suiciding V.G. which is what S. as well as H. do' (p. 15). When, in the middle of his argument, Derrida shifts to fetishism, the tone of Sontag's notes indicates a certain impatience – '(Freud now!)' (p. 7) – as if to remark that the theoretical reference was unnecessary since, at the start of the lecture, Artaud and the phantom had already questioned the idea of the pair. Nevertheless

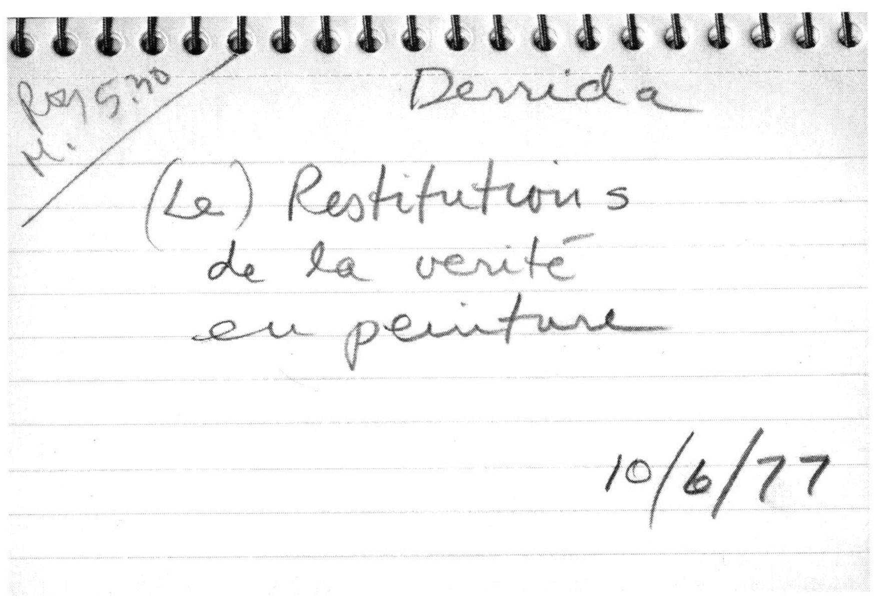

12. Susan Sontag Papers, Notebook (the 'Derrida Notebook'), with notes on Derrida's '(Le) Restitutions de la vérité en peinture', 10 June 1977, initial page. Box 134, Folder 10.

she continues to take down the drift of his argument and see his point – 'no disc. of fetishism w/o shoes and feet' – following Derrida with interest on this track: 'fetishist interest in shoes is always one shoe' (p. 7). Betting on the pairness of the shoes ('parier sur la paire égale') minimises or hides the fetishistic side ('diminuer (cacher) le coté fetishiste') (p. 7). She catches up with Derrida's argument that attribution, in fact, is appropriation; it is a discourse of 'declarations of property, performances or investitures of the type: this is mine, these shoes or these feet to someone who says "me" and can thereby identify himself, belong to the domain of the nameable' (Derrida, 'Restitutions' 306). Derrida's critique of the limits imposed on the meaning of the work of art by the fetishistic desire of philosophical and critical discourse must have sounded rather familiar to Sontag, who had resisted the instrumental use of the work of art and the stifling 'excavation' of the text. She knew the litany on p. 8 of her notes, 'penis in vagina/ foot in shoe/ hand in glove.'

When Derrida, in the first part of the lecture, mentions Schapiro's efforts to depart from Heidegger's allegorical instrumentality of the artwork, in her notes Sontag inserts herself in the debate as an active and responsive reader of Heidegger: the 'decoupage de texte de H. made by S. (+ by me) est bien problematique convenablement cadré'. Her association with Thek had given her permission to reclaim a luminous encounter with the work of art that stopped just before the delivery of its truth-content. The notes on Derrida offered a new opportunity for self-assessment. Her self-insertion in the debate – '(+ by me)' – recontextualises her in a line of thinkers who have used the work of art as a starting point for a critique of modern philosophy.[38]

Vincent Van Gogh was Paul Thek's favourite painter. Perhaps it was Thek's spiritual longings – his commitment to '[a]gape as charity, as the love that consumes, as the great communal banquet' (Wilson, 'Beatitudes' 118) – that made him sympathise with the artist, who identified with the wretched of the earth.[39] In his correspondence with Sontag, Thek called himself Vincent. When she does not answer his letters, he tries to elicit a response by attaching a self-portrait as Vincent Van Gogh and signing himself playfully and affectionately 'Vincent Wishful'.[40] The detail may shed further light on Sontag's notes on Derrida. Obviously, *this* Vincent is not the artist of Heidegger's essay, but it certainly is the one known to Sontag. It might not be wrong to assume that her knowledge of Thek's practice and her collaboration with him entitled her to claim an active role in the wider philosophical debate on the work of art.

Indeed, Thek's 'Vincent' adds a special resonance to Sontag's notes on Derrida. Sontag and Thek had reclaimed a luminous sensuous encounter with the work of art. Their collaboration had given her a second birth as a critic. She and Thek were united in the task of subtracting the work of art from the aggression of thought. This is why the notes on Derrida come alive, almost unfolding as a parallel world to deconstruction. In the comparison, the Sontag/Thek collaboration seems an alternative discourse on 'restitutions of the truth in pointing (*pointure*)'.

The collaboration with Thek actually brought Sontag closer to Benjamin. Soon, the celebration of transparency ceded to a concern for the rigidification of objects, and interpretation, once disposed of, made a comeback.[41] From the vantage point of Thek's 29th bather, the aesthetic was largely the domain of unappropriated meaning. Later, however, it would comprise the problem, as she put it in a comment on Kafka, in a notebook dated 1964, of a 'strictly external, functional, conventional reality' confined to the 'objective', in which anything spiritual can only be introduced by way of interpretation.[42]

The surface

From *Against Interpretation* onwards, Sontag refused to put her feet in the shoes. If she and Thek had resolved not to assimilate art to philosophical thought, the resolution was only strengthened when she encountered Jasper Johns and, in 1965, forged a friendship with him. Through Johns she became aware of Robert Rauschenberg's experiments and began to think about criticism itself as an experimental form of discourse which, in the encounter with the work of art, resists its assimilation and rather lets thought stand back to receive art's 'stare' ('Aesthetics of Silence' 16).

Her collaboration with Thek had encouraged the visionary investment in a conceptual tabula rasa, a surface of pure forms to be experienced only with the senses. This erotics of art certainly reclaimed the modernist autonomy of art, in other words, art's capacity to pose a parallel reality to the historical one. But the horizon of floating forms in flux was not entirely new. The processual, transient, evanescent luminousness of the thing itself updated a familiar intellectual model. The notion of the world as a cultural surface may date back to her student days at Chicago, when Sontag was encouraged to view texts, authors and thinkers as 'ideal models in an a-historical space' (McQuade 273). This a-historical space is not extraneous to some of the premises of the New Criticism, especially to the assumption that discursive production is the result of the encounter with artefacts 'naked of context' (Brooks iii). The New Criticism rearranged literature into a flat plane of verbal icons, existing among objects and people, which are terms of attachment insofar as they are exempt from market value (Wellek, *History* 159). The flat plane was a response to a certain anxiety about the secondary status of criticism in relation to the texts it explicated. The new surface of verbal icons sought to remedy the gap between creative artefact and critical commentary by placing centre-stage the metaphor of citation, of connection through repetition. The verbal icons formed a lush fabric of allusions, references, citations and traces; they projected a space of allegorisation in which each poem, each work of art, each idea can be met as the product of citations, of imagery carried over from other imagery (see, for example, Brooks 97). The interpreter and the thinker, therefore, share a similar fundamental experience – the experience of the 'lost piece of evidence' (Gombrich 6). The ancient priest in his solitude resorted to exegesis, the technique of finding meanings, having at his disposal only a basic text to read, to meditate on and to interpret. Devoted exegesis yielded discourse as it helped him 'composing his sermons day in day out on given texts which had to be applied to the changing events of the community' (Gombrich 14). Similarly, the modern interpreter must proceed in the manner of the iconologist for whom allegorisation is part and parcel of representation. There is no work without a subject; we generally know what the work before us represents. But in the a-historical space the iconologist must help establish the missing links 'across long and obscure paths', joining widely diverse works and retracing a historical connection where none was apparent before (Argan 18). This may mean reckoning with the danger of allusions, memories, dreams, condensations and other individual factors in meaning-making.

Sontag sided with the iconologists. Being against 'elaborate systems of hermeneutics, aggressive and impious theories of interpretation' ('Against Interpretation' 6–7) meant pursuing the missing links of meaning across long and obscure paths. She was animated by the desire for a more nuanced style of interpretation 'that would serve the work of art, not usurp its place' (12). The art of Jasper Johns and Rauschenberg caused her to refine the notion of surface and brought her to a new level in her search. If Johns gave her an erudite insider reintroduction to the modernist avant-gardes (they spoke about Stein, Duchamp, Schoenberg) and revived her fidelity to the autonomy of art, the reintroduction combined with the experience of Rauschenberg's surfaces to produce a new event in Sontag's mind. Those surfaces came to resonate with her 'solitary' critical post-philosophic trajectory, which assumed the dissolution of thought in the open space of the environment.

The stream

After seeing *Axle* in 1965, Sontag took notes on Rauschenberg's 'cinematically organized fragmented surface'.[43] She was drawn to this surface because it translated into cumulative listing without hierarchical connections: 'Rauschenberg – a pillow, a stuffed eagle, a shirt, a clock'.[44] They might have reminded her of Whitman's levelling sensualism, but there was something different: a Rauschenberg canvas meets the eye as a surface that is 'more potent than [the] object represented'.[45]

Rauschenberg's composite paintings, also called 'combines', thrust to the fore the notion of surface because they had no syntax. The combines incorporate heterogeneous materials and objects (see Krauss). When the object is not materially imported, it is photographed or combined with other media. The first impact Sontag recorded is fragmentation and a dynamic shock effect, like that of cinema. But she was struck by the power of his surface because the artist used objects or reproductions of objects that functioned as catalysts for the collective, historical imagination. In this sense, Rauschenberg's surface stood for something similar to what Benjamin, speaking of photography, had called the 'optical unconscious' ('Little History' 512). His paintings, midway between objects and images, had the capacity to trigger individual and even private associations. His technique served to evoke not so much the object's concreteness on canvas as its weight in the imagination of the viewer.

Mark Ormond singles out *Orphic Ditty* as representative of the 'visual experience of a Rauschenberg painting' (3). Part of the 'Salvage Series', *Orphic Ditty* (1984) continues the approach that Rauschenberg had developed in the mid-1950s, with the invention of a pictorial surface that incorporated objects and images from everyday life (Ormond 5).[46] Executed on a single piece of beautiful raw linen,[47] it is divided into two narrow lateral panels headed by a milk can, a photographed object that has been painted over, and a central panel showing a mythological detail, an unusual representation of Orpheus playing a rudimentary harp instead of the lute. The repetition of the object creates a tripartite narrative made of the two side panels and a central area occupied by a rustic scene placed in symmetrical opposition to a mythological detail, the photograph of a grotesque probably taken by the artist.[48] On the panel to the left, what to the naked eye appears as a non-figurative blotch is revealed on closer scrutiny as a scene of urban construction turned upside down.[49] On the panel to the right, colour veils more than reveals, just as in the combine paintings of the mid-1950s. The instrument of Orpheus in the mythological detail rests on the ground, a fact that indicates an earth-bound song, a ditty rather than the music of the heavenly spheres, but also alludes to Dürer's *Melancholia I*, and places Rauschenberg's Orpheus 'under the Sign of Saturn'. The whole canvas depends on 'a personal souvenir' (Ormond 7) which determines its structure and the arrangements of the other disparate elements. But, as Ormond argues, it is precisely its singular, biographical reference that ensures its public readability: 'Rauschenberg manipulates memory, or the act of recalling the past at the present moment. While the artist creates for now, the imagery recalls those aspects of material culture that may be a shared memory of those with common experience' (6).

As Sontag herself experienced, in the typical encounter with Rauschenberg's art meaning is decentred, it radiates out and disseminates without any seeming point of origin. But his technique also stimulates 'a rich array of sensations' (Ormond 6) on to which the individual viewer can mount a 'mental and visual dialogue on canvas' (6). Eventually, the internal time of the canvas and the privatised objects, layered with collective affect, flow into the public time of history and interpretation. The point, however, is that the surface impacts the viewer with a double layering, with another plane of meaning. More than understanding, Rauschenberg's art demands attachment. On the one hand, his objects defend the modernist distance or negativity of art, its utopian power to recreate the world; on the other hand, more than the modernist abstracting eye, they promise access to an 'optical unconscious' that recalls the thinking plane itself, which, in her early notebooks, Sontag had conceived as an 'ignored', asyntactical sensibility.[50] 'Rauschenberg – a pillow, a stuffed eagle, a shirt, a clock': one thing, another and another. The asyntactical stream is the environment of the 'cosmophage' (Koestenbaum) – the world eater – someone who takes in the world as flux, process and transience, as a sequence of segments and pieces, one after another after another. Rauschenberg's 'cinematic fragmented surface' reflected the image of the thinker that Sontag was becoming: part of a larger whole, the thinker merging with the writer, and the writer as sensitive membrane, an I-skin: 'I write what I can: that is, what's given to me and what seems worth writing, by me . . . My books aren't me – all of me – And in some ways I am less than them' ('Singleness' 259).

In this sense, writing is a 'daring' enterprise: 'By extension, there was that one, the one who had dared to become a writer. And I, the one with the standards, who happily made sacrifices to keep her going, though I didn't think all that much of what she wrote' ('Singleness' 260). 'Singleness' closes with a rejection of self-objectification: 'Now I think there is no escaping the burden of singleness. There's a difference between me and my books. But there's only one person here. That is scarier. Lonelier. Liberating' (262). Unity of purpose and intent, though scarier, is liberating because, even more consciously, Sontag occupies that position of exposure to the stream of stimuli that will never be written, and ultimately will exceed books.

For the cosmophage, the cognitive power of thinking becomes a 'summer project': it is reconciled with bliss, as ideas are reconciled with aesthetic pleasure.[51] In another, powerful self-portrait Sontag comes forward feeling that she has to apologise for the stream of thinking, for the vertiginous conjoining of hermeneutics and aesthetics, reflection and bliss, on the same flat plane ('Writing as Reading'). The sequence must inevitably be translated into writing in order to be read by others, and to be thought again. The notion of surface evokes the stream of thinking, revealing that thinking is thinking again. Thinking is repetition and the problematic boundary between thinking and an inscription in excess of books calls attention to that.

'About Hodgkin' defends the stream of thinking unapologetically, but does so through the mask of Paul Valéry. Sontag quotes Valéry's opener for his essay 'About Corot': 'One must always apologize for talking about painting' (152). The essay is composed of a sequence of potentially autonomous segments which are given a unity under the same title 'About Hodgkin'. The British painter, whose surfaces convey a directness and spontaneity that follow from a slow process of reflection, provides the opportunity for the unrepentant and defiant apology of the cosmophage in her search to bridge the distance between idea and form, cognition and beauty, aesthetics and hermeneutics. It is a fragment about Venice:

> There is a price to be paid for stubbornly continuing to make love with one's eyes to these famous tourist-weary places. For not letting go: of ruined grandeur, of the imperative of bliss. For continuing to work on behalf of, in praise of, beauty. It's not that one hasn't noticed that this is an activity which people rather condescend to now.
>
> Indeed, one might spend a lifetime apologizing for having found so many ways of acceding to ecstasy. (159)

The correspondence between the surface of art and the plane of thinking here is complete. Like Rauschenberg's surface, Sontag's writing meets the viewer/reader with provocative enigmas.

Like *écriture*

In her collaboration with Thek, Sontag had come to realise that 'freedom could only mean freedom from interpretation' (Weibel 42). The project 'against interpretation' issued from her bond to modernism understood in its profound affinity with a living practice of thinking and writing. This idea of modernism traverses her journals. One is struck by an early journal entry of 1961 consisting of a brief quote from Albert Camus (1913–60), the acclaimed author of *L'Étranger*: 'Each time that one (that I) surrender to one's vanities', begins the quote copied by Sontag, and continues expanding on the joy of writing: the writer warms himself to the thought of living alone and unknown.[52] It was to develop this idea of modernism that Sontag reviewed Cesare Pavese's diary. She talks of the shape of the artist's life, made of renunciations and denials, and of the asceticism that it exacts. In 'The Artist as Exemplary Sufferer', Pavese, a man of letters (*uomo di cultura*), embodies Camus's joy by standing for a syncretism of identities: 'poet, novelist, short story writer, literary critic, translator, and editor with one of Italy's leading publishers (Einaudi)' (43). In the Pavese essay, Sontag locks the ideal of modernism as the name of a true writing superior to others into the active fantasy of a literature that defends us 'against the attacks of life' (Pavese qtd. in 'The Artist as Exemplary Sufferer' 42). Pavese 'transforms his suffering into art' (42), therefore prolonging and carrying over into the present Sontag's belief in art 'as a medium of spiritual transformation' (Sayres, *Elegiac Modernist* 104), inseparable from a certain heroism of the self and from the choice of hardship. She quotes the Italian writer: 'To choose a hardship for ourselves is our only defense against that hardship . . . Those who by their very nature can suffer completely, utterly, have an advantage.'[53]

Thek's influence depended on his capacity to embody the modernist artist of her essay on Pavese. In the private space of Sontag's collaboration with Thek, she lectured on Nietzsche and he supported her as a post-philosophic aphoristic thinker. However, his willingness to transform his life into an experiment in the service of art, to access layers of meaning beyond historical reality (and this included sexual promiscuity and the use of drugs), was also a source of anxiety. Like Thek, Sontag believed in self-creation: she believed in shaping her life and using her body and her sexuality in ways that were functional to intellectual illumination. Her relationships with women, for instance, are profoundly linked to the experience of intellectual empowerment and difference.[54] Apparently, though, self-creation could not conquer the great fear of loss that was the motor of Sontag's production: loss of self and loss of the capacity to think.

If, with Thek, she might be said to have embodied modernism, Jasper Johns's erudite reintroduction to modernism gave her a more scholarly distance from the idea. After Johns, modernism became an object of critical investigation in her journals and in her published work. Johns introduced her seriously to the ideas of Marcel Duchamp, to the notion of painting as a 'mental act' that makes us see things anew. He introduced her to the work of André Breton and surrounded her with the ideas of Gertrude Stein and the music of Schoenberg.[55] The array of references afforded her a mental environment secure enough to contrast her usual anxiety of intellectual impoverishment, while the connection with the world of the historical avant-garde, through conversations with Johns, renewed her sense of freedom: '"Nothing" is true; everything is possible.'[56] She began to formalise the correspondence between painting and critical thought, understanding Johns's non-perspectival plane and '"flat" anti-metaphoric' standpoint – his 'literalness' – in terms of 'the critical theory of Roland Barthes'.[57] During one of her visits to the artist in his retreat of Edisto Beach, she wrote in her journal: 'subject: painting + écriture'.[58] The reorientation towards the 'Cage&Stein' axis[59] felt like a radical change before which 'all preexistent vocabularies are a prison'.[60]

From the safety of a more theoretical distance from modernism, Sontag could assess her own critical trajectory and its consequences for her self-image. She placed herself in the camp opposite Lukács and those critics who, in the wake of Hegel and Marx, condemned modernists because they lacked devotion to art.[61] After the encounter with the New York avant-garde, her devotion reached a more refined level. Appearing as the site of 'real thinking',[62] Rauschenberg's surfaces assisted Sontag in the transfer of the idea of modernism as a living-thinking-writing continuum to the present. The New York School combined with the work of Benjamin to provide Sontag with a framework for the investigation of photographic surfaces. In her work on photography, modernist abstraction reveals the problematic beautifying impulse of photography but ultimately makes way for another, weaker modernism confused with and enfolded in the mortality and transience of Being.

Chapter 6

Aura, Dread and the Amateur

I wanted to be pure flame.

Susan Sontag, *The Volcano Lover*

Positions

Sontag's progression towards Benjamin is strange, fascinating. More than finding him, she finds herself. Encountering Benjamin translated into a clear sense of belonging to a theoretical tradition; above all, it gave her a more nuanced narrative of the critical act.

Sontag had earned her place as a literary critic by emancipating herself from firmly held beliefs in the critical establishment. This, however, took some time. Despite her youthful rebellion, in her first book of essays she was still working with a rather traditional notion of interpretation. She thought that 'great art induces contemplation' and that 'the reader or listener or spectator [. . .] must be detached, restful, contemplative, emotionally free, beyond indignation and approval' ('Against Interpretation' 27). For the most part she echoed René Wellek, who defined the aesthetic object as that which the reader does not attempt to reform, possess, or consume, because it is something that induces contemplation or amorous attention (Wellek and Warren 327). She transformed Wellek's amorous contemplation into 'dynamic contemplation' ('Against Interpretation' 27), but she was still under the influence of a traditional view according to which interpretation was commentary aimed at evaluating bad and good literature, bad and good art. Her difficulty is palpable in the contradictions in her claims. On the one hand, she dutifully stands by accepted academic opinions on the value of art: 'The greatest artist attains a sublime neutrality' (26). On the other hand, extolling 'transparence', she rejects hermeneutical depth.

Benjamin was in the avant-garde of critical thought: earlier than other thinkers and in more nuanced ways, he 'strove to relate a new image culture [. . .] to a modernity that involves new forms of subjectivity and social organization' (Andrew viii). One of the primary signs of his influence on Sontag is her effort to place the critic and his task in the forefront of these new forms of subjectivity. Perhaps it would not be wrong to say that Walter Benjamin did for Sontag what she did for Thek; he 'rearranged [her] head'.[1] The world he left her, rearranged by the reproducibility of the work of art, must have felt like the flat, fragmented plane of a Rauschenberg canvas. This meant the possibility of new literary genealogies. In an undated talk, 'The Avant-garde and Contemporary Literature', she wrote: 'the whole spectrum of the world culture is available to us through the modern processes of technological reproduction in a sense in which it never was at any other period in any other culture'.[2] Technological reproduction had rendered inoperative the procession of ruptures and destructive gestures implied in the narrative of the avant-garde. It had shifted the emphasis to a spatial rearrangement of works of art in 'a continuous parallel between contemporaneity and antiquity' which recalls T. S. Eliot's simultaneous order of tradition.[3] But Sontag's simultaneous order of potential literary contiguities and reconfigurations not only compromises the notion of the avant-garde, but also makes obsolete the intellect that must decode their emergence. This altered order unremittingly relocates the thinker and interpreter before the world reduced to surface, but a surface that is not the equivalent of the a-historical plane she had been used to since her formation at Chicago. The disassembled chronology of works of art, far from emanating the anxiety of solitary exegesis, is rich with the promise of conceptual invention. Before the surface, reflection and wonder converge, and so do, in a chain of confluences, understanding and appreciation, hermeneutics and aesthetics.

The imaginary rearrangement has far-reaching effects that extend to everything beyond works of art. Benjamin had celebrated a new sense of the proximity of everything through the image of a crowd desiring to be close to images. In his landmark essay on technological reproduction, 'The Work of Art in the Age of Mechanical Reproduction' (hereafter the Art Work essay), the masses, with their 'ardent [. . .] bent toward overcoming the uniqueness of every reality by accepting its reproduction', form a political image that asserts the more general proximity of things in the new imaginary rearrangement of the world (*Illuminations* 223).[4] While Benjamin's representation of the proximity of things resonated with a Marxist equality of things and with the Marxist concern for commodity fetishism, from Sontag's point of view it repaired and healed a deeply felt split between mind and world.

The experimental montage of 'One-Way Street' (1928) was a compelling introduction to the new landscape. There, the proximity of everything – people as well as things – forms a panorama that emphasises, as Michael Jennings notices, 'the progressive decay of the perceptual and cognitive apparatus' (25). The world as assemblage of parts (people near commodities near artworks) not only celebrates the proximity of things but also foregrounds a concern for mass psychology and the fear of a regression of intellect. Before the panorama, the observer minutely records the influence of commodities, but his philological sampling only more vividly implies the violence of their spectacle. In 'Imperial Panorama', as Benjamin travels in Germany and observes the material world, he is struck by 'the violence, incomprehensible to outsiders and wholly imperceptible to those imprisoned by it, with which circumstances, squalor, and stupidity here subjugate people entirely to collective forces, as the lives of savages alone are subjected to tribal laws' ('One-Way Street' 452–3). The new proximity of things can certainly be understood in Marxist terms, as dictated by commodity fetishism, that is to say, by the fact that commodities 'stand in relationship to one another and to men'.[5] But the point is that it raises the question of 'mass instincts [that] have become confused and estranged from life', and consequently the question of a narrowed space for thought (451). This landscape that Benjamin presents in 'Imperial Panorama' is dominated by the ebb and flow of warmth and repulsion issuing from commodities, a fact that compels an epistemological turn: 'all things, in an irreversible process of mingling and contamination, are losing their intrinsic character while ambiguity displaces authenticity' (454). In the essay on Naples (1925), Benjamin had used the term 'porosity' to indicate the 'great process of intermingling' (Benjamin and Lacis 421) which the technological reproduction of the work of art had only further brought to the fore. Beyond the new proximity dictated by commodity fetishism, in Benjamin's book of jottings or *Denkbilder* the Marxist frame serves to contain and keep at bay a neo-reality of instincts, spectacle and violence, glimpsed as if in a delirium by an utterly disoriented spectator. The new proximity, in fact, means a labyrinth of hidden, unclear, aggressive affects. Benjamin's observer can master the disorientation with the instruments of reason – he forges new concepts (porosity; effacement of boundaries) – but the thinker essentially vacillates before a world that fades into illegibility.[6]

As she read 'One-Way Street', Sontag marked Benjamin's point that 'ambiguity displaces authenticity'.[7] The predicament of ambiguity resonated particularly with her own experience of the clash between mind and world. Her exposure to the New York School of painting had given her a new awareness of the body oriented in space. In her search for embodied knowledge, Sontag welcomed Benjamin's effacement of boundaries and his defence of porosity as a value of modernity. Above all, Benjamin's deeply ambiguous landscape of technological reproducibility confirmed the inevitably experimental position of the philosopher in the Cioran essay. As we have seen, the essay argues that 'the traditional forms of philosophical discourse have been broken' ('Thinking Against Oneself' 78). Benjamin's observer enacts the metamorphosis of the philosopher and the possibilities that remain: an incomplete and aphoristic discourse. Sontag's beholder was en route to a similar transformation.

The transformation joins Sontag to contemporary philosophers. Jacques Derrida described the impasse of the speculative mind (Sontag, 'Thinking Against Oneself' 79) in terms of a position at the limit of philosophy: 'I try to keep myself *at the limit* of philosophical discourse. I say limit and not death, for I do not at all believe in what today is so easily called the death of philosophy etc.' (*Positions* 6). Derrida's position at the limit, between philosophy and not-philosophy, at the place of a mutual incorporation of disciplines, is comparable to what Sontag calls the 'metamorphosis [of philosophy] into other forms' ('Thinking Against Oneself' 78). The beholder who receives the 'stare' of experimental art strives for this position ('Aesthetics of Silence'). The position is an effect of a different perception of mental acts. These no longer flow from a mind reaching out to the world, but come from outside the mind, where thought, scattered and dispersed in a thousand plateaus, is pinned to the subject's affective relation to space and movement. Sontag saw Benjamin as a spatial thinker. His work led her to a more experimental practice based on the assumption, which she shared with Deleuze, that thinking is a pressure from the outside.[8]

Eros and Thanatos

First of all, the encounter with Benjamin freed Sontag from a confining view of the critical act. Initially she conceived of criticism as a secondary kind of writing associated with rumination and opposed to the 'first idea' of literary productivity, taken to be synonymous with freshness, youthfulness, novelty. The New Criticism had not been successful in emancipating the critical act from prejudice. While wishing to dignify the critical act, the New Critics also perceived it as closely allied with Thanatos;[9] they mistrusted the interpreter 'sifting and measuring the ashes' of the text (Brooks 20). Benjamin's ideas on modernity, technological reproduction and photography liberated Sontag from the reductive view of interpretation as isolated exegesis and, importantly, from the phantom of the 'rough grip' of the interpreter's hand as it rummages through the cinders of the text ('Against Interpretation' 10).

The sort of exertion of learning involved in solitary exegesis felt inadequate to the young Sontag, but contradictions persisted. At the same time that she dutifully stood by accepted academic opinions on the value of art – 'The greatest artist attains a sublime neutrality' ('Against Interpretation' 26) – she also wanted criticism to see more and argued for an aesthetic experience beyond hermeneutics (14). The contemplative beholder which she initially assumed was incapable of this critical leap; it seemed more an ideal abstraction of the reader, a projection of the autonomy that the critic wished but did not have in the milieu in which Sontag came of age as a public intellectual. When she flaunted the erotic materiality of the signifier in her essay-manifesto 'Against Interpretation', she displayed all her disaffection for 'a philosophically naive criticism' ('Nathalie Sarraute' 103).

The contradictions in Sontag's writing (she equally refused solitary commentary and theory-building) betrayed frustration. Sontag's beholder could freely encounter all sorts of aesthetic artefacts and signs, but he had no narrative to account for the encounter, no narrative, that is, that might not resemble the kind of aggressive theories that she rejected. The Sciences of Man had reduced art to a statement, to sociological and historical documentation, and her formalist notion of the critical act was to no avail because it did not account for the failure in reciprocity between the speaking subject and the semiotic universe around her. Benjamin passed on to Sontag a viable narrative of the critical act, which, through the notion of the aura, steeped it in the notion of the answering gaze. After Benjamin, she could think of the work of art outside of the restricted realm of a purely theoretical aesthetics and from the wider perspective of reception, at the intersection of different disciplines and artistic media. Above all, he had established a tie between meaning and the gaze that felt closer to psychoanalytic views of subjectivity than to dialectical views of history, and, for this reason, touched the core from which her productivity flew, that is, the link between intellectual power and loss.

'What is aura, actually?'

Benjamin's genius depends on the idea of 'the anticipated reciprocity of the gaze' (Hansen 187). This central motif emerges only if we recognise his highly ambivalent attitude towards the aura. The destruction of the aura has been associated with equality and democracy, but this political closure of meaning, as Miriam Hansen has argued, obscures Benjamin's ambivalence towards a key concept of his work. In the writings of his middle and later period he 'actually tries to redeem an auratic mode of experience' (Hansen 186). As one of the terms in a fascinating dialectic of the gaze, the aura allows Benjamin to think of history as an unconscious dynamic beyond the dogmatic constraints of historical materialism.

In 'On Some Motifs in Baudelaire', Benjamin writes: 'The person we look at, or who feels he is being looked at, looks at us in return. To experience the aura of a phenomenon means to invest [*belehnen*] it with the capability of returning the gaze' ('Some Motifs' 188). The aura is a 'cognitive mode' that ties the expectation of an answering gaze to the retrieval of buried knowledge (Hansen 192–3); it aims at 'making the past look back at us' (194). While in Benjamin's work on Baudelaire this expectation is overshadowed by the historical experience of the loss of 'the ability to look' ('Some Motifs' 189), in his essay on photography, 'Little History of Photography' (1931), Benjamin invests the technological apparatus with the power to return the gaze. In conjunction with early photographs, he writes: 'There was an aura about them, a medium that lent fullness and security to their gaze even as it penetrated that medium' (515). The 'fullness and security' of the subject's gaze is the effect of technique and will soon decline, especially in later photography where people 'look out at the world in so excluded and godforsaken a manner', much as Kafka does in one of his childhood portraits (515). But piercing through the fog that surrounds early photography, Benjamin glimpses a generous apparatus that reciprocates in ways the Other might not.

Later in the essay Benjamin historicises the aura, which becomes a political vector: it refers to the subject's social standing, and its disappearance means the disappearance of the 'imperialist bourgeoisie' (517). Nevertheless, at this stage of the text the aura still alludes to the conceptually promising if undescribed correspondence between the photographed subject and technique. Benjamin's brief history of photography in the end disposes of the tie, but when he calls the world shown by photography the 'optical unconscious'

[*Optisch-Unbewussten*] (512), comparing it to the psychoanalytic unconscious, he is still pursuing the promise of a removed knowledge that might not necessarily make sense. Despite the disappearance of the tie, therefore, the history of photography becomes the history of the unsuccessful erasure, of a faded reciprocity: the gaze of the subject answered by the gaze of the apparatus. Its 'magical value' (510) depends on the power of the apparatus to assuage the dread of the direct human gaze of another. This is why, as Hansen writes, if technology 'epitomized in the very structure of the apparatus, the decline of the human capability to return the gaze' (Hansen 203), it also kept that capability alive. The history of photography is the history of the repression and insistence of 'the art of regarding' (Benjamin, 'Che cos'è l'aura?' 25).

In the middle of the essay on photography Benjamin stops to ask, once again, the question about the aura, as if discussion in the first part of the text could not suffice: 'What is aura actually?' (518). He replies: 'A strange weave of space and time'; 'the unique appearance [*Erscheinung*] of a distance' (518). His answer, this time, calls to mind the very process of interpretation, by which an aesthetic artefact is encountered after it has ruptured the shell of the meanings that have encased it in the past. Benjamin names the event of sense at a particular time and in a particular place. The 'strange weave of space and time' suggests a meaningfulness that can be reconstituted through the displacement of the object and its decontexualisation. This is why Benjamin defines the aura as 'the unique appearance of a distance' (518).

There follows an example taken from nature. It explains the aura in terms of the transitory moment of accord between beholder and object, when the nuances that make up the fruition/experience of the object become part of the object, as if to form a patina around it: 'While resting on a summer's noon, to trace a range of mountains on the horizon, or a branch that throws its shadow on the observer, until the moment or the hour become part of their appearance – that is what it means to breathe the aura of those mountains, that branch' (518–19). The fruition of the object in its immediacy can appear as a distance because the accord between the beholder and the object depends on a gaze that has taken in all the past layers of moments of accord. The aura tracks the disappearance and reappearance of the discursive worlds surrounding aesthetic objects. It evokes the 'patina of interpretation', the *zeitgeist* that changes with each generation (Praz qtd. in Wellek, *Storia* 358), but also affirms the discontinuity that inaugurates interpretation, the loss of evidence that it always requires (Gombrich 6–7).

In the natural setting, Benjamin extends a shadow connecting the tree to the beholder, as it were, as if to rhetorically extend the remotest trace of the answering gaze from the past, with its fullness and security, to the lived experience of the present. The next lines anticipate the famous passage that in the Art Work essay would describe the destruction of the aura: 'Now, to bring things *closer* to us, or rather to the masses, is just as passionate an inclination in our day as the overcoming of whatever is unique in every situation by means of its reproduction' ('Little History' 519). In the Art Work essay the passage is repeated almost word by word, but with a difference. The destruction of the aura, which in the Art Work essay is announced by the imperative 'need to possess the object in close range in the form of a picture, or rather a copy' (*Illuminations* 223), in 'Little History of Photography' affirms the *possibility* of interpretation. After photography, interpretation is the manifestation of the object – in a movement of externalisation – not an accrual of semiotic layers. Objects lie fixed and confined in a peripheral shell and a new interpretation cannot but amount to a prying of the object from its shell (*Illuminations* 223). Photography helps to free the object of its membrane of meanings; based on an almost tactile proximity of what stands before us, it replaces the expectation of an answering gaze with a renewed hermeneutic accord between the subject and what goes unnoticed, unremarked, forgotten.

Distance and proximity

Benjamin aims technology against history, working with the idea that we exist, in our symbolic and material essence, in the gaze of another, that we are born to the world only when another casts his or her gaze on us, when he or she returns our gaze. The history of a repression, photography is the negative of Hegel and Marx's history. The optical unconscious – this mythical modernity seemingly produced by the loss of the aura – is a visual field where the trace of the early possibility of regard is not lost. It excavates in the depth of history another order – the broken, intermittent order of restitution and of the reparative gaze – which cannot be reduced to a dialectical clash of forces.

Photography's optical unconscious counters history; more exactly, it counters history's capacity to sediment, like an eternal present, in the exchange of gazes. In the fragment 'What is aura?' (1937),[10] Benjamin links the concept of the aura clearly to removed layers of social affect.

The aura registers the impact of social conflict, of chronically hostile social relations in a hopelessly polarised world. He describes the historical phenomenon of the rigidification of the gaze:

> The one who is looked at or believes that he is looked at // raises his gaze // responds with a gaze. To experience the aura of a phenomenon or of a being is to realize his capacity for returning the gaze. This capacity is full of poetry. ('Che cos'è l'aura?' 25)

The social bond articulated through the gaze is both historical and 'full of poetry', lost in another time: 'When a man, an animal, or a thing raise their gaze to us . . .' 'When' suggests both the diachronic depth of history and the fleetingness of the moment, the insurgence of a now. The specular poetry of the gaze causes a continuous flat plane of history and affect to open before the mind's eye. The theoretical potential of the aura transforms the gaze: 'It ceases to resemble the gaze of the beloved who, under the gaze of her lover, raises her eyes, and rather begins to resemble the gaze that those who are despised return to those who despise them, the gaze that the oppressed return to those who oppress them' (25). At a certain point in this narrative of decay, history appears, but its rise marks the closure of any symbolic possibility apart from the most somatic, corporeal enactment: 'From this gaze every distance is erased' (25). The ossification of the conflict between scrutinised object and scrutinising subject becomes a 'disposition of the gaze' (25), and, as such, a mass phenomenon when class struggle intensifies. Benjamin's modernity depends on this perception. The ossification bans from sensibility the expectation of the gaze of another, it turns it into a forbidden practice, a prohibition. The history-laden exchange of gazes closes the space of symbolisation; the two poles of the materiality of history and of poetry coincide and the closure of their distance is experienced as blocked potential, as an arrested time of despair that transforms life itself: 'it is the gaze of those who have woken from any kind of dream', whether the nocturnal dream world of the unconscious or the daydreaming of reveries and unforeseen new ideas (25). Despair, however, is also the beginning of any real critical and imaginative pursuit. It throws open the doors of the world, precisely with the relocation of the thinker *in* the world: 'the alert eye does not lose the art of regarding when, in it, the dream dies' (24).

Benjamin seems to entwine historical knowledge, even though rigidified in the present of the evil gaze, with dreams and the unconscious, the domain of a language of transport that may not be so well understood or heard: the returning gaze 'dreams, it transports us in its dream' (25). But the reciprocity of the gaze (aura) exceeds even the psychoanalytic domain. Benjamin's observer is beyond the domain of dreams: he is 'the alert eye that does not lose the art of regard when, in that eye the dream is turned off' (25). The thinker begins here, in this dark night of illegibility, where the historical and psychoanalytic levels have withdrawn, where symbolic space closes except for the most somatic gestures (see the discouraging, enigmatic gestures in the essay on Naples) and the body finds itself divested of meaning. No longer a combat of forces, history means being covered in a gaze, and the evil effect of this desire. In this dense, visionary fragment, dream and history compenetrate to form a new opening: 'The aura is the appearance of a distance, no matter how close it is' (25).

Thus, the aura is destroyed, but it also persists and, persisting, it transforms intellectual experience. Photography is the negative of history. It meets the eye with empty spaces, shifting the divinatory power of the intellect on the side of the twilight of becoming and perishing, of a historical unconscious that speaks in the play of the gaze. Modernity is the climactic completion of history in the transition from the gaze of the beloved (returning the gaze of the lover) to closure and danger. When the dream dies, the gaze hardens into a perilous, evil scrutiny of non-equals mutually locked in dread. Only then does the 'alert' eye of the thinker have a chance. Benjamin casts inquiry into modernity in terms of this dread-bearing gaze. Although Sontag had not read this fragment, she shared with Benjamin the conviction that the critical act originates in a movement of proximity and distance in relation to a zone of illegibility and, ultimately, in the gaze as a locus of seduction and dread.

Differently from the moving image, photography encourages a type of absorption which underscores the promise of technology to counter the loss of the aura, that is to say, the loss of the reciprocating gaze.[11] In the still image, the 'here and now' with which reality 'has seared the subject' places centre-stage the contradictions of the aura ('Little History' 510). We might grasp Benjamin's aura through Kristeva's concept of 'the specular'. The specular is the place that 'absorbs primitive pulsional frayages, unsymbolized aggressivities' and transforms the drive into desire (Kristeva, 'Ellipsis' 240).[12] Flowing from unsymbolised aggressivities, the specular translates aggression into seduction: 'Once installed in the specular, seduced by the image that the father holds out, seduced consequently by "my" image, I seduce others: "I" can entice others by addressing the aggressive drive as a desiring appeal to them' (Kristeva, *Intimate Revolt* 72). Crucially, the specular indicates a repository of 'the earliest point of departure of the signs, narcissistic identifications, and phantasmatic trances of one identity speaking to another' (72). It helps explain what I mean when I locate the origin of the critical act in a zone of illegibility. Kristeva writes that the specular is also a point of departure for thought, for intellectual speculation: When 'facilitation and fear burst into view', the 'start of speculation becomes the fascinating specular' (72).

Encouraged by Benjamin, Sontag turned to photography as a fresh ground for inquiry. She was attracted to photography because it was more aphoristic than any post-philosophical writing could be; it was more fragmentary than any sequence of fragments and notes, more decontextualised than any decontexualised sign. *On Photography* opens under the sign of this freedom:

> Still, the book is not a wholly satisfactory scheme for putting groups of photographs into general circulation. The sequence in which the photographs are to be looked at is proposed by the order of pages, but nothing holds readers to the recommended order or indicates the amount of time to be spent on each photograph. (5)

Photography means photographs, that is to say, an eternally unfinished series of images. As such, it is an ideal depository of a different kind of intellectual speculation. Kristeva describes the specular in terms on an unfinished series of images: the specular 'flow[s] from frayages (rhythms, somatic waves, color frequencies) toward that impossible target where the eternally unfinished series of images is supposed to converge, a convergence which would finally constitute an "I" identical to itself' ('Ellipsis' 240). The I identical to itself is the I that, freed from the dyadic relation to the mother, recognises itself in the glance of another: '[f]rom that point on, the I would be able to attract others by addressing the (aggressive) drive toward them in the form of a (desiring) call' (240). Similarly, the infinite fragmented series of images separates Sontag's thinker from the dyadic embrace with thought, from the plenitude of meaning. In her shift towards photography, following Benjamin, she experiences thought and intellectual speculation – the capacity to think which she referred to as the capacity to move the world – as flowing from a mix of seduction and dread. This is what she meant when, in 'Under the Sign of Saturn', she called him a chronic *triste*, when she noticed that the stones of Marseilles were the bread of his imagination, and when she conjoined herself to him under the sign of Saturn.

The work of art: the event of undialectical surfaces

It is in Benjamin's Art Work essay that specular seduction is at work most explicitly. In fact, the essay itself may be considered as an example of 'thought-specular', a term by which Kristeva means the 'visible signs that designate fantasy and denounce it as such' (*Intimate Revolt* 73). It is information that 'no longer refers to the referent (object) but to the attitude of the subject vis-à-vis the object' (73). We need to concentrate less on the referent, the destruction of the aura and its definition by Benjamin, and more on Benjamin's attitude *vis-à-vis* that destruction. This means concentrating on the image that Benjamin chooses to describe the decay of the aura.

At the centre of the Art Work essay there is an event 'as much for thinking as for perception' (*Illuminations* 223):

> Namely, the desire of contemporary masses to bring things 'closer' spatially and humanly, which is just as ardent as their bent toward overcoming the uniqueness of every reality by accepting its reproduction. Every day the urge grows stronger to get hold of an object at very close range by way of its likeness, its reproduction. (223)

The image of the masses – their irresistible disposition 'to possess the object in close range in the form of a reproduction' – certainly has an argumentative function, but it is also a parodic sequel to the narrative of the gaze that Benjamin had presented in 'Little History of Photography'. The images amplify the disposition to overcome uniqueness to a mass instinct; reproduction becomes the urge for an intimacy with images – 'to get hold of an object at very close range', as if to remark emphatically on the disappearance of the returning gaze. The masses in the Art Work essay are the most concrete and vivid image of the event that, in the 1937 fragment 'What is aura?', would mark the closure of the space of symbolisation, and the subsequent rise of the thinker as observer in a zone of illegibility.

In 'Little History of Photography', Benjamin had lingered on the hermeneutic accord between observer and observed. Repeated in the Art Work essay (*Illuminations* 222), that accord is broken in favour of the urgency of tactile proximity to the reproduced image. Of course, this moment in the text is wholly functional to Benjamin's political argument about the revolutionary effect of the tabula rasa on old meanings in the age of standardisation. The fact remains that there is something theatrical in it. The masses are jubilant (their 'ardent' desire, their bent, the 'urge' that 'grows stronger'). They display not only the bliss of reproduction, but also, mixed with that, another kind of bliss at the closure of any distance between observer and observed, mind and the world, ultimately between materiality and abstraction. Therefore, Benjamin is not only describing the decay of the aura, he is also exhibiting this ambiguous bliss: he is objectifying and looking at it. He makes a point of showcasing the closure (and perhaps this explains the repetition, almost word for word, of the decay of the aura in 'Little History of Photography' and in section III of the Art Work essay). Since he is talking about an event in perception and thinking, Benjamin joins the masses in the event, as if the thinker were part of an affective milieu he cannot call himself out of. The crowd's ever-growing passion for reproduction – their ardent desire to hold images close – points to photography as that intellectually unoccupied territory that in 'Little History of Photography' Benjamin had called 'a lodging that has not yet found a new tenant' (519). The jubilation at empty spaces for the exertion of interpretation here glosses over the conflicting play of the gaze, which all along had accompanied the idea of the aura, and glosses over as well the realisation that the divinatory power of interpretation is intimately bound up with this conflict.

Now that the specular has turned into spectacle, the affect that binds the masses becomes almost like another gaze, the gaze of the Other, under whose parodic insistence the new idea surges. Benjamin's crowd and their gaze make perhaps for a more political version of the painted women under whose parodic gaze Freud, a few years before Benjamin (1919), lost on a sunny southern European piazza, found a new concept: the uncanny – the familiar unfamiliar.

Adorno perceived Benjamin's preference for expression over the concept, and faulted him by the standards of the dialectical method. He criticised his grand 'theory of reproduction' for being undialectical (*Aesthetic Theory* 72).[13] In fact, in Adorno's reading the image of the crowd moves to the foreground the cultic context, the community unified and cohered around totems. He concludes:

> The failure of Benjamin's grandly conceived theory of reproduction remains that its bipolar categories make it impossible to distinguish between a conception of art that is free of ideology to its core and the misuse of aesthetic rationality for mass exploitation and mass domination, a possibility he hardly touches upon. (73)

What is missing from Adorno's criticism is an appreciation of the theatrical and parodic quality of Benjamin's prose. The undialectical intimacy with reproduction, in Benjamin's essay, exhibits precisely the confusion of the two 'antagonistic demands of observation and interpretation' that are at the basis of dialectical mediation also called the 'double-edged method' (Adorno, *Minima Moralia* 74).

Observation becomes confused with interpretation, the space between annulled in the name of that porosity which Benjamin had discovered in the essay on Naples. What to Adorno seems undialectical may be understood as psychoanalytical. The image of the masses and their ardent desire for tactile proximity with photographic reproductions points to the realm of drives. Benjamin's image refers us to a level prior to the image, a place from which, as Kristeva writes, flow 'unnamable fears, sounds . . . pulsations, somatic waves, waves of colors, rhythms, tones' (*Intimate Revolt* 72). The image of collective bliss is therefore the specular itself, the repository where aggression is transformed into seduction. The Art Work is not just an essay, but the shelter of a different intellectual speculation, which Adorno called Benjamin's 'grand theory'. It does preserve the open secret of theorising, the infectious joy of productivity, in front of the world.

Benjamin hints at the work of the specular in a letter to his friend Gershom Scholem, which he sent while he was writing the Art Work essay. In the letter, he speaks of his reflections on the work of art in terms of a pure intimacy, of which he is jealous and which he wants to keep secret: 'Ich halte sie sehr geheim, weil sie zum Diebstahl unvergleichlich besser als die meisten meiner Gedanken geeignet.' [I am keeping these reflections very secret, because they are incomparably better suited to theft than most of my ideas.][14] The aura is not in itself the secret, but it seals the place of the secret, where intellectual speculation starts by intercepting the locus of the unsymbolised. This locus in Benjamin is the empty lodging of photography, occupied, that is, only by phantoms that elude and vanish the moment we reach for them, where the self-identical I of the critical theorist is deferred, where theoretical construction is aggression turned into seduction.

Given to us while they hold reproductions close, captured in their incapacity for distance (the distance of abstraction), the masses help plant a mix of terror and seduction in the regime of the copy. The prominent seduction of the image, where aggression is transformed into desire, protects the secret of which Benjamin is jealous: the secret of productivity itself, the secret of the thinker enclosed in the erotic membrane of thought. Under the paternal eye of the masses, Benjamin's critical theorist is seduced by his image and can consequently 'entice others by addressing the aggressive drive' as his desiring call to his readers (Kristeva, *Intimate Revolt* 72).

It is on to this scene that Sontag arrives as she moves towards Benjamin.

Beginner

Photography emanates all the ambiguity of Benjamin's concept of the aura. Like the specular place from which Benjamin's aura issues, Sontag's notion of photography is aggressive and seductive; like the aura, it is reparative and destructive:

> Images which idealize (like most fashion and animal photography) are no less aggressive than work which makes a virtues of plainness (like class pictures, still lifes of the bleaker sort, and mug shots). There is an aggression implicit in every use of the camera. (*On Photography* 7)

Like Barthes, Sontag thought that photography and death commingle like no other art (Barthes 32–3), but when she calls photography a 'death mask' (*On Photography* 154) it is to indicate less a concept than an attitude. Her notion of photography is the depository of the conflicting desires she lists in 'Fragments of an Aesthetic of Melancholy':

> The desire to dissolve the self into the world; the desire to reduce the world to matter, something one can inscribe oneself on, sink into, be saturated with . . . The desire to compete with one's own image, to become image; artifact; art; form . . . (6)

The list goes on:

> The desire to become fully visible, to be seen (at last) as one is; to be honest; to be unmasked.
>
> The desire to hide, to be camouflaged. To be elsewhere. Other. The desire to impersonate someone else, but that is not other enough. The desire to escape from a merely human appearance: to be animal, not a person, an object (stone? wood? metal? cloth?), not a person; to be done with personhood. . .
>
> The desire to be emblematic. Impervious to age and the distress of flesh.
>
> The desire to accede to the ruins of time, to be reconciled with the depredations of time; to *become* a ruin. (6)

Thinking is infinitely fragmented in the play of two poles, two conflicting gazes: on the one hand, the see-er, corresponding to the thinker, on the other hand, the see-ee in the position of the looked at, of form. This is why in 'Fragments of an Aesthetic of Melancholy' Sontag's list results in the seemingly incomprehensible oscillation between the desire to inscribe oneself on the world and the desire to be image, artefact, form. She calls the first gaze the gaze of the 'professional see-er'; it enters into conflict with a second gaze, the gaze of the 'amateurish see-ee' ('Certain Mapplethorpes' 234). The first gaze corresponds to the thinker she had created, fashioned herself to be: 'and it is my fantasy, and my privilege, perhaps my professional bias, to feel that the world awaits my seeing' (233). The word 'fantasy' here is synonymous of a poiesis of the self, while the word 'seeing' condenses her experimental post-philosophical turn towards art and the image. This gaze corresponds to the vigilant consciousness, to the head and the I in control of the mental station. The second gaze is brought into the arena of contemplation and reflection by the fear triggered by a photographic session, a fear, she remarks, that remains inexplicable for someone who has spent five years writing about photography and is a photographed celebrity (233).

The fear is triggered by the inequality of positions between observer and observed. The 'photographer's look is looking in a pure state'; it is a gaze that wants her (to be) as an image: 'it desires what I am not – an image' (234). She cannot respond in kind 'unless I were to decide to be photographed with my head behind my own camera' (233). As in the essay on Cioran, the author at hand, in this case the photographer Robert Mapplethorpe, becomes a pretext to overview the state of a field of knowledge – photography – but also her choice of photography as an object of inquiry:

> When I am photographed, this normally outgoing, fervent relation of consciousness is jammed. I yield to another command station of consciousness, which 'faces' me, if I have agreed to cooperate with the photographer . . . Stowed away, berthed, brought to heel, my consciousness has abdicated its normal function, which is to provide amplitude, to give me mobility. I don't feel threatened. But I do feel disarmed, my consciousness reduced to an embarrassed knot. (233)

A double-sided art of reflection and fear, photography is keyed into a place where the unthought takes over and consciousness is diminished; it is linked to a place where thought flows from the work of fantasies, what Sontag herself, in an early essay, had called 'a substratum of hidden thoughts and feelings' ('Nathalie Sarraute' 106). She made the same point but in a slightly different way when, in *Regarding the Pain of Others*, she wrote: 'Narratives can make us understand. Photographs do something else: they haunt us' (89).

In the Mapplethorpe essay Sontag comes close to holding up and analysing the place from which her thought flows when it pauses on topics like photography and reproduction. Significantly, the essay opens with the question of technological reproduction – her photograph as an 'image-replica' – which she connects to the fear of being robbed of something (233). In choosing these topics, in courting them, thought unfolds as a clash between faculties: thinking and seeing, seeing and interpretation. In the Cesare Pavese essay, 'The Artist as Exemplary Sufferer', she had welcomed the difficulty or hardship that must be central to the modernist artist. Now we can see that, as a site of productivity, modernist hardship is not so different from post-philosophical fragmentation, which seems to reduce thinking to 'passionateness', to the interminable pursuit of evanescent moods.[15] Hence her insistence on calling herself a beginner, an amateur:

> I'm a fierce learner . . . I feel I'm in flight from the books, and the twaddle they generate. Sometimes the momentum is more pleasurable. I enjoy beginning again. The beginner's mind is best.
>
> It's the beginner's mind I embrace and permit myself now, when I am very far from a beginner writer. ('Singleness' 260)

Totems

Sontag remarks on the distance that separates her from Benjamin's time and does not ignore the historical changes. After Benjamin, one ought to acknowledge that technological reproduction 'has its history – rather, is inserted into history'. Contrary to what Benjamin thought, its 'artifacts become "historical," not merely contemporary'.[16] Technological reproduction cannot 'make everything into an eternal present'; it cannot abolish history.[17]

Sontag outlines the changes in *Regarding the Pain of Others*. Here, she is concerned with the effect of the proximity of images, indeed with what seems a definitive closure of the space from which critical thought flows. No longer an opening towards the locus of the unsymbolised, photography appears restrictive, inadequate, repressive in fact: it no longer leans towards the hidden substratum of history but decides what history is by a process of severe abridgement that wipes out the memory and therefore the symbolisation of significant events:

> The familiarity of certain photographs builds our sense of the present and immediate past. Photographs lay down routes of reference, and serve as totems of causes: sentiment is more likely to crystallize around a photograph than around a verbal slogan. And photographs

> help construct – and revise – our sense of a more distant past, with the posthumous shock engineered by the circulation of hitherto unknown photographs. Photographs that everyone recognizes are now a constituent part of what a society chooses to think about, or declares that it has chosen to think about. (*Regarding* 85)

Echoing the 'phantasmatic poverty' and the 'inability to judge' that Kristeva denounces in the society of the spectacle (*Intimate Revolt* 68), Sontag presents photography as a homogeneous surface – a *doxa*. In *Regarding the Pain of Others*, modernity, from Wordsworth to our time, forms an arc of moral torpor. But the fact that she notices our inability to transform being affected into moral action does not mean that she condemns photography. Quite the contrary, she revives its power by insisting on a reality that cannot be eroded by images, that indeed awaits to be intercepted:

> The view I proposed in *On Photography* – that our capacity to respond to our experiences with emotional freshness and ethical pertinence is being sapped by the relentless diffusion of vulgar and appalling images – might be called the conservative critique of the diffusion of such images.
>
> I call this argument conservative because it is the sense of reality that is eroded. There is still a reality that exists independent of the attempts to weaken its authority. The argument is in fact a defense of reality and the imperiled standards for responding more fully to it. (*Regarding* 109)

Images are necessary. They are the allies of literature and art in preserving the scene of hardship from which 'real thinking' flows.[18] The impoverishment of fantasies, says Kristeva, 'threatens to abolish inner depth itself, this camera obscura that has constituted the psychical life of the living being for millennia' (*Intimate Revolt* 68). For Sontag, the impoverishment of the space of thought, reduced to stipulation and triggered by visual totems, comes with a loss of history.

History and the maze

The divergence of critical thought and history became an important concern for Sontag in the 1990s. She devoted to it her novel *The Volcano Lover*, which she saw as her most satisfying book, the emblem of her intellectual pilgrimage ('Singleness' 260). The emphasis on beauty and collecting, the setting in the distant past at the time of the Neapolitan Revolution, the theme of the public intellectual divided between ideas and historical change all point to the fact that Sontag chose fiction because it gave her more freedom to continue the meditation on the work of art, reproduction and the legacy of Benjamin. The novel has been rightly seen as an allegorical portrait of Benjamin (Peucker). Benjamin is present in the protagonist, the Cavaliere, a collector who, in seeing 'reality as things', translates Benjamin's baroque and surrealist imagination (Sontag, 'Under the Sign of Saturn' 120). But the novel is especially informed by Benjamin's aphoristic mind, by his experimental position in the landscape of the city, by his pursuit of a critical theory of illuminations that aims at altering the order of history. Benjamin's theory is very much the *donnée* of the novel, which can be read as a phantasmagoric alternative 'essay', a historical fable about the reconstruction of the past in terms of thought's eternally present demand to become action.

In a remarkable fragment of the *Passages*, Benjamin tropes the sidewalks of Paris as the lava of Naples:

> As a social formation, Paris is a counterimage to that which Vesuvius is as a geographic one: A threatening mass, an ever-active June of the Revolution. But just as the slopes of Vesuvius, thanks to the layers of lava covering them, have become a paradisiacal orchard, so here, out of the lava of the Revolution, there bloom art, fashion, and festive existence as nowhere else. (qtd. in Buck-Morss 66)

Paris and Naples exert the same seduction that is typical of the volcanic landscape. *The Volcano Lover* takes its cue from Benjamin's troping to rewrite the fundamental hunger for sameness that prompted him to celebrate the copy. His hunger, as we have seen in the discussion above, is inseparable from the mix of seduction and dread wherefrom flows intellectual speculation. For this reason, it is also inseparable from a tension between affinity and difference, between the dyadic embrace of self-identical plenitude, on the one hand, and the evil gaze of historical depth, on the other. Sontag's way of putting it was to quote, in 'Under the Sign of Saturn', Benjamin on Marseilles: 'These stones were the bread of my imagination' (121). She remarks, in Benjamin's own terms, on his experimental philosophical position, and, indirectly, on the site of hardship and conflict through which Sontag herself experienced the capacity to think. *The Volcano Lover* is the outcome of her listening for the profound tension which in the Art Work essay Benjamin had spectacularly resolved with the undialectical surface of the jubilant masses.

In the passage quoted above, the sediments of culture, the irresistible propulsion forward towards sociality, art, fashion of Paris's volcanic landscape, recall the 'tremendous shattering of tradition' brought on by the technique of reproduction in the Art Work essay (*Illuminations* 221). Paris's negative capability distils rags, poverty, even the nuances of grey and bad weather into art, as proven by the poetry of Baudelaire, while making the beholder feel, as Benjamin put it in an hashish-induced illumination, like an 'enraptured prose-being [. . .] in the highest power' [*geniessende Prosawesen hochster Potenz*] ('Hashish in Marseilles' 220). For Benjamin, these slopes are a maze: they evoke the bliss of the thinking-writing continuum, the joy of productivity which began with 'the mere act of unwinding a ball of thread' (220). But at the core of Benjamin's fragment, the 'dangerous, threatening mass', interrupts the blissful continuum. The image of the mass evokes the troubling conjoining of violence and the forward movement of history, pointing to the tension between thought and history. It is this tension that Sontag plays up in *The Volcano Lover*.

The novel is set at the time of the Neapolitan Revolution of 1799. In comparison to its French counterpart, the Neapolitan Revolution was rather short-lived; it merely brought to the fore the problem of an illiterate mass chained to material poverty and impervious to ideas, language and symbolisation. If understood as a social, rather than a geological, referent, as history rather than 'fossil' (Buck-Morss 66), the Vesuvius of Naples brings Benjamin's critical trajectory to a halt. In Sontag's novel the nuances of Paris and Naples are not the same. What keeps them separate is precisely Sontag's experiment here – to craft a novel in which human agency is planted in the struggle of history. The possibility of revolution, which delivered Benjamin's imagination to 'the rhythmical bliss' ('Hashish in Marseilles' 220) of prose productivity, in Sontag is undermined by a threatening mass before which imagination stops, discouraged.

The novel's protagonist, the Cavaliere, is a reader and collector ostensibly modelled on Lord William Hamilton, a British diplomat at the Neapolitan court of King Ferdinand and his wife, Maria Carolina of Austria, at a time when Jacobin sympathies were spreading to southern Italy. He shares Benjamin's sensibility, attracted as he is to minor and blemished objects: he knows how to recognise 'something unappreciated, neglected, forgotten' (*Volcano* 71). Like Benjamin, he 'liked finding things where nobody was looking' ('Under the Sign of Saturn' 121). Like Benjamin, he is a pioneer: he 'starts to collect it, or to write about it, or both. Because of these proselytising efforts, what no one paid attention to or liked many now find interesting or admirable' (*Volcano* 71). In the prismatic figure of the Cavaliere, the collector, the photographer, the reader, the tastemaker are all intertwined, as is also Sontag, the writer and intellectual. The Cavaliere is an aesthete in multiplicity: 'there are so many objects' (231). He enjoys the spectacle of diversity but elevates himself above the vulgarity of indiscriminate acquisitiveness. His detachment and his scepticism enable him to rank and evaluate, to judge. He is a figure for the critic, sharing with him a 'fastidious' (222) temperament and an authority that 'lies in his ability to say: no – not that' (222).

Just as the Cavaliere evokes Benjamin, and just as in this evocation Sontag includes herself, he is also a degenerated version of Benjamin's collector and Sontag's vehicle of self-critique. In this fable, she continues the work of *Under the Sign of Saturn*: in a different genre, she continues to write about those who thought against themselves; she continues to insert herself into that tradition. The Cavaliere is seduced by images of crafty perfection and physical beauty. With him, collecting is reduced to an appetite of the eye; it parallels thinking as a style of 'possessing', something that Sontag longed to avoid:[19] 'Correggio's art. And Venus's groin. You can really possess – even only for a little while' (*Volcano* 71). The avid, promiscuous gaze, which Sontag knew to belong both to the photographer and to the collector, and in which she and Benjamin as theorists of photography participated, prevails in the Cavaliere: 'There are so many objects. No single one is that important. There is no such thing as a monogamous collector. Sight is a promiscuous sense. The avid gaze always wants more' (71). As a decayed version of Benjamin's (and Sontag's) beholder, the Cavaliere stands for an autonomous appetite that ends up being divorced from critical thought.

For most of the novel, the spotlight on the Cavaliere, who uses beautiful objects against history and its violent chronology, prevents us from seeing other scenes that remain in the shadows. Her masterful knowledge of the theatre guides Sontag to turn the lights at the novel's end on those marginal scenes. At that point, the appearance of Eleonora de Fonseca Pimentel induces a sudden awakening.

Fonseca was one of the protagonists of the short-lived Neapolitan Revolution. She wrote, directed and published the newspaper of the Republic, *II Monitore Napoletano*. Her concern was to change the minds and hearts of the destitute bent by need. She was sentenced to be hanged in Piazza Mercato on 20 August 1799, on the same day as her best friend Gennaro Serra di Cassano. The same people for whom she wanted a life of the mind cheered vulgarly at her death.[20]

As she makes her appearance, Sir William Hamilton withers to '[a]n upper class dilettante enjoying the many opportunities afforded in a poor and corrupt and interesting country to pilfer the art and make a living out of it' (*Volcano* 418). She asks: 'Did he ever have an original thought, or subject himself to the discipline of writing a poem, or discover or invent something useful to humanity, or burn with zeal for anything except his own pleasures and the privileges annexed to his station?' (418). When compared with this woman's genuine convictions, the Cavaliere pales to an aesthete, the symbol of a critical thought too caught up in a reflexivity that verges on solipsistic theatricality (his ultimate aim is 'to get himself known as a connoisseur', 418). Instead, Fonseca, a Neapolitan of Portuguese descent, values the mind as it awakens from torpor. She equates writing with the capacity 'to change hearts and minds' (417). She wants 'to be pure flame' (417). She challenges what in *Regarding the Pain of Others* Sontag called a thinking reduced to stipulating, assisted by images of 'collective instruction' (*Regarding* 85).

In the conflict between the critical alternatives represented by the Cavaliere and Fonseca, Sontag produces a powerful allegory of the present. In her allegory, Sontag, the woman of letters, and Benjamin, the collector, engage in a fictionalised skirmish around important questions about the relation between aesthetics, thought and action. How can an aesthetic subject also be a critical subject? Can thought walk the path of critique, which is the path of negativity, without imploding in melancholic incorporation? Must the critical theorist become, like Benjamin, a chronic *triste*? Can critique, which is versed in the undoing of established ideas (and, for this reason, exposed to the risk of utter inwardness and self-reflexivity), deliver itself to the capacity for belief? What does it mean in post-philosophical (and post-ideological and post-historicist) times to become attached to ideas, to believe in an idea? These questions would not be there without the monologue of Fonseca. The book's close reads like an essay by itself, in Sontag's favoured dramaturgical mode.

Like the author of *Regarding the Pain of Others*, Fonseca looks at the social map and sees, on the one hand, a circle of privilege, and on the other those 'whom birth or revolt have cast outside' (*Volcano* 418). Like her author, she thinks the vista is 'disgraceful', suggesting that social justice is also a matter of aesthetics, of taste. But Fonseca is not interested in aesthetic distance; she cares about how ideas rise and spread: 'I do not think I was wrong to consider education the most imperative task. What is a revolution if it does not change hearts and minds?' (418). Her tragic destiny makes her choose between history and the nuances of thought. That the cruel opposition cannot be overlooked – not even in Benjamin's refined tradition – becomes clear when we realise that Sontag's heroine feeds on the contradictions implicit in Benjamin's essay on Naples.

Fonseca's faith in the receptivity of Naples' *popolaccio* to the faculties of thinking and feeling contrasts with Benjamin's ambivalence towards the southern European city. In his essay on Naples, co-authored with Asja Lacis, Benjamin bends the city to the exigencies of the materialist dialectician educated by photography. Naples attracts and repels. At first, everything is 'dispersed, porous, and commingled' (Benjamin and Lacis 419). Porous like the stone on which it is built, Naples can make the same aesthetic promises as Paris. For example, it can promise a knowledge that comes in flashes, correspondences between the shape of things and enrapturing intellectual affections, first and foremost incompleteness and fragmentation: 'For nothing is concluded' (416). Its architecture enables the alert eye to discern a new erosion of boundaries between public and private (419), sacred and profane (416). However, if in the case of other cities the spatial proximity of things assists in the mental transit from images to critical speech, Naples resists the passage. It somehow remains unlovable. Its masses, in particular, resist the modern porosity that the city architecture yields to the mind of the observer. Intensely conscious of the supreme theatricality of life, the city's inhabitants seem to exist solely for the camera: 'Even the most wretched pauper is sovereign in the dim, dual awareness of participating, in all his destitution, in one of the pictures of Neapolitan street life that will never return' (417). If not contained by the reverie of the political gaze, this extreme theatricality turns the city into a vista of 'epistemological despair' (Buck-Morss 54).

The essay closes on such a note, consigning us an international *flâneur* suffocated by the 'impenetrable' correspondences of gestures and touch, 'hopelessly lost' in a space before prose and the critical faculty, where both wane (Benjamin and Lacis 421). In *The Volcano Lover*, Sontag elaborates on Benjamin's ambivalent treatment of Naples. Setting the novel in the past affords her the necessary distance from a theoretical present concentrated on the critique of the subject and on its deconstruction. The entrance of Fonseca enables her not only to turn the spotlight on the question of agency but also to suggest how the long arc of thought uniting critical theory to later theory can easily vacillate in the face of history. Sontag, who had always refused to be associated with feminism, gives us in *The Volcano Lover* one of her most feminist works.[21] The public intellectual of the present speaks through the mask of Fonseca, the Enlightenment woman of letters, who is made to represent all those who have not been delivered by thought from the fetters of history, including the author of the novel:

> For all my certitude, I feared I would never be strong enough to understand what would allow me to protect myself. Sometimes I had to forget that I was a woman to accomplish the best of which I was capable. Or I would lie to myself about how complicated it is to be a woman. Thus do all women, including the author of this book. (*Volcano* 419)

Critical thought can create us; history remains less friendly. It can strip us of our symbolic garments in the blink of an eye.

Continuing Benjamin's discourse, Sontag touches on the still-unsolved problem of the link between theory and history at a safe distance from a present that would rather dispose of the problem as a modernist ruin. At the time of *Regarding the Pain of Others*, the volcanic slopes of New York had never been closer to Fonseca's Naples. Her point, however, is not a sterile polemic against poststructuralist theory and its deconstruction of all dichotomies radiating from the primary philosophic dichotomy of mind and body: essence and substance, voice and writing, original and copy, being and seeming. Rather she includes herself in that turn of the critical mind but in the deflective style of the amateur, of '(literature's) servant'.

In another novel, *In America* (2001), the theorist reappears in the guise of the performer, whose ultimate role is that of Hamlet. Shakespearean actor Edwin Booth says:

> [Hamlet] does know 'seems.' He knows nothing else. That's his problem. Hamlet would give anything, anything, not to be an actor! He is waiting to break through seeming and performing, and just be, but there is nothing on the other side of seeming, Marina. Except death. (*In America* 373–4)

The comment applies to Sontag, for whom the name of Benjamin is synonymous with a wide tradition of theory (which would include Lacan's *désêtre* and Butler's performativity) which combines negativity (the undoing of the power that social meanings exert on us) with the destitution of social meanings as symbolic semblances and poses. For Sontag, the problem is that the critical act, so conceived, is made inoperative by that impoverishment of the attitude towards images which she denounces in *Regarding the Pain of Others*.

We might now begin to understand the bliss that Sontag celebrates in her essay on Hodgkin. Now that essay appears as the perfect companion piece to *Regarding the Pain of Others*. The painter's slow art provides relief from the battlefield that photography has become in its totemic abridgement of history. She praises the fact that the artist shuns the maniacal registering of the seen: he 'doesn't sketch, doesn't take photographs, doesn't do anything obvious to commit to memory the scene or an interior or a view or a face – instead trusting what will happen when the sight of something has burrowed itself deep down in memory, when it has accumulated emotional and pictorial gravity' ('About Hodgkin' 158). He is not impatient to put his images out there: 'He labors over them as if painting could still be a vehicle of self-transcendence' (160). The painter's labour recalls Barthes' taxonomy of jubilation (Sontag, 'Remembering Barthes' 170) minus the self-absorption. Hodgkin's qualities provide a counterpoint to a certain collective formalistic rigidity. Our use of images to perform rites of collective assent endangers our capacity to think: it reduces thinking to crystallisations of predictable ideas; it severs us from the possibility of the new; it represses the joy of unforeseen thoughts.

Chapter 7

Interlocution

> Even if it communicates nothing, the discourse represents the existence of communication; even if it denies the evidence, it affirms that speech constitutes truth; even if it is intended to deceive, the discourse speculates on faith in testimony.
>
> Jacques Lacan, 'Function and Field of Speech and Language'

The facts in the archive

Sontag became aware of Benjamin's work in the early 1960s. The first mention of his name occurs in a thin spiral notebook dated on the cover September 1963. Inside, however, the entries show abrupt chronological leaps from 1963 to March 1965; the entries continue to April 1965, then jump back to 1964. Tucked between a cluster of pages dated 1964 and an entry for April 1965 is the first reference to Benjamin. We find his name written next to ideas from *The Antiquiertheit des Menschen* (1957) by philosopher Günther Anders. The fragment expands on 'the technique of reproduction', on 'a spectral and mortuary cosmos' superimposed on the world by mass culture and by the vanishing of 'the aura surrounding things', which has caused men to shift to blindness and passive reception.[1] The chronological leaps suggest that Sontag, who often used her journals as notebooks to try out ideas or interests she would develop in her published essays, might have gone back in 1964 and 1965 to the notebook begun in September 1963 to fill the remaining blank pages with new entries. Similarly, she might have gone back to the ideas of Anders and added the name of Benjamin and marked the passage as meaningful, with an asterisk, at a later stage, as she gained a firsthand knowledge of his oeuvre and began to engage with him more systematically.

In a notebook dated 1964, Sontag takes notes on Benjamin, cinema and the abolition of tradition.[2] The notebook, however, also contains notes from 1962. In this notebook we encounter a Benjamin page in which she lists a bibliography of his work taken from the French edition of his selected writings, *Oeuvres Choisies*, translated from the German by Maurice De Gandillac (1959). At the top of the page, she reminds herself to read the two works that Benjamin had published in 1928, 'One-Way Street' and the book on 'Baroque Drama'.

We can therefore assume that, while Sontag became aware of Benjamin's work between 1962 and 1964, she may have begun to read him systematically only in 1964. In any case, Benjamin seems already to be there in the extensive rewriting of her essay on Lévi-Strauss, 'The Anthropologist as Hero' (1963). Moreover, he must have been in the back of her mind as she completed 'Notes on "Camp"', which appeared in 1964 in the autumn issue of *Partisan Review*, and while she was thinking about the Frankfurt School and planning to write on Adorno and the Marxist thinker György Lukács.

In fact, at first she appraised Benjamin comparatively, within the early Frankfurt School tradition and next to Lukács. In the postscript to her essay on Lukács (1965) she complains that the critics who descend from Hegel and Marx have not been willing to admit that art is autonomous. She finds Benjamin guilty, too:

> Even the extraordinary Walter Benjamin, who wrote with equal brilliance on Goethe, Leskov, Baudelaire (but not, be it noted, on any 20th century writers) succumbed to this bias. The cinema, the only wholly new major art form of our century, was singularly misunderstood and unappreciated by Benjamin. ('Literary Criticism of Georg Lukács' 91)

At this early stage, Sontag took her distance both from 'strongly apolitical aestheticians' like McLuhan and from Marxist ideology. Despite her admiration for Benjamin, whose work, at this point, she still knew only partially, she navigated the world of ideas with one compass: a fidelity to modernism and its tenet of the autonomy of art. Against Lukács, she concludes:

> Only when the historicist critics (and all their progeny) are able to accommodate into their views a large measure of devotion to works of art, as above all, works of art (rather than as sociological, cultural, moral, or political documents) will they be open to more than a few of the many great works of art which are of the 20th century, and will they develop – this is mandatory for any serious critic today – an intelligent involvement with the problems and objectives of 'modernism' in the arts. (92)

Benjamin belongs to a specific constellation of influences that, apart from Adorno, includes Paul Thek and Jasper Johns, and the combines of Robert Rauschenberg. This constellation, together with the incredible range of material that Sontag read, forms the backdrop of her search for a new sensibility which seemed to elude her more prestigious colleagues. She wrote in her journals: 'How revealing to meet [Richard] Eberhart, [Paul] Tillich, Dwight MacDonald, Mary McCarthy!'[3] When she finally met the most prominent public intellectuals of her time, she was disappointed: 'The word on the page may not reveal (may conceal) the flabbiness of the mind that conceived it. All thoughts are upgraded – get more clarity, definition, authority, by being in print – that is, detached from the person who thinks them.'[4] She realised that she was on a quest for a thought that felt less like a 'potential fraud'.[5] She used the term 'sensibility' to indicate an order of things that escaped her teachers and peers. She turned to literary criticism because in that realm she saw the potential to assess the phenomenon of modernism in a new way, especially its effects on the critical act. The question of being open to modernism – and the task of criticism in its wake – had been there since her collaboration with Thek, but it became even more central as she wove her impressions of the New York School experiments with her critical theory readings.

Between 1964 and 1965, as she read Benjamin and connected his ideas with those of others (hence his name added next to the Anders quote from April 1965), the journal entries record a frenzy of activity. The role of the intellectual (Gramsci), American experimental art (Rauschenberg and Johns), film, popular culture: multiple, potential strands of inquiry emerge, which must have seemed interwoven, even though she did as yet not know how.

Thinking as remembering

One moment stands out, the entry for 3 September 1964, for our understanding of the tie between Sontag and Benjamin. The entry consists of Sontag's notes after seeing *The Devil is a Woman*, the 1935 movie directed by Robert von Sternberg, with Marlene Dietrich. She is struck by the production: 'Dietrich is "mounted" inside her costumes, her huge hats – behind the confetti, the streamers, the doves, the grilles, the rain . . . Décor is "surcharge," both beautiful and parodic.'[6] The image validates her personal insight into what seems a new cognitive framework: the spiritual encased in the material.

It accompanies her efforts to break away from the prevailing abstraction of philosophical thought. While she shared these efforts with Frankfurt School critical theory, she also departed from it. The dialectic of Enlightenment assumed a uniform rationality that encases, that is oppresses, the world, enforcing domination (Jarvis 22). But the structure of encasement that strikes Sontag is less dialectical and more parodic: it amplifies the material and its seductive spectacle. The fast, phantasmagoric style of enumeration and accumulation of 'Notes on "Camp"' is further from Adorno's 'immanent critique of the most advanced forms of logic and epistemology' (Jarvis 12), and closer to Benjamin's 'philological attitude' (Adorno and Benjamin 291).[7] Like Benjamin before her, she becomes interested in the spell cast on the observer by a world 'confined to the "objective"', as she writes in the same notebook that contains both the entry on Dietrich and her reading list of Benjamin books.[8] The entry is important because it captures Sontag in the position of the thinker fascinated by a duplicitous materiality that both imprisons and reveals, with the result that meaning remains in excess, ignored and asyntactical.[9]

It is after the Dietrich entry that she reminds herself to read Benjamin's 'One-Way Street' and his book on 'Baroque Drama', and drafts a bibliography of his work.[10] Prefiguring Benjamin's notion of the ruin and of baroque allegory, the Dietrich entry marks Sontag's first moment of identification. Even before she had become fully aware of his theory of interpretation, her own sense of the spectacle of a surcharged material reality prepared her to appreciate Benjamin's dissident magical sampling of materiality.[11] Like him, she lingered in that region where the spell cast by the spectacle of the material is not yet thinking but promises exceptional writing, the joy of productivity which begins when you know that you are an Ariadne lost in the maze, unrolling a ball of thread. The distance between philosophy (the moment of theoretical construction) and language (the sampling of material reality) was for Benjamin 'an antagonism of which I would not wish to be relieved not even in my dreams' (Adorno and Benjamin 291). Before she knew his work well, Sontag discovered herself to be jealous of a similar antagonism. As we have seen, she, too, oscillated between mind and world. The antagonism was for her a matter of life, 'like breathing in and breathing/ out, systole and diastole'.[12] Benjamin courted philosophical danger, tarrying before that material facticity which in Sontag's Dietrich entry and in the essay on camp manifests as a parodic spectacle deferring theoretical construction. The fragmentation of the essay format into notes further underscores the deferral. By the time Sontag did read his theory of baroque allegory, she must have felt that reading Benjamin was like remembering her own insight.

Promesse du bonheur

Images help to track the shifts in what societies consider to be meaningful. They leads us to the mental structures through which we establish meaning and can assist in conceptualising those structures, even in transforming them. The structure of encasement that captured Sontag's attention resonates with Benjamin's allegorical landscape of stiffened signs (ruins). The echo of his theory of interpretation only steered her further towards the work of the image. Unlike the moving image, which yields meaning through shock and distraction, photography encourages absorption. It is, therefore, imaginatively closer to a landscape of floating signifiers cut off from hermeneutic meaning. The lost evidence of meaning can only be enlivened by the iconologist-interpreter.

But what is photography? *On Photography* does speak about the photographer and the use of the camera, but Sontag's interest is primarily the artistic importance of photography.[13] Photography alters linear chronology and the sense of the passage of time. We have seen that Sontag's photography makes the aesthetic promise of modernist abstraction and concomitantly renews the philosophical promise of negativity to project an order behind the historical level. We have also seen that photography functions as the compelling repository of unsymbolised ideas and unforeseen thoughts, of, in Wilfred Bion's formulation, unthought thought. In the post-philosophical scenario of broken discourse, photography made the philosopher's yearning for truth still possible, on condition of not usurping the work of art.

First perceived in contrast to modernism, incapable, like Lukács, of fully appreciating its consequences for critical theory, Benjamin ends up facilitating Sontag's fidelity to the autonomy of art. From the distance of time and generations, he lent significance to the link between knowledge and bliss, to a critical thought that would practise an unprecedented proximity to the artwork without usurping it (the argument of Derrida in his reading of Heidegger's reading of the pair of boots painted by Vincent Van Gogh) ('Restitutions'). From the distance of time and generations, Benjamin became the Other she wrote with, one who is and is not there, the imaginary master whose disciple she was.[14] Adorno wrote that art is the 'critique of praxis as the rule of brutal self-preservation at the heart of the status quo and in its service', adding that it 'opts for a form of praxis beyond the spell of labor' (*Aesthetic Theory* 14). Sontag agreed with Adorno's defence of negativity, that is to say, of art's potential to be 'the social antithesis to society' (14), but felt that Benjamin's astonishment was actually closer to '[a]rt's *promesse du bonheur*' (15).

The concept of photography incorporates the negative, antisocial and utopian potential of modernist aesthetics. As such, it becomes the repository of fundamental unsymbolised aggression which critical theory transforms into seductive reflection once it is aimed at the knot of power and knowledge: 'To photograph is to appropriate the thing photographed. It means putting oneself into a certain relation to the world that feels like knowledge – and therefore, like power' (Sontag, *On Photography* 4). Transferred from Benjamin's Art Work essay to Sontag's reflections on photography, the ever-growing need to bring images close shows up as the urgent need to appropriate the world. In fact, photography divides the world into parts 'that anyone can make or acquire' (4). Sontag does begin by speaking of the photographer and of his use of the apparatus, but soon enough the photographer's ambition to reduce the world to so many mental objects parallels the ethical dilemma of the critical theorist. The critical theorist, much like the iconologist, must face the problem of the lost evidence of meaning. Before the unstoppable trajectory of history that 'sap[s] the traditions and shatter[s] the living wholes in which precious objects once found their place' (76), does the critical theorist choose the same rapacious gesture? Rephrasing Benjamin's *Verfall der Aura*, Sontag describes waves of tradition that destroy meaning because they shatter the hermeneutical texture of objects. In the face of this hermeneutical destruction, it is no longer possible to conceive of intellectual inquiry as a reconstruction of wholes. The thinker 'may now in good conscience go about excavating the choicer, more emblematic fragments' (76). Issuing from such emblematic fragments, reflection takes on a necessarily allegorical character when, far from happening in a void, it (reflection) assumes its ethical responsibility to be within history and society.

Benjamin emblematises this type of allegorical excavation. Sontag focuses on Benjamin as collector to best capture the danger of thinking in the modern world: appropriating and collecting the world rather than understanding it (*On Photography* 82). While the German philosopher's sympathies for Surrealism make him aware that the challenge of the thinker is neither to reduce reality to a philosophical system nor to appropriate it, his critical path also points to a possibly fatal divergence between seductive material facticity and theoretical construction. His project was 'a work of literary criticism that was to consist entirely of quotations and would thereby be devoid of anything that might betray empathy' (77). Like the photographer, Benjamin displays 'a disavowal of empathy, a disdain for message-mongering, a claim to be invisible' (77), but unlike the photographer, he does not accept passively the 'cumulative de-creation of the past' (77). His thought revolved on 'an excruciating idea of fastidiousness' which was 'meant to permit the mute past to speak in its own voice, with all its unresolvable complexity' (77).

Therefore, his thinking-collecting has a higher purpose. Photography, instead, has disseminated Surrealism's posture of alienation to the most advanced parts of the world, encouraging a free-wheeling, anything-goes aestheticism of the mind that – 'partly jubilant, partly condescending' – does not hesitate to sum up reality as an array of casual objects (80). After Atget, photography has cultivated an 'inveterate fondness for trash, eyesores, rejects, peeling surfaces, old stuff, kitsch' (78). Separated from its 'most original and important critic' (76), the concept of 'photography' translates the modernist energies of Surrealism into the conservative arm of collective consciousness. It also signifies an infinite surface where past and present become confused, where the present is transformed into the past and history into an eternal present (77). From such a locus, an aggression flows that strips the mind bare.

W. B. (lodgings)

Sontag's overt homage to Benjamin in *On Photography* is limited to a selection of quotations, which includes only two fragments from his work. The list of quotes is appended to the collection of essays and dedicated to 'W. B.' The first Benjamin quote is from 'Little History of Photography', and alludes to the moment when the author, looking at pictures by the great master Atget, muses on their historical documentary value (*On Photography* 184). But Sontag leaves out the fundamental part of the Atget passage. There, Benjamin explains that the reason for their documentary value is that Atget's images present reality as if emptied of meaning, as if cut off from a familiar hermeneutical depth. Benjamin suggests the transformative power of photography with the metaphor of the absent, immaterial tenant when he writes: 'the city in these pictures looks cleared out, like a lodging that has not yet found a new tenant' ('Little History' 519). Sontag leaves out, in other words, the idea of photography which most attracted her, and which she had taken from her master, that is to say, photography as an unoccupied conceptual space. The second quotation from Benjamin in the appendix to *On Photography* regards the idea of which Benjamin was jealous, the destruction of the aura. Sontag quotes his image of the masses desiring the copy in a somewhat altered version of the 1969 translation of the Art Work essay: 'The need to bring spatially and humanly "nearer" is almost an obsession today, as is the tendency to negate the unique or ephemeral quality of a given event by reproducing it photographically. There is an ever-growing compulsion to reproduce the object photographically, in close-up' (*On Photography* 191).[15] What she omits, how she quotes, how she discusses him, how she names or does not name him in the anthology of quotations – everything contributes to raising the question of their collaboration, of their parallel thinking lives across time and generations.

More than expounding on Benjamin's work, Sontag is thinking with Benjamin. He is the phantasmatic master by her side, the immaterial tenant of a thought that mirrors hers and lights hers up. The initials in the dedication, 'Homage to W. B.', seal, on the public space of the page, her intimacy with the other thinker; they extend to Sontag's readers the shadow of the symposium of two taking place in the notebooks. Ultimately, the initials frame Sontag's work on photography as a private, informal meditation with him, alluding to the master–disciple relation that instead she explicitly names in the notebook. 'I see what I'm trying to do! Re-write, up-date, and surpass Benjamin's essay "The W-o-a in the Era of Tech. Reprod." Right on,' she writes in 1977, when her work on photography was completed.[16] She must then proceed to dethrone the master: 'Benjamin is neither a literary critic nor a philosopher but an atheist theologian practicing his hermeneutical skills on culture.'[17] His fall from grace may confirm a master–disciple dynamic, but his influence, quite different from any blithe mastery, seems other than the logic of schools.

Measuring the distance of the present from her predecessor, she finds that the promise of Benjamin's photography has metamorphosed into a surface of things that repels the act of understanding and almost fascistically insists that the viewer gulp down the world. Well-to-do countries wear a fashionable surrealist surface that is a parodic mental image of the reduction of thinking to an appropriative gesture: thinking is taking, grabbing and possessing. This image of contemporary planetarity flows from the locus of dread at the centre of Sontag's philosophical life, an interior theatre where the primary mind/body opposition redoubles as a clash of forces that leaves the thinking I naked of its symbolic vesture and power. The fantasy of intellectual impoverishment had done its work of connecting Sontag to the world, prodding her on in her need to 'move the world' ('The Idea of Europe' 286). The detachment of photography from Benjamin's promise turns the light on Sontag's own 'scene of crime', to use the same phrase that Benjamin had used to describe his discovery of Atget's 'empty' photography. What, then, does it mean to rewrite, update, surpass Benjamin?

From bliss to bliss

Contact with Benjamin's mind had kindled Sontag's ambition to write philosophically: 'I want to write an essay like/ a fist. I want to write an essay/ where the date (year) it's written/ isn't important. Philosophical, not historical; not culture-criticism' she wrote on 20 March 1977, before doing substantial work on her essay on him.[18] His example linked her more steadfastly to her aboriginal impression of modernism. Modernism first appeared to Sontag as the idea of a literature against the world, of writing and thinking as 'techniques of life'.[19] Benjamin revived the memory of Camus's enjoyment of the fantasy of a productivity that subsists in obscurity; it revived Pavese's living thought (*il mestiere di vivere*). He represented the unassimilated energy of the avant-garde, which persisted through the late modernist writers that Sontag valued.[20] But he also helped her lodge this fidelity in her strongest philosophical passions.

Because of the promise he saw in photography, because of his dissident disposition to linger before interpretation, Benjamin – nomadic, uprooted and displaced – could easily confuse himself with the over-wakeful, intoxicated, ruminating poet of Nietzsche's fragments:

> But everything that suffers wants to live, to become ripe and joyful and longing.
>
> – longing for what is farther, higher, brighter. 'I want heirs,' thus speaks all that suffers, 'I want children, I do not want *myself*' –
>
> But joy does not want heirs, not children – joy wants itself, wants eternity, wants recurrence, wants everything eternally the same. (Nietzsche 262)

The astonishment of the observer, itself an object of critical reflection in aphoristic writings like 'One-Way Street', causes its author to appear to Sontag closer to Nietzsche's joy than to Adorno's labour. Benjamin's 'hunger to taste what is the same in all places and countries' ('Hashish in Marseilles' 221), his eagerness to trope difference as affinity, must have sounded like a version of Nietzsche's joy. While, under Adorno's paternal eye, Sontag cultivated his ideal of the critical theorist, she received from Benjamin the promise of critical gestures that, like artistic gestures, might deliver a certain plenitude of meaning. Moving the world means acceding to ecstasy. Critical theory means 'the imperative of joy' (Sontag, 'About Hodgkin' 159). Critique is the movement from bliss to bliss.

When photography is detached from its prime theorist, when it no longer makes sense as the dwelling of a phantasmatic tenant, Sontag's work with the master comes to an end. Even before she wrote her essay on Benjamin, there are signs that she had emancipated herself from the master–disciple relationship.[21] Her need to devalue Benjamin, the valued object, only means that the disciple takes his place, so that it is now Benjamin, the object of her inquiry, who comes to seek her, the subject of thought. From this new stage comes 'Under the Sign of Saturn', her great essay on the German philosopher.

Hunger

In 'Under the Sign of Saturn', Sontag refers to that moment in 'Hashish in Marseilles' when Benjamin writes about his 'hunger to taste what is the same in all places and countries'.[22] She quotes Benjamin: 'These stones were the bread of my imagination' ('Under the Sign of Saturn' 121). Her aim in doing so is to argue for his non-conformity, for his philosophical difference. Far from being an isolated trait, Benjamin's hunger rules Sontag's entire essay, which is about a hunger 'transmuted into philosophical argument' (125). Benjamin's allegorical method – 'the process which extracts meaning from the petrified and insignificant' (125) – is intellectual productivity *as* hunger; it is reading as delirium, writing as obsession (125). The best way of acquiring books 'is by writing them' and the best way of understanding a book is by copying it (125). She alludes to and/or directly quotes from moments in Benjamin's work which cast intellect in terms of hunger. His hunger for work impresses those who approach him. The defiant Benjamin that Sontag gives us projects a formidable continuum of thinking-writing that she can grasp only in terms of 'cardiac sufficiency' (130), of the literal equation of physical strength and moral force.

At the heart of her essay, she quotes Benjamin on Karl Kraus:

> If style is the power to move freely in the length and breath of linguistic thinking without falling into banality, it is attained chiefly by the cardiac strength of great thoughts, which drives the blood of language through the capillaries of syntax into the remotest limbs. (130)

Sontag comments: 'Thinking, writing are ultimately questions of stamina' (130). The leitmotif of hunger creates exactly the effect of a resilient labour, of an unstoppable continuum of thinking-writing, as if Benjamin's addiction to work were itself the emblem of philosophy's 'uninterrupted labor' of knowledge, of criticism, of destruction (Groys 93), of its capacity for incessant metamorphosis and migration. She quotes Benjamin from the essay on Surrealism: 'Thinking which is an eminent narcotic' ('Under the Sign of Saturn' 127), to suggest that art and thought are united in this addiction which symbolises not only the modernist quest for the new but also the transmutation of things into philosophy (127). She speaks of the melancholic's devouring need to turn everything into material for the writer, of his addiction to a fluid continuum of thinking and writing that seems more valuable than life itself. She emphasises the need to be solitary: 'The need to be solitary – along with bitterness over one's loneliness – is characteristic of the melancholic' (128). She describes him as she would describe herself in 'Singleness' (1995).[23] Benjamin's interest in reproduction and the copy – the vivid correlative of his hunger – does not lead Sontag to conclude, like Boris Groys, that Benjamin is an anti-philosopher (Groys 91–104). Technological reproduction does not translate as 'a slap in the face' (Groys 104); it does not imply the impossibility of the copy to produce, diasporically (departing from the original), the new and the unexpected. Although Sontag was disappointed in Benjamin and called him a clever 'theologian',[24] she did not think that the loss of aura in total reproduction amounted to a 'sacral topology' of truth (Groys 104). Benjamin's hunger stood for the hope in a composite type: 'modern artists and intellectuals' who can be both ('Under the Sign of Saturn' 126), in a composite critical-artistic act of the mind.

Benjamin's model for this composite type was Baudelaire, with his 'impassioned pledges to work more, to work uninterruptedly, to do nothing but work'; either that or the fear of doing nothing at all ('Under the Sign of Saturn' 126). The poet's addiction became his gift to the philosopher, hence Benjamin's joy: 'Benjamin, always working,

last section

The writer always

positions

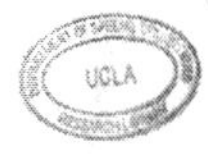

end of essay: melancholy
secret positions

Benjamin's method is allegory. He says that allegory is the way of reading the world typical of melancholics. Baudelaire: "Nourri de melancholie, la genie de Baudelaire est une genie allegorique." In allegory, there is an emblematic stiffness. The stiffness of the physical object, the emblem, corresponds to the mental stiffness of the allegory.

Benjamin's method is allegory. Trauerspiel is read as an allegory of historical pessimism---an allegory about the nature of allegory. As he reads ~~Goet~~ Goethe's Elective Affinities as a book about symbolism.

Benjamin's work can itself be read as an allegory. An allegory about the spatial imagination. An allegory about that tragic-comic figure of modern cultural history, The Last Intellectual---his ruins, his defiant visions, his reveries, his unquenchable pessimism.

End of Trauerspiel: "Empty-handed does allegory go away. (p. 233) X X

Benjamin was fascinated by the Mulusána tale. "New Melusina" is a meditation on duplication, on miniaturization.

~~It can be re The The story~~ The world is reduced to a thing, an object in the most literal sense. The hero is obliged to carry the box around. The little world in the box is like a picture, a tableau. The world is reduced to

13. Susan Sontag Papers, 'Under the Sign of Saturn', no date. Loose ms pages with holograph corrections (the 'defiant visions' page). Box 54, Folder 4.

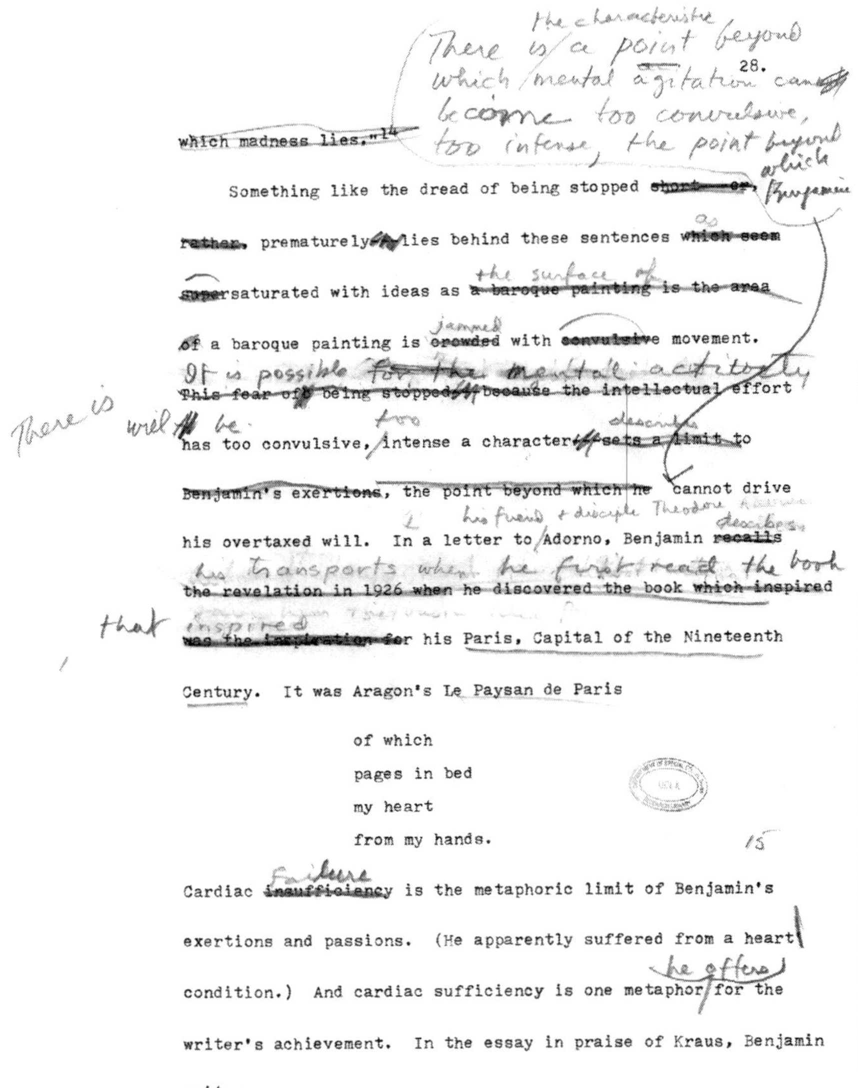

28.

which madness lies."14

Something like the dread of being stopped short — or, rather, prematurely — lies behind these sentences which seem supersaturated with ideas as a baroque painting is the area of a baroque painting is crowded with convulsive movement. This fear of being stopped — because the intellectual effort has too convulsive, intense a character — sets a limit to Benjamin's exertions, the point beyond which he cannot drive his overtaxed will. In a letter to Adorno, Benjamin recalls the revelation in 1926 when he discovered the book which inspired was the inspiration for his Paris, Capital of the Nineteenth Century. It was Aragon's Le Paysan de Paris

of which
pages in bed
my heart
from my hands.

15

Cardiac insufficiency is the metaphoric limit of Benjamin's exertions and passions. (He apparently suffered from a heart condition.) And cardiac sufficiency is one metaphor for the writer's achievement. In the essay in praise of Kraus, Benjamin writes:

14. Susan Sontag Papers, 'Under the Sign of Saturn', no date. Loose ms pages with holograph corrections (the 'cardiac failure' page).

always trying to work more . . .' (127). It is the absolute proximity to Baudelaire, his object of inquiry, that sustained Benjamin, Sontag argues, suggesting a close connection between the object of inquiry and the style of transposition. Style is the thing. And Benjamin let himself be shaped by his object of inquiry. She looks to his notebooks as evidence of the pure desire and pure cardiac labour that philosophy had become for Benjamin. She mentions the 'quotations and excerpts from daily reading which Benjamin accumulated in notebooks that he carried everywhere and from which he would read out loud to friends' (127). In the notebooks, thinking unfolds as accumulation. To be sure, it is 'a form of collecting': 'Thinking was also a form of collecting, at least in its preliminary stages. He conscientiously logged stray ideas . . .' (127), but the quotes in his notebooks also resist the acquisitiveness and appropriative drive of collecting. His quotes testify to a 'living matter' that resists the force of the finished concept.[25]

More than a personal trait, then, melancholia is the necessary angel of all those who engage in a similar flight from interpretation, from the force of the finished concept. In fact, those who are under the sign of Saturn are a new type of philosopher, for whom thinking and interpretation become conjoined. Benjamin's hunger is symptomatic of the realisation that 'all human knowledge takes the form of interpretation' (112); he 'understood the importance of being against interpretation whenever it is obvious' (122). An effect of the modern conviction that nothing is straightforward (122), his addiction to work, his hunger, is the sign of the nomadic thinker, unsheltered, 'weighed down by his passions'. Benjamin, 'drawn to whatever had to be deciphered' (124), could ultimately say, with Sontag, 'I write what I can; that is, what's given to me' ('Singleness' 259).

The aim of 'Under the Sign of Saturn' is to pursue Benjamin's standard of proper 'philosophical style': immersion, total concentration (128); claiming 'freedom to concentrate on work' (128); the 'fullness of concentrated positivity' (130); stamina, strength; and 'his reveries', a way of harnessing dreaminess to the working material (126). She finds out that his writing 'was torture to execute. It was as if each sentence had to say everything, before the inward gaze of total concentration dissolved the subject before his eyes' (129).[26] To be born under the sign of Saturn means this philosophical style of concentration, immersion, reverie and strength, which is summed up by the concrete image of the notebook: 'For the character born under the sign of Saturn, the true impulse when one is being looked at is to cast down one's eyes, look in a corner. Better, one can lower one's head to one's notebook' (126).

Venice

In Sontag's journals Benjamin and Venice are tied mysteriously. Venice in the winter, 'metaphysical,/ structural, geometrical', like a black and white photograph,[27] aptly illustrates Benjamin's 'cartographic' imagination: 'A kind of seeing-for-the-first-time'.[28] Unlike Proust, Benjamin describes 'graphically, on a map'.[29] Sontag thinks of his writing as 'a metaphysical landscape': 'Like a "metaphysical landscape." (And metaphysical interior? de Chirico.) Things rather than people. City.'[30] Winter Venice reminds her of a text of enigmatic graphic marks: 'Every figure is a silhouette.'[31] It is like Benjamin's 'freeze-frame baroque' ('Under the Sign of Saturn' 129), which aims for 'the stiffness of the object looked at'.[32] Venice, like a photographic negative, has the same effect as Benjamin's allegory: 'The most absolute language, the most hermetic/ mysterious or allegorical.'[33] Metaphysical and abstract, 'drained of color',[34] Venice is the best introduction to Benjamin's mind and to its capacity 'to drain symbolism out of some things, like the Kafka stories, or Goethe's elective affinities; and pour it into others'.[35] Ultimately, just like a photographic negative, Venice is as cartographic as Benjamin's writing because it enables Sontag to understand his inclination 'to go against the usual interpretation'.[36] She adds: 'Not against interpretation, as such. (How could he? All thinking is/ interpretation, in the largest sense – as Nietzsche said). But/ against interpretation,/ wherever it was obvious; wherever it was accepted.'[37]

In the published version of Sontag's portrait of Benjamin, the rich visual and sensory support that Venice provides to her insight into the philosopher's style disappears. We are given only the conclusive points. She retains the 'metaphysical landscape' of his writing, severed, however, from any reference to Venice ('Under the Sign of Saturn' 116). But in her notes, not only her reflections on Benjamin are informed by her image of Venice; the composition itself is like a pilgrimage from city to city which culminates in Venice.

The composition unfolds in a series of stations: at each station is a piece of his thought, as if the valued object were like the dismembered body of Osiris that Sontag–Isis re-members. The labour of Sontag is precisely to recognise the pieces of a loved body of ideas across the landscape of cities. In February 1978 she reads 'The Writer as Producer' in New York and takes notes. She muses on Benjamin's role as modern philosopher through the words of Socrates in Phaedrus: 'I am a lover of learning and the men who dwell in the city are my teachers, and not the trees or the country.'[38] In May 1978 she reads him (the new volume *Reflections*) in Madrid, finding him 'less/ extraordinary, less mysterious'.[39] A few days later, on 23 May, she is in Munich taking notes on Benjamin the intellectual labourer, who 'wrote radio dialogues in the early 20s – + hundreds of reviews'; the man who used his sexuality for critical illumination: 'Spent/ a lot of his time chasing women; frequented prostitutes – bourgeois romance/

about crossing into forbidden class-territory through sex.'[40] On 25 May 1978 she is in Venice. She continues to think about him and jots down a plan for the essay mainly through thematic blocks which connect his life and his thought. The day before she drafted the essay outline, 24 May 1978, she wrote:

> Venice makes me weep. Walking alone in
> the Piazza San Marco in the early
> morning. So I went into the cathedral,
> sat among the five or six faithful,
> heard the mass, and took communion.[41]

In the essay on Hodgkin, Venice is the city of productive repetition: 'rising out of the sea, in winter perhaps, semideserted, what you appreciate is that it will not have changed' ('About Hodgkin' 159). Like a black-and-white text of enigmatic graphemes, Venice makes a more ample space for the mind, promising the observer infinite possibilities of meaning, an infinite productivity. Before a text like Venice, Sontag can catch herself 'imagining the imagined' ('About Hodgkin' 159). Venice is her own hunger to taste sameness in every place. This 'sameness' is not some topographical truth sealed in the ruins of old places ('ruined grandeur') but that mix of happiness and anxiety which every time, and in every place, raises, for the observer, the question of aesthetic experience: the question of a discontinuity between an interior ecstasy and the bliss of productivity. In the essay on Hodgkin, the 'imperative of bliss', of which Venice reminds the observer, named a thought intimately linked to aesthetic experience, which nevertheless continues to flow elusive and ungraspable. It can only manifest as a lifetime of apologies for 'having found so many ways of acceding to ecstasy', that is to say, as the repetition of what does not become writing but promises – time and again – the act of creation, the exquisite joy of productivity.

The Venice of the May 24 journal entry, as she is thinking about Benjamin and preparing to commit to paper the structure of her essay on him, affords Sontag a cathartic release: 'Venice makes me weep.' Preparing to write about Benjamin, and thus explaining him to herself and to others, coincided with experiencing herself not as a body-object in a landscape of other objects, but from within her body, as an incarnated being 'traversed by desire and fear, feeling an entire range of impressions linked to the flesh because they are constitutive of the substance of the flesh, an impressionable substance that begins and ends in what it feels' (Henry 5). In her solitary wandering she rushes impulsively to the event of the Eucharist, to take the bread of communion, the ultimate symbol of the mystery of the flesh, as if to stop the hunger (his? hers?). The secret of the thinking life is a living thought that the master did not hand down to the disciple readily conceptualised; rather, it flows like 'an invisible life which eludes the grasp of thought' (Henry 23) and risks becoming nothing, 'mood', 'tone', 'passionateness', an anachronistic dissidence.[42] An interior writing of nothing, suspended between joy and anxiety.

Tactus intimus

One evening in early December 1973, during a party at Elizabeth Hardwick's house in New York, Susan Sontag heard Hannah Arendt conversing with other guests, among them Mary McCarthy, Mme Stravinsky and historian Arthur Schlesinger. In her notebook, she reported only a fragment of what she had heard: 'Hannah Arendt said that Benjamin/ was the only person Scholem ever/ really loved . . .'[43] By that time, Sontag's interest in Benjamin was long-standing. As we have seen, she had begun reading him in the early 1960s, and had gone on to work with his ideas in her essays on photography, defining herself after the master and conceiving of her research as a prosecution of his. Finally, a year after the publication of the essays on photography, in autumn 1978 she completed an essay on Benjamin, which, in a revised form, would give the title to her fourth collection, *Under the Sign of Saturn* (1980).

Under the Sign of Saturn was a long time in the making. For a few years Sontag thought of it as one with the book on photography, but for most of the time Benjamin's name did not appear in the table of contents. In November 1971, in New York, she first drafted a table of contents that included unwritten essays on Adorno and Arendt.[44] At various stages between 1971 and 1976 she revised the table of contents in which essays on Adorno and Arendt promised to become staple features of the collection, until in October 1976 the new draft of contents shows that she was no longer sure whether she would write on Adorno. Illness entered the table of contents and, some time in the summer of the same year, she included Benjamin. It is, therefore, at a difficult time, a year after she discovered that she had breast cancer and felt that her body had colonised her intellectual life – 'the body drifting downwards, sinking or plummeting, leaving the self stranded, evaporating'[45] – that Sontag turned to Benjamin. The great men she wrote about in this collection form a modernist philosophical tradition of critique which elsewhere she had called 'thinking against oneself'. As she wrote in the journals, they described her 'as I have described them. The pathos of intellectual avidity, the collector (mind as everything), melancholy and history, arbitrating the moral claim versus aestheticism, and so forth. The intellectual as an impossible project.'[46] Saturn was her metaphor for a philosophical and critical tradition whose Archimedean point was no longer Adorno, but Benjamin.

To Benjamin scholars, the phrase that Sontag chose for her title, 'Under the Sign of Saturn', will unfailingly recall the German philosopher's self-description in the fragment 'Agesilaus Santander'. In both versions of the fragment, the philosopher writes: 'I was born under the sign of Saturn – the planet of slow revolution, the star of hesitation and delay –' ('Agesilaus Santander (First Version)' 713; 'Agesilaus Santander (Second Version)' 715).[47] Sontag refers to this 'amazing text' to point out Benjamin's tendency to secretiveness and dissimulation indicated by the enigmatic title ('Under the Sign of Saturn' 118). She proceeds to outline, in a few wide brushstrokes from a palette of predominant greys, the character of a problematic man who could only entertain 'veiled relations with others', a man agitated by 'feelings of superiority, of inadequacy', by the 'baffled feeling, of not being able to get what one wants' (118). His 'argument', however, is 'more daring' than the simple 'pathology' of melancholia (119) in that he believed that the only transactions between himself and the world 'always take place with things' (119). Far from describing only the limits of the man, Saturn is a metaphor for a life devoted to meaning. Benjamin himself took the metaphor from Panofsky's study of Dürer's *Melancholia I* (1923, with Fritz Saxl), which he discusses in the *Trauerspiel* book. The remarkable fact is that a year after the completion of her essay on Benjamin, in her journals Sontag applied the phrase 'under the sign of Saturn' to herself.

In early December 1979, while re-reading Panofsky on Dürer's Melancholia, she muses:

> My first novel is a portrait
> of Melancholy, I discover –
> re-reading Panofsky's essay
> 'Symbolism + Dürer's Melancholia I'
> The Melancholy humor . . . was
> supposed to be coessential with
> earth and to be dry and cold; it
> was related to the rough
> Boreas, to autumn, evening
> [. . .]

> Not for nothing was I born
> under the sign of Saturn –
> Without knowing I knew.[48]

Sontag repeats Benjamin's self-objectification as if it applied to herself. It is not insignificant that the latent knowing ('without knowing I knew') that conjoins the two thinkers emerges *après-coup*, after Sontag had been reading the German philosopher for more than ten years and after she had finished her essay on him. To say it in the terms of Benjamin, 'the now of knowability' ('Theory of Knowledge' 276) occurs in the private space of the journals, after she had published on him. The repetition, in fact, suggests a knowing in excess of her public work on Benjamin. It is as if a circle were closed and the sense of a critical knowledge emerged that manifests in a fashion other than critical commentary: she *is* where he knew. The journal entry thus invites us to think more carefully about the terms in which we might best describe what appears to be unequivocally a privileged connection between Sontag and Benjamin. The entry demands that we ask: What is between them? What goes between them?

Styles of theory

The sense of something 'between' Sontag and Benjamin places them in a relation that exceeds the notions of encounter (in Gadamer's sense), repetition or recognition, but might be advantageously described as interlocution. The notion of interlocution was fleshed out by Lacan in his essay 'Function and Field of Speech and Language' (1953). There he writes: 'there is no speech without a reply, even if it is met only with silence' (40) He is, of course, referring to the psychoanalytic setting in which the notion of locution, the speech of someone, is well delimited not only by the presence of an auditor (analyst) but also by its function: it involves someone telling one's history, speaking about oneself, putting out there a construction of oneself for another (the task of the psychoanalytic cure being to exhibit the construction so it can be understood as such). Such a setting is emblematic of a situation in which a locutor assumes his being and, insofar as this assumption is constituted in language, he or she addresses the construction of his being to another. In this setting, the speaker's being is constructed and reconstructed *for* another, and can also be taken away *by* another.

Locution, therefore, is always interlocution: speech between two. As such, interlocution extends well beyond the psychoanalytic setting. It seems fundamental to the activity of critique, especially as Benjamin understood it: a 'transaction with things' (Sontag, 'Under the Sign of Saturn' 119) that gets to their truth, not to commentary. As Benjamin writes in his essay on Goethe's *Elective Affinities*, 'Critique seeks the truth content of a work of art; commentary, its material content' (297). Much like psychoanalytic interlocution, critique alternates construction and reconstruction in a process during which the distinct sense develops of a more visible text overshadowing another less legible text. Benjamin compares critique to paleography, the scholarly interpretation of earlier, especially ancient, writing and forms of writing, and the critic to the paleographer. Fusing the traditional yearning of the philosopher for wisdom and the interpreter's exegetical passion, critique is the pursuit of truth in a play of distance and proximity. Like the paleographer in front of a parchment 'whose faded text is covered by the lineaments of a more powerful script which refers to that text', the practitioner of critique seeks truth in the surface of the material contents. He 'would have to begin with commentary', that is to say, with the 'more powerful lineaments which refer' to the faded text. Critique aims for the weaker text; it wants to enable the speech of an illegible text. This is why, in his fragments on *Erkenntnistheorie*, Benjamin writes that truth reaches the seeker 'catastrophically' ('Theory of Knowledge' 276), that is to say, along a trajectory of interruption and loss, in a movement of construction and dissolution. Along this trajectory, truth exists in the 'now' of knowability (in logical time, not in atemporal time): it is out there in the world, 'authentic and unbroken'; it 'contains *unbroken* only itself' ('Theory of Knowledge' 277). Only in this being enclosed, he says, 'it is nexus' that is, link, connection, articulation. Benjamin makes us see the welling up of thinking, in a flash, as a frayed knowing, as a bridge thrown across a reality that is real but discontinuous, disconnected, simply inaccessible. Knowing seems limited to symbols, to symbolic concepts which irradiate other meanings. His truth resembles less the noetic grasp of the concept and more a rhythmic alternation; as he will say of the aura, it is 'the appearance of a distance, no matter how near/close it is' ('Che cos'è l'aura?' 25).

The image of a double layering of writing conveys the notion of meaning as truth. Material surfaces shine with the lustre of truth, which they might yield secretly, privately, to the practitioner of critique. It is a matter of devotion, fidelity, passion. Hence Sontag's emphasis on Benjamin's solitary, nomadic life. When she proceeds to apply to herself Benjamin's assumption of his being constituted in speech – 'I was born under the sign of Saturn' – as if it were addressed to her, she takes away his being, becomes conjoined with his life across historical time. She accepts her position in their interlocution, the position of the other to whom his construction of being is addressed.

It would seem fitting to talk about interlocution for someone like Benjamin, whose writings, as his friend Scholem said, hide a secret truth (interlocution is about truth, not about representing reality or conceptualising):

> Hunter vielen Schriften Benjamins stehen persönliche, ja persönlichste Erfahrungen, die in der Projektion auf die Gegenstände seiner Arbeiten verschwunden oder aber gänzlich verschlüsselt worden sind, so dass sie dem Aussenstehenden nicht erkennbar oder auch nur erahnbar werden konnten. (Scholem, 'Walter Benjamin und Sein Engel' 37–8)
>
> Behind many of Benjamin's writings stand personal, indeed most personal, experiences which by projection into the objects of his works disappeared or were put into code, so that the outsider could not recognize them or at least could do no more than suspect their presence. (Scholem, 'Walter Benjamin and His Angel' 54)

This is the fact, adds Scholem, of his greatest theoretical achievements, whether the theory of baroque interpretation in the *Trauerspiel* book or his masterpiece in aesthetic criticism, the essay on Goethe's *Elective Affinities*.[49] Benjamin's secret truth is the law of writing: the absence of representation. The destruction of the aura marks precisely the insurgence of the concept of the trace, of a writing of traces.[50] Benjamin's writing of traces is a process of erasure that evokes representations which have been removed (Green 25). The exhibition of manifest non-representations is the basis of Benjamin's writing of erasure, a prime example of which is provided by the undialectical surfaces of the Art Work essay. As we saw in Chapter 6, even in its published form, Benjamin's most popular essay manages to keep his idea 'geheim' – secret somehow.

The point of talking about interlocution is to try and shape into words Sontag and Benjamin's common stake in a certain relation to thinking. What Scholem said of Benjamin could just as well apply to Sontag. Describing Benjamin's theoretical style, in his 1965 lecture on his friend delivered at the Leo Baeck Institute in New York, Scholem emphasised 'the rejection of any systematic approach in all his work published after 1922' ('Walter Benjamin' 9). Benjamin's style of theory, argued Scholem, had 'screened the center of his personality from the view of many' (9). For the first time since Benjamin's death, his friend wished to have it 'defined clearly': 'Benjamin was a philosopher. He was one through all the phases and in all the fields of his activity' (9). Scholem insists on his friend's strategy of indirection:

> on the face of it [Benjamin] wrote mostly about subjects of literature and art, sometimes about topics on the borderline between literature and politics, but only rarely about matters conventionally considered and accepted as themes of pure philosophy. Yet in all his domains he derives his impulse always from the philosopher's experience. (9)

Similarly, Sontag has screened her centre, which manifests only indirectly in some memorable moments of her journals and notebooks. One of them is when she transfers Benjamin's being to herself.

We can now return to that entry for December 1973, where Sontag reports the words she had heard at Elizabeth Hardwick's party from Hannah Arendt, who had told the guests that 'Benjamin/ was the only person Scholem ever/ really loved.'[51] Sontag records Arendt's words without further commentary, as if to remark silently on a knowledge that she possessed as well but which remained private. Publicly, in fact, it had been Arendt who had first introduced Benjamin to a wider English-speaking audience and thus had the opportunity to put her imprint on his image.

In her 1969 introduction to *Illuminations*, Arendt had presented Benjamin simultaneously as an unlucky outsider, hovering on the outskirts of academic schools, and as the ultimate embodiment of the Frankfurt School, especially of its rejection of commercialism and the reduction of culture to profit and merchandise. In an orientalising move, Arendt turns Benjamin into the exotic antithesis of the culture industry, one who defied the laws of visibility and success with his posthumous fame: 'Posthumous fame is one of Fama's rarer and least desired articles, although it is less arbitrary and often more solid than the other sorts, since it is only seldom bestowed upon mere merchandise. The one who stood most to profit is dead and hence it is not for sale' (Arendt 1). Arendt's Benjamin is a necessary supplement, simultaneously idealised and annihilated, reduced to no identity in particular: neither a literary critic nor a scholar, neither a philologist nor a theologian, neither a historian nor a philosopher (Arendt 4). Sontag's Benjamin, instead, is a philosopher who, like her, longs to write philosophically in the post-philosophic world.

The archive keeps track of her enterprise through a progressive descent towards lightness. The mind reaches for something that always slips away. After the publication of *Under the Sign of Saturn* in 1980, she notes:

> If there is a unifying theme of
> my work it is naive. The theme
> of moral seriousness, of
> passionateness. A mood, a tone.[52]

Benjamin helps her make sense of her own pursuit of elusiveness as quite other than a chancy meandering or, worse, as the clever exertion of skills acquired through a first-rate education. Through him she sees herself as more than an amateur thinker, a journalist, an eternal beginner. Sontag must have felt she knew Benjamin because he undid the rigidity of the world and helped her move beyond traditional philosophical metanoia (Groys ix), the requirement of the production of universally self-evident discourses to transcend the limits of any particular gender and cultural identity.[53] But as he did so, he also consigned to her the knot of truth, solitude, knowability that we hear in her journals, where thinking is a descent, where she does not want to write essays because she does not want to be dogmatic, where she strives to be other than the subject supposed to know.

In the text of 'Agesilaus Santander', the angel has 'claws and pointed, razor-sharp pinions', but is extremely patient and moves 'on that road to the future along which he came', all the while remaining turned towards the human gaze in which he hopes ('Agesilaus Santander (Second Version)' 715).[54] When Sontag assumes Benjamin's self-objectification, she becomes that gaze, that reader, that other who encounters Benjamin the philosopher addressing himself to her, telling her 'Look at yourself', at the same time that she addresses herself to him, asking him 'Show me'.[55] Benjamin's autobiographical fragment continues:

> As soon as this man encountered the woman who held him in thrall, he at once determined to lie in wait for her on her journey through life and to wait until she fell into his hands, ill, aged, and in ragged clothes. In short, nothing could weaken the man's patience. And the wings of this patience resembled the wings of the angel: they needed but a few movements to hold him stationary in the face of the woman whom he was determined not to abandon. ('Agesilaus Santander (Second Version)' 715; modified translation)

As the two who know each other without knowing, Benjamin's man and woman illustrate an interlocution, a specific form of reciprocal legibility. In Sontag's and Benjamin's *jeu d'écriture* (Green 27), Benjamin seems the blank book of her thinking-writing, the silent pre-reflexive cogito of her reflection. Far from being limited to them, their interlocution extends to critical activity, encouraging us to ask fundamental questions: What does it mean for a thinker to understand another thinker? What does it mean to write about him or her? How is that done best?

Coda (to the Gentle Reader)

UCLA, 26 August 2011. Something happened to my notes on Box 175, the box containing the research materials for *Regarding the Pain of Others*. All the notes have gone. The Leica ads, Fenton and First World War photography materials, the Elizabeth Bishop poem . . . the anthropological gaze – everything gone. I am trying to reconstruct the notes, but it is not simple. In the attempt to remember, I realise that Sontag's research relied above all on newspaper and magazine articles, in particular *The New Yorker* and *The New York Times*. But there was also an article in Italian bearing in its title the phrase *il dolore degli altri* – the pain of others. I remember thinking that her writing fed on other languages. (She read her favourite authors in different languages, and she wrote about translation.)[1] The Italian article spoke of the distance between the observer and the object of the gaze in photographs of pain. Because it remarked on the sheltered position of the observer in those images, it might have been germinal to a key idea of her last book on photography: the haunting hiatus between victim and perpetrator, who have become the poles in the cruel theatre of art-related critical reflection.

Sontag had always been concerned with the reduction and simplification of the world; she had oscillated between the lure of rigid formalistic face-to-face between the viewer and the viewed (the amorous contemplation of her earlier writings on interpretation), and the destabilising stare of what is in excess of our understanding (especially after the encounter with New York avant-garde art). Photography had offered an opening, a truce. It had strewn the distance between the thinker and the world with the cyclical return of the vulnerability of Being, transforming the distance into an unlimited vista of floating signifiers voluptuously severed from the burden of meaning. After the *Verfall der Aura*, after the semantic shell of things had been shattered, intellectual inquiry was no longer conceivable as a reconstruction of wholes. The thinker may now excavate the more emblematic fragments (*On Photography* 76). Jubilation appeased for a while some frightening inability of the mind. But soon the excavation of fragments came perilously to resemble a form of collecting, a form of accumulation and hoarding that felt too much like a taking and a possessing which left the mind dejected, lonely, without aim. Signs no longer returned their 'gaze'; they no longer lent themselves to productive allegory, but hardened in the distance, not just thin but harshly inhospitable marks ('One Hundred Years of Italian Photography'). In Sontag's later work, it is as if the circle closed: the impasse of the rigid formal notion of critical act that caused her to shift towards Benjamin seems to return, but this time the rigidity is greater. The problem of understanding, which is that great distance between viewer and viewed, evolves into the combat of victim and perpetrator, the deadlock of two actors. The act of the mind, always at risk for Sontag, can be imagined only as a silent, life-taking corporeal enactment of reciprocal positions.

I am struck by the fact that from the distance of time she went back to look at the Vietnam photographs: the photograph of the girl running naked next to that of the man killed by a general who died in the 1980s, at the age of 67. There was a debate on whether violence, in that case, was justified because the victim had killed people. I remember an article on Robert Capa discussing the authenticity of the photograph of the militiaman during the Spanish Civil War. I remember an insightful article in the *New York Times* signed by a certain Boxer, and the flyer for the photographic exhibition in Prince Street on the tragedy of the Twin Towers – a great democracy of images because everyone could send in his or her photograph which would have then been scanned and exhibited next to images by great photojournalists and professional photographers. Then I remember an important detail: Sontag revised the jacket copy of *Regarding the Pain of Others*. Her edit, in the opening paragraph, concerns the idea that observing the tragedies of others is a trait of modernity. The edit clarifies that her book is yet another step in her ongoing cartography of modernity.

On Photography had investigated the convergence of seeing and understanding. *Regarding the Pain of Others* continued that investigation, choosing to dwell on an extreme form of seeing. Not only does it confirm that we understand through the gaze, but it further proposes that the extreme gaze on the pain of others might be a metaphor for the hermeneutic distance between any observer and any observed. The risk that harrowing pictures lose meaning over time because of the relocation of a photograph to another context – a relocation to which all objects and all people may be subjected – is proof that images need words. But such a dependence is only a reminder of the urgency to put ourselves in the place of others for any act of understanding to happen. Harrowing images suggest that understanding might be the capacity to vanquish the distance that separates us from the observed, a capacity that contrasts with photographic seeing, which is, instead, reifying and dissociative. The pain of others seriously tests style, in Sontag's sense, as an aristocratic distance from the world.

Among the research materials, there is a photograph of a dead soldier who seems to continue to look at us from the other side of life. Once again, the image evokes the distance between the observer and the observed, who is represented as the impotent victim of violence and pain. In Sontag's research materials this distance is insistent, as if the exertion of thought and language could not be conceived as separate from it, and therefore cannot be considered as severed from the safe and protected condition of the one who regards. In harrowing photographs, this sheltered condition is severely questioned by the regarded. As a subject of language and thought, the observer must be ready to be changed or affected by what he or she regards. The word 'other' or 'others', though invoked repeatedly, seems to lose the meaning that it has accrued through decades of cultural criticism. It suddenly appears as a prop in that theatre of the mind in which Sontag saw that thought becomes 'a stipulating' (*Regarding* 86). In pictures of violence, the gazes of others meet ours with questions of a common condition, of a proximity which that theatre of the mind denies. Suddenly, reading Sontag opens to an unforeseen question, which exceeds the familiar terms of cultural criticism: the question of the neighbourliness of others, which is the question, more properly, of the Neighbour, and the kind of achievement that this position might be. Her cartography of modernity introduces us to a new wilderness of criticism, an unsheltered 'zone-Concept' in which culture, language, thought and meaning, estranged from us, need a new beginning – perhaps, a new lexicon.

Sontag's 'photography' allows us no easy escape from the intimate dialogism of the subject, neither does she seem to wish to throw away the philosophical notion of subject. She is caught in a spot where the great tradition of the dyadic intimacy of self and other (Levinas's face-to-face of the lovers, or Benveniste's structural I–you of discourse) clashes with another knowing regarding a multitude of bodies that recoils from everything that we know: 'What multitude of bodies,' exclaims, many decades before Jean-Luc Nancy, the modernist writer Anna Maria Ortese: 'all is body, only body, motionless body' (Ortese 101); while to the French-adopted Russian

Jewish philosopher Vladimir Jankélévitch, the multitude appears as a vast grey and indistinct ocean of unnamed and interchangeable others (with no hope of ispeity). Sontag exposes the impasse of the I–you model but is not willing to dispose of it. She stakes her hope for the renewal of thought in a face-to-face that still seems to promise a space for thought; one, however, that is entangled with will, conflict and life-forms.

But all this is perhaps for another book. When researching, it is paramount to be in the company of a set of terms, to inhabit a certain sensibility, to spend time with it. In the long run the company may feel like a confinement. Yet no matter the devotion, it is perhaps not uncommon to feel that after finishing a book, writing has passed us by. This sense of a loss might be proportional to the desire to reach our readers, crossing their horizon lightly, with a fraction of the lightness with which the sailing boat crosses my view now (a moment and it's gone). Writing passes us by as it is being written: once I was convinced that this was the condition of the bilingual writer, a sort of self-exiled thinker always short of words. Now, perhaps, I know that it is the condition of writing.

Notes

Introduction: The Archival Relation

1. Jerome Boyd Maunsell, *Susan Sontag* (London: Reaktion, 2014), is an accessible biography that has the merit of integrating materials from the Sontag archives, availing itself also of the two-volume publication of her journals edited by her son David Rieff; Daniel Schreiber's *Susan Sontag: A Biography* (Evanston: Northwestern University Press, 2014) is a translation, by David Dollenmayer, of the original volume first published in German in 2007.
2. Susan Sontag, *Reborn: Journals & Notebooks 1947–1963*, ed. David Rieff (New York: Farrar, Straus, and Giroux, 2008) and Susan Sontag, *As Consciousness is Harnessed to Flesh: Journals & Notebooks 1964–1980*, ed. David Rieff (New York: Farrar, Straus, and Giroux, 2012). I began my research in Sontag's papers at UCLA before the second volume was published.
3. For an introduction to the extraordinary array of art forms she dealt with, and the many performances and productions she was involved with, one might begin with E. Ann Kaplan's insightful essay, 'Sontag, Modernity, Cinema'.
4. Susan Sontag Papers, Box 84, Folder 43, Charles E. Young Library, Special Collections, UCLA. Henceforth, all materials from the Susan Sontag Papers will be referenced to simply with the box number followed by the folder number.
5. Box 125, Folder 5.
6. Box 128, Folder 1.
7. Box 128, Folder 3.
8. In his introduction to the collection of essays *Modernism and Theory*, Stephen Ross is careful to provide the facts. First, theory's philosophical roots are either modernist (Heidegger, Husserl, Sartre, Wittgenstein) or shared by modernism (e.g. Kant, Hegel, Schopenhauer, Nietzsche, Kierkegaard). Secondly, theories emerged in modernism: 'formalism (Russian and New Critical alike) emerges alongside modernist art's

emphasis on technique and significant form' (2). Furthermore, 'psychoanalysis is a quintessentially modernist theory' and 'Bakhtin, Bergson, William James, and Wittgenstein are all modernists,' states Ross (2). This also means that 'phenomenology, existentialism, third-wave feminism, queer studies, postcolonial theory, Lacanian psychoanalysis [. . .] do not merely parallel the development of modernism, but partake of it' (2).

9. Box 128, Folder 5. Sontag, *As Consciousness* 438.
10. Box 134, Folder 10. See my discussion in Chapter 5.
11. Box 123, Folder 10.
12. Box 128, Folder 8. Sontag, *As Consciousness* 519.
13. Box 128, Folder 1.
14. Boris Groys inserts Sontag's beloved Nietzsche in a line of antiphilosophy that 'dispenses with the heroic philosophical act and substitutes it by ascribing philosophical dignity to practices of ordinary life' (xi).
15. I make an exception to the rule of limiting my discussion to Sontag's critical essays and include *The Volcano Lover*, a novel, because it is there that, through the figure of an Enlightenment woman of letters, Sontag speaks against the end of history.
16. Idit Dobbs-Weinstein (Vanderbilt University), 'Negative Dialectics as a Radical, Secular or Jewish Species of Negative Theology', keynote address, 6th International Critical Theory Conference of Rome, 6–8 May 2013, John Felice Rome Center of Loyola University Chicago.
17. A concern expressed by Pamela Fraser, Roger Rothman and Randall Szott in their call for contributions to a new volume 'Reframing the Critical: Art, Theory and Instruction', http://bams.ac.uk/2013/10/15/cfs-reframing-the-critical-art-theory-and-instruction/ (accessed 1 February 2016).
18. One of the pioneering essays in a new kind of affirming criticism is Eve Kosofsky Sedgwick's *A Dialogue on Love*. Here the deconstructive practice of one of the foremost feminist queer critics, at a vulnerable moment of her life, is counterbalanced by the emergent notion of tenderness. Sedgwick also launched the notion of reparative reading in her now popular essay 'Paranoid Reading and Reparative Reading, or, You Probably Think This Essay Is About You'.
19. Box 125, Folder 4.
20. As philosopher Roberto Esposito points out, in modern thought community and melancholia are joined in an ineluctable tie. From Hobbes to Freud, thought that opens itself to the world is structurally melancholic: it assumes violence as the originary form of interhuman relations (82). Rousseau's passion to communicate the self to others is countered by the melancholy acceptance of an absent community (84). Similarly, for Lacan the formula for community is being alone together.

21. The essay is a paean to the paradox at the heart of communities that are also intellectual and artistic circles and, as such, schools in which everyone creates alone together.
22. In her later work Sontag insists on the notion of parallel, simultaneous and unequal worlds. See especially her homage to Nadine Gordimer, 'At the Same Time: The Novelist and Moral Reasoning'.
23. In our regime of technological reproduction and intimacy with images, Sontag tracks the ways in which thinking and the aesthetic act of looking have become conjoined, even confused one with the other. As revealed by the specific example of photographs of atrocities, 'regarding' can never just be the act of looking, but contains and carries in itself the call to think differently, with concern.
24. In 'A Sketch of the Past', Woolf uses the opportunity of a childhood memory to describe the life of the mind. The memory is 'highly sensual'. Meaningfulness happens when the object of inquiry seems to extend its hermeneutic layers from the past to us, and this event becomes part and parcel of the meaning of the object.

Chapter 1

1. Nelson perceives 'mutually sustained and countered impulses toward intimacy and abstraction' in Sontag's work, as if the desire for knowing something deeply were inseparable from the experience of a distance.
2. For Badiou the discourse on difference and the proliferation of identities are completely functional to the 'homogeneous surface' of capital and the market, since identities can be only if they are counted and computed subjects, subjects who, like the man in Kafka's well-known parable, are before the law in a manner that remains extraneous to the notion of singular life. In *Regarding the Pain of Others*, Badiou's *doxa* will translate as ready-made ideas, and his questioning of democracy (is democracy, he asks, only this homogeneous surface of *doxa* or there is something else?) into Sontag's concern with the reduction of thinking to stipulating. She exposes herself to the pressure of the surface and realises that the task of the thinker must begin anew.
3. On the basis of this shared truth effect Groys draws out the similarity between philosophy and traditional art. Just as philosophical texts, unlike scientific texts, rely on a truth effect that is 'not dependent on empirical verification', so art relies on a similar truth effect hinged on its own inner structure: 'the ability of an individual artwork to generate, emanate, irradiate the "aesthetic experience" is generally also regarded as an effect of its own, inner structure' (Groys ix).
4. For example, in 'On Paul Goodman', the opening chapter of *Under the Sign of Saturn*, she speaks of 'some need to strip down, to close off for a while, to make a new start with as little as possible to fall back on'

(3). Years later, the same need recurs in her piece on Sarajevo, 'Waiting for Godot in Sarajevo', and is the defining trait of the heroine of her last novel, *In America*.

5. The master scene of the thinker as the vulnerable beholder that Sontag offers to the gaze of her readers can be traced to a stark vista full of hardship and solitude, where the clamour of an ineluctable collision can be heard. At this stage, Sontag differs from Hans-Georg Gadamer, who is concerned with a similar issue. The latter argues for a hermeneutic moment that is so comprehensive as to include aesthetic experience. Sontag, instead, assumes an ongoing conflict between the two. See Gadamer, 'Aesthetics and Hermeneutics'.
6. In *Susan Sontag: The Elegiac Modernist*, Sohnya Sayres speaks of a conflict between meanness and repression, on the one hand, and human growth and pleasure, on the other (55). She traces this conflict to the extreme lives of the modernists Sontag favoured, like Artaud, who impacted on her with the sense of an acute conflict and 'a spectacle of flagellation' (105).
7. Two essays by Lonzi, in particular, 'La solitudine del critico' (1963) and 'La critica è potere' (1970), resonate with Sontag's position in *Against Interpretation* (1966), whose lead essay was written in 1964. Lonzi's work enables insight into Sontag's vulnerable beholder. All translations from Lonzi are mine.
8. Lonzi's individual, unlinked from groups, not defined or constrained by/in a social identity, will become, in the hands of Giorgio Agamben, the 'Whatever' (il Qualunque), which refers to singularity, to 'being such as it always matters' (*The Coming Community* 1).
9. As Sontag moves closer to Johns and the New York School, in the autumn of 1966, she writes in her diary: 'The only arts where there's real thinking going on today are painting and music. None in literature!', Box 125, Folder 5. The investment in the new is palpable in her notes on a 'new sensibility' as she navigates an astonishing array of stimuli – from Pavese to Miró's 'biomorphism' to the experimental New York artists like Rivers, Lichtenstein and Warhol and the 'new development' of plastic-based paints. Box 124, Folder 11.
10. Jerome Maunsell notices 'the jagged, electric movements of her own aphoristic essay style' (88).
11. The mutual stimulation of art and theory is best illustrated, for Sontag, by art in media other than the literary, especially film.
12. Box 124, Folder 11.
13. In his *Introduction to Antiphilosophy* (2012), Boris Groys distinguishes between two processes of reproduction: 'one topologically determined, which guarantees the continuity of the original in time, the other topologically undetermined, diasporic, profane, which does not guarantee this continuity' (102). For Sontag, criticism is another name for a diasporic plane that Benjamin, according to Groys, did not admit because

he sealed truth topologically. The whole world is reproduction, and reproduction is 'a pure power that equalizes everything and abolishes all differences' (Groys 104). That is why Sontag, in her notebooks, will conclude that Benjamin is an 'atheist/ theologian'. Box 128, Folder 3.

14. Especially the experimental art of Robert Rauschenberg and Jasper Johns, both of whom will feature prominently in her journals after 1965, right after she had finished her essay 'Against Interpretation' (1964).
15. For example, when he says that in the Oedipus myth the parts of the myth mean nothing ('The Anthropologist as Hero' 80).
16. Luigi Pignat, *Poor People in Udine*, 1909 (Naldi 54).
17. Vincenzo Balocchi, *Passersby*, Malandrini Collection (Naldi 113).
18. Sontag wrote on Abbott's photography in a key passage of *On Photography* (67–8). See my detailed discussion in Chapter 4.
19. Anonymous, *State Examinations in Milan*, 1927, Malandrini Collection (Naldi 98).
20. Paul Strand, *The Family Luzzara, Italy*, 1953, also included in Naldi, is owned by Aperture Foundation, Inc., Paul Strand Archive.
21. She neglects the fact that in his poetry the celebrated Italian intellectual had stood powerless – except for a fleeting homoerotic power – before the fantasy of a national abyss deserted by language and symbolic activity. 'La terra di lavoro' (1956).
22. 'Hamm: I love the old questions.
    (With fervour.)
    Ah the old questions, the old answers,
    there's nothing like them!'
23. 'Body-thinking' is a phrase that Kenneth Burke, Sontag's mentor at Chicago, used to describe her enterprise in her first book of essays, *Against Interpretation*. Box 82, Folder 47.
24. Box 124, Folder 11.

Chapter 2

1. Around 1976 Sontag was reading Jauss at the same time as gluing especially beloved fragments from Adorno's *Minima Moralia* in her notebooks. Box 127, Folder 10.
2. According to Jauss, Gadamer and Adorno share an ambivalence towards the beautiful, the former because he opposes art as truth even to aesthetic self-enjoyment, and the latter because of the doctrine of negativity and the failed crossing to communication. They and their followers 'recognize nothing but the veiling or repression of ruling interests in the ambiguous power of the beautiful and believe they can escape the vicious circle of "false consciousness" only if they set aside for "true consciousness" a place beyond the seductions of the economically subservient arts and all the manipulations of distorted

communication' (41). They expel or suspend art 'with the purpose of ushering in their purity in a state of nondomination' (41). But Jauss deconstructs their 'new opposites' as a return and assertion of the 'unavowed Platonic legacy' (41).

3. Box 128, Folder 3. Sontag, *As Consciousness* 411. For immediacy, here and elsewhere I have chosen to retain the lineation as it appears in Sontag's notebooks.
4. Box 128, Folder 3. Sontag, *As Consciousness* 411.
5. Jauss works against the grain of a tradition of aesthetic theory – Adorno, Gadamer, Brecht – which revolves around the prohibition of pleasure and the inhibition of the beautiful. Although she was sympathetic to Adorno, Sontag shared the same concern.
6. The other two categories are poiesis and catharsis.
7. The solitude and insularity that Jauss attributes to Adorno's interpreter might also apply to our age of hermeneutic universalism, when interpretation seems to have replaced reality. In Richard Shusterman's words, a 'host of global hermeneuts' maintains that 'simply to perceive, read, understand, or behave at all intelligently is already, and must always be, to interpret' (133).
8. Box 123, Folder 10.
9. Box 82, Folder 47.
10. In 'The Work of Art in the Age of Mechanical Reproduction', Benjamin contrasts the 'man who concentrated before a work of art is absorbed by it' with 'the distracted mass' that 'absorbs the work of art' (*Illuminations* 239).
11. Box 125, Folder 1. Sontag, *As Consciousness* 19.
12. In fragment 74, 'Mammoth', of her copy of Adorno's *Minima Moralia*, Sontag underlines the part on Karl Hagenbach's experiment to create an open zoo 'with trenches instead of cages' (115). Adorno comments: 'They deny the animals' freedom only the more completely by keeping the boundaries invisible, the sight of which would inflame the longing for open spaces' (115). In pencil, Sontag writes: 'typical Frankfurt thinking (comes from N.)'. Box 212, Folder 2.
13. Sontag had wanted to write about Adorno for a long time, but although the planned essay features in the drafts of the table of contents of both her second and third book of essays, it made its way into neither. Her second book of essays was drafted in Pesaro, Italy, in June 1967. The original plan was to have three sections: one on literature; a second on theatre and film; a third on culture, aesthetics, philosophy. The Adorno piece was to have found a place in this last section, together with Cioran, Pornographic Imagination, Theories of Interpretation, Psychotechnics, Silence (Box 125, Folder 5). While the final version of *Styles of Radical Will* would include essays on silence, the pornographic imagination and Cioran, Adorno was left out. Four years later, in the winter of 1971 Sontag was in New York reading Adorno's book

The Jargon of Authenticity. She drafted the contents of her third book of essays, which includes a planned essay on Adorno, together with essays on Arendt and Vertov (Box 126, Folder 10). In July 1973, in Paris, while working on *I etc.* she came up with another revised draft of the table of contents of her third book of essays, which includes an essay on Adorno to be written in 1974 (Box 126, Folder 10). In the summer of 1974 a new version of the 'possible table of contents' for her third book of essays, drawn up while she was in Europe, shows that Arendt is still there while Adorno has gone, supplanted by four chapters on photography (Box 127, Folder 9). In 1975 she is still planning to write on Adorno but has doubts on him as an elite intellectual. She opposes his difficult style to the lucidity of Benjamin, and his privileged position to the marginal existence of the latter (Box 127, Folder 9). She continued to take notes on Adorno, but in the autumn of 1976, the year she found out about her cancer, Adorno disappears from her table of contents. Leni Riefenstahl is in, with Peter Hujar, Illness, Simone Weil and the Arendt essay, now called 'Arendt + Jews'. The history of the unpublished essay is nevertheless proof of a sustained engagement with Adorno's work.

14. Page numbers from *Minima Moralia* are from this edition.
15. In her notebooks, she also refers to Adorno, with SW [Simone Weil] and Artaud, as 'my amphetamine'. Box 128, Folder 3.
16. My translation.
17. She also annotates it: 'Hegel vs N.[ietzsche].'
18. Box 127, Folder 10.
19. Box 124, Folder 10.
20. Box 127, Folder 10.
21. Box 127, Folder 10.
22. Hence the disassembling and destruction of meaning which we have seen in the essay on Lévi-Strauss.
23. Apart from Cioran, she includes Kierkegaard and Nietzsche, whom Groys classifies as anti-philosophers.
24. Box 128, Folder 8. Sontag, *As Consciousness* 518.
25. We may think here, by way of example, of Damien Hirst's *After Max Ernst. The Hat Makes the Man* (2004), modelled on a collage dated 1920 by the German surrealist Max Ernst. The collage is composed of cutout images of hats from catalogues linked by *gouache* and pencil outlines to create abstract anthropomorphic figures. Hirst produces a sculpture which repeats the work of the master; it puts it 'out there' again. See Paldam.
26. With one difference, perhaps. As Sontag writes: 'Untempted by the same kind of fame or emotional rewards that can descend on the poet, the philosopher can perhaps better comprehend and respect the modesty of the inexpressible' ('Thinking Against Onself' 91).
27. Box 153, Folder 8. Graduate student notes on Nietzsche.
28. Box 128, Folder 3. See my discussion in Chapter 6.

29. Box 128, Folder 5. Sontag, *As Consciousness* 438.
30. I thank Peter Carravetta for calling my attention to the fact that, in the mid-1970s, the anthropologist Edward T. Hall, author of *Beyond Culture* (1976), theorised 'proxemics'.
31. Box 128, Folder 8.
32. Box 125, Folder 4. Sontag, *As Consciousness* 166.
33. The co-founders of The Living Theater, Julian Beck and Judith Malina, knew personally the first translator of Artaud's work into English, Mary Caroline Richards. It was through Richards that Beck and Malina had seen, by 1959, the English text of Artaud's 'The Theater and Its Double'. For a good source, see Tytell.
34. Sontag's work on Artaud was later included in *Under the Sign of Saturn* (1980).
35. Box 126, Folder 10.
36. Box 128, Folder 3. Sontag, *As Consciousness* 419.
37. Box 128, Folder 3.
38. Note 17 in the original publication became note 20 in the essay 'Force and Signification' (303).
39. The notion of the total work of art is also discussed in a later piece on Wagner, 'Wagner's Fluids'.
40. For the debate spurred by this controversial point, see Judith Butler's response 'Photography, War, Outrage', later revised as 'Torture and the Ethics of Photography'.

Chapter 3

1. Box 124, Folder 11.
2. For a good account of Sontag's involvement in the circle of New York intellectuals, see Horowitz, 'Sexuality and a New Sensibility'. I thank Dan Horowitz for sharing an early draft of his work.
3. Sontag, 'Is The Reader Necessary', revised and published as 'Nathalie Sarraute and the Novel', in *Against Interpretation*. See Poague and Parsons 138.
4. Lionel Trilling first talked about the deep places of the imagination in his most influential book, *The Liberal Imagination*. Trilling argued that the American writers of the 1930s and 1940s, such as Theodor Dreiser and Sherwood Anderson, 'had not penetrated the deep places of the imagination as had the pioneering figures of European literary modernism' (Krupnick 60), a position that Sontag would embrace.
5. A keyword in Trilling's book, *The Liberal Imagination*.
6. For a different account of Sontag's positioning within the New York public intellectuals, see Lopate, *Notes on Sontag*. According to Lopate, Sontag 'for the most part ignored all that past history of factionalism and bad blood' (49). In his account, which stresses a difference

in degrees of political belief, she sides with the New rather than the Old Left: 'her politics emphasized anti-imperialism and sexual freedom, while de-emphasizing the working class or any Marxist economic analysis' (49).

7. Diana Davies, *Susan Sontag, 1967*. Diana Davies Papers, Box 7, Folder 13 ('Women and Peace') and Box 28, Folder 9, Sophia Smith Collection, Smith College, Northampton, MA. Writer Paul Blackburn read at the same event.
8. See Posner; Etzioni and Bowoditch; J. Hillis Miller; Small; Novick; and Andrew Ross.
9. Sontag's essay on Benjamin, 'Under the Sign of Saturn', was first published as 'The Last Intellectual' in *The New York Review of Books*. See Poague and Parsons 237.
10. I do not know the title of the book she is reading from.
11. In 'The Aesthetics of Silence', Sontag expresses reservations that anticipate contemporary attacks on this scene of utterance. See Parker and Sedgwick.
12. The phrase, part of the title of Liam Kennedy's early study of Sontag, is taken from Sontag's essay on Canetti, 'Mind as Passion'.
13. To view the image, go to http://www.metmuseum.org/exhibitions/listings/2006/tribute-to-susan-sontag (accessed 1 February 2016).
14. Diana Davies Papers, MS 309, Sophia Smith Collection, Smith College.
15. See especially 'Analytical Philosophy and Language' (1963), Benveniste's response to British philosopher J. L. Austin on the topic of performative utterances. I discuss the essay in detail in 'Enunciation Performed (From Benveniste to Performativity)', unpublished.
16. Davies's photograph dwells on a speaking subject who wishes to designate herself with the first-person pronoun. The iconic banner of the feminist pioneer Susan B. Anthony points to the silent image of the past that is enfolded in the living speech of a present illustrated by the marching women. Perfectly blended in the visual Babel of urban space, the weave of past and present descends on the city to ruin ever so slightly its ideal topography of forward-moving social time, faulting the present as a time behind time, transferring to the women's utterances the capacity of graffiti to make scratches on the surface of social conventions, especially when these have become the drab armour of grey norms.
17. In 1972 she published 'The Double Standard of Aging', in which she explores the intersection of gender and power, and explains why culture punishes women, setting for them higher aesthetic standards than it does for men and encouraging them to indulge in a narcissistic regard for the image. In 1973 she published 'The Third World of Women', in which she compares sexism with chattel slavery and appears to share Virginia Woolf's conviction that gender discrimination bespeaks fascist leanings and is therefore a moral issue. The essay went through different

rewrites. Its ideas develop from Sontag's answers to a questionnaire: 'At What Stage Is Now the Struggle for Women's Liberation.' Sontag's answers were published in French as 'Réflections sur la libération des femmes (réponses à un questionnaire)', *Les temps moderne* 29 (December 1972) (the text was edited for a Dutch edition of a pamphlet format of 'The Third World of Women'; Poague and Parsons 62), under ten subheadings that correspond to the ten-question format; finally, Sontag's answers to the questionnaire appeared as an interview included in a South American collection on feminism, 'Entrevista a Susan Sontag', *El feminismo: Nuevos conceptos* (Poague and Parsons 167). For the history of the publication of this important questionnaire, the best source probably remains the Sontag Papers at UCLA. Finally, her work on photography led to a profound gender-marked ambivalence. See 'Certain Mapplethorpes'.

As for Sontag's complaints about the simplifications of feminist discourse, in the early 1980s, in a piece known as the Salmagundi interview, she responded to Adrienne Rich, who had attacked her essay on Leni Riefenstahl for disregarding feminist values. Sontag clarifies: 'It's not the appropriateness of feminist criticism which needs to be rethought, but its level – its demands for intellectual simplicity, advanced in the name of ethical solidarity. These demands have convinced many women that it is undemocratic to raise questions about "quality" – the quality of feminist discourse' ('The Salmagundi Interview' 333). For a re-evaluation of Sontag's relationship with feminism, see Showalter.

18. Gloria Steinem, 'Letter to the *Saturday Evening Post*, 20 Sept. 1956', Gloria Steinem Papers, Box 32, Folder 1, Sophia Smith Collection, Smith College.
19. The fascination with what their culture perceived as exotic played an important role in their intellectual formation. In 1956 Steinem longed to say something about 'the peculiar fascination and crucial position of India' (letter to the *Saturday Evening Post*, 20 September 1956). Once in India, the young American felt transformed by the cultural contact, darkened her hair and dressed in a sari. Sontag, in her turn, had a connection with China through her parents, who were fur traders and lived there. Peter Hujar photographed her in 'Chinese wear' in 1966. For a discussion of Sontag's trips to Asia and the writing they inspired, see Ching.
20. See, for example, *Steinem speaking at UN Women's Solidarity Rally*, December 1975, photographer unknown. Gloria Steinem Papers, Sophia Smith Collection, Smith College.
21. Gloria Steinem Papers, Box 218, Folder 5, Sophia Smith Collection, Smith College.
22. See images of Gloria Steinem in the Gloria Steinem Papers, such as *Gloria Steinem Speaking (1970?)*, unknown photographer, or *Gloria Steinem Speaking (1975)*, contact sheet, by photographer Cary

Herz, Gloria Steinem Papers, Box 218, Folder 5; and *Gloria Steinem Speaking, 29 October 1979, New York Rally (anti-pornography march)*, by photographer Dori Jacobson, Dori Jacobson Papers, Sophia Smith Collection, Smith College.

23. The Peter Hujar photograph was taken in an interior in 1975. At the same time, demonstrations for International Women's Year were going on outside, with crowds flooding the streets demanding in unison the passing of the equal rights amendment. Hujar's Sontag provides a private counterpoint to this public scenario.
24. Originally published in *Art in America* 74.9 (1986): 115–23, later used as the introduction to the volume *'Verushka': Trans-figurations* (1986), from which I am quoting.
25. Diana Davies Papers, Box 10, Folder 35, Sophia Smith Collection, Smith College. Published in *Photojourney: Photographs by Diana Davies* (1989).
26. Diana Davies, *Kate Millett*, contact sheet. Diana Davies Papers, Box 10, Folder 35, Sophia Smith Collection, Smith College.
27. For a comparison of Sontag with feminist intellectuals outside the US, see also Wiseman.
28. Giorgio de Chirico, *The silent statue (Ariadne)*, 1913, oil on canvas, Düsseldorf, Kunstsammlung Nordrhein-Westfalen. See Fagiolo Dell'Arco 88.
29. For an interesting discussion of the myth, see Lyons, especially the chapter 'Ariadne and Dionysos', 124–8.
30. Of the statue's metaphysical silence, the painter said: 'nessuno prima di me lo tentò' [no one else attempted it before me] (qtd. in Crescentini 54).
31. See also these other images in the series: *L'Aprés-midi d'Ariane*, 1913, oil on canvas; *La lassitudine dell'infinito*, 1912–13, oil on canvas; *La Nostalgie de l'inconnu*, 1915, ink on paper; all included in Fagiolo Dell'Arco. The myth of Ariadne is central in De Chirico's early years. The painter was attracted by the myth of Daedalus connected to the Labyrinth, to the Minotaur, Theseus, Ariadne and the final intervention of Dionysus. In the myth Theseus, who was given the key to the Labyrinth, abandons Ariadne but she subsequently becomes the lover of Dionysus. Ariadne 'represents the enigmatic connection between the first stage of the search for knowledge and the second stage of Dionysian bliss' or Nietzsche's 'gay science' (Fagiolo Dell'Arco 84). In Nietzsche, the myth is connected to the spirit of knowledge and therefore to enigma and mystery.
32. *Melanconia*, oil on canvas, 1914. Fagiolo Dell'Arco comments that here the title clarifies the myth of Ariadne. Moreover, the inscription 'Et Quid Amabo Nisi Quod Enigma Est?' connects the theme of knowledge to melancholy.
33. See Crescentini 514. Crescentini also remarks on the connection with Nietzsche's literary-philosophical Ariadne (see Nietzsche, *Also sprach*

Zarathustra, qtd. in Crescentini 152, 129). Like Dürer's *Melancholia I*, Nietzsche's Ariadne stands halfway between the inaugural, liberating cognitive moment of gaiety and the rapture of enigma, on the one hand, and the abyss of melancholy, on the other. My claim is that for De Chirico silence is different from a crepuscular Bacchic abandon and closer instead to a discourse on the cultural responsibility of the interpreter.

34. The Sontag archives preserve the 1977 translation of Benjamin's *German Baroque Drama* by John Osborne, published by NLB, with Sontag's annotations. Benjamin drew on Erwin Panofsky and Fritz Saxl, *Dürers 'Melancholia I'. Eine quellen- und typengeschichtlichen Untersuchung* (Leipzig: Teubner, 1923).
35. In her journals, Sontag writes about 'rereading Panofsky's essay "Symbolism and Dürer's 'Melancholia I' "' (Box 128, Folder 5), probably referring to the ideas on *Melancholia I* presented by Panofsky in *The Life and Art of Albrecht Dürer*, a reprint of an earlier work in two volumes, *Albrecht Dürer*, first published in 1943. Sontag's ideas resonate strongly with Panofsky's discussion of Dürer's *Melancholia I* in the chapter 'Reorientation in the Graphic Arts: The Culmination of Engraving, 1507/11–1514' (*Life* 132–71). See especially pp. 157–71.
36. Box 128, Folder 1. Sontag's quote is probably from the chapter 'Of Accidie: On Mortification' by Cassian of Marseilles.
37. As Panofsky writes, the legibility of the world ends, but the alienation brought on by the world's illegibility seems as important. Dürer's Melancholia becomes a reference point for the modern form of secular ascesis which is required by thought.
38. Box 128, Folder 5. Sontag, *As Consciousness* 495. For an in-depth discussion of this point, see Chapter 7.
39. See Benjamin's Erkentniss Theorie, 'Theory of Knowledge' 276.
40. For this function of melancholy, see the study co-authored by Raymond Klibansky, Erwin Panofsky and Fritz Saxl, *Saturn and Melancholy*. The study is divided into four parts, with Part IV entirely devoted to Dürer's engraving *Melancholia I*. Part II, 'Saturn, the Star of Melancholy', explores representations of Saturn in the literary and pictorial traditions, while Part III, 'Poetic Melancholy' and 'Melancholia Generosa', traces the transformations of melancholy which, from subjective mood, in the post-medieval tradition and in the Renaissance becomes associated with the man of letters and his pursuits, and goes on to preside over the rise of the modern notion of genius.

While working on him in the late 1970s, Sontag joins Benjamin 'under the sign of Saturn', that is to say, in the realisation that, in the humanist tradition since the Renaissance, Saturn, despite all his menace, had been '"iuvans pater" of men of intellect' (and women of intellect), endowing them with extraordinary power (Klibansky et al. 254). It is not a coincidence that, in 'The Aesthetics of Silence', Sontag had quoted

Keats: 'thought beyond thought'. Keats, in fact, scorned traditional melancholy understood as a subjective mood; his new 'romantic' melancholy conveyed the longing of thought to be closer than ever to reality; it was a 'harsh and alert melancholy, whose very yearning for the eternal brought it in a new sense nearer to reality' (Klibansky et al. 238).

Chapter 4

1. Box 124, Folder 6.
2. Box 82, Folder 47.
3. The lead essay 'Against Interpretation' was originally published in 1964 in the *Evergreen Review*.
4. Box 124, Folder 11.
5. Offering the example of T. S. Eliot's 'Prufrock', David Ayers writes that the experience of the reader is that of 'being plunged into an obscure involvement with the "character" and language' (19).
6. Szondi died prematurely in the early 1970s and could therefore only witness the most popular phase of deconstruction.
7. Box 126, Folder 10.
8. Box 124, Folder 11.
9. Box 134, Folder 10.
10. The tie of knowledge to this ban is the main concern of Derrida in 'Archive Fever': 'this archontic dimension of domiciliation, with this archic, in truth patriarchic, function, without which no archive would ever come into play or appear as such' (Derrida and Prenovitz 10).
11. Ricoeur differentiates among three principal kinds: 1) the documentary trace, a type of 'external' mark strictly pertaining to the archive as a social institution (the material stored in the archives, which I take to be what I found in 'the boxes' at UCLA); 2) the cortical trace, pertaining to the biological organisation of the brain, consisting of external marks for the brain; 3) the psychical trace, the sort of inscription which I discuss in this chapter. Ricoeur's work on archived memory concerns the historian's craft but can have a bearing on other kinds of readers, and anyone who encounters an archive is a reader.
12. See her essay on Leni Riefensthal, 'Fascinating Fascism' (1974), in *Under the Sign of Saturn* (73–105).
13. Box 128, Folder 3.
14. Box 128, Folder 1. Sontag refers to Jameson's book *The Prison House of Language*.
15. Box 84, Folder 43.
16. Box 127, Folder 9.
17. Box 127, Folder 9.
18. Box 127, Folder 9.

19. Sontag begins to work through the implications of the idea of modernism as intellectual property to be guarded by a few, and begins to dissociate herself from the melancholy narrative of its end in the age of consumer culture.
20. Box 127, Folder 9
21. Box 127, Folder 9.
22. Box 127, Folder 9.
23. Box 127, Folder 9.
24. Box 127, Folder 9. In Sontag's notes, her interest in camp illustrates this streamlining of modernism: 'History of camp taste in the last 10 years [1964–74] illustrates the perils of extending to everyone the invitation to exercise the faculty of taste, that invitation which, generalized, is the basis of a consumer society' (Box 127, Folder 9). Her notes suggest that it was her interest in modernism to lead her to study fascist aesthetics. See 'Fascinating Fascism' and 'Syberberg's Hitler' in *Under the Sign of Saturn*.
25. Box 127, Folder 9.
26. The song is 'It's Alright, Ma (I'm Only Bleeding)'. Box 126, Folder 10.
27. Box 127, Folder 9.
28. A list of books to read, probably drafted in 1973, includes Derrida's *Marges* in French and Foucault's *Birth of the Clinic*, mixed with titles on photography and a book on Saturn (see Fig. 1). On the inside cover of a notebook dated 1976–1977, she lists Jauss, 'Literary History as a Challenge to Literary Theory', in *New Directions in Literary History*, and Jacques Derrida, 'White Mythology', *New Literary History* (1974).
29. As we shall see in Chapters 6 and 7, Benjamin is the figure who presides over her rediscovery of the complexity of modernism in light of the new theorists. He connects the modernist past and the postmodernist present because he did not share the traditional disdain for mass culture. Box 127, Folder 9.
30. She even plans to write an essay about speed and velocity as the only new category of twentieth-century consciousness. Box 127, Folder 10.
31. Box 127, Folder 10. Sontag, *As Consciousness* 397.
32. It was published as an article entitled 'Photography: The Beauty Treatment', *The New York Review of Books*, 28 November 1974, 35–9.
33. This is why, in her public work, Sontag talks about the didactic democratisation of beauty. This is also why, in her journals, at about the same time, she spoke, in a critical tone, of modernism as the question of the intellectual (Box 127, Folder 9) and of the intellectual as 'an impossible project'. Box 128, Folder 8. Sontag, *As Consciousness* 518.
34. Box 125, Folder 4.
35. The original version of the chapter, with the title 'Shooting America', was published in *The New York Review of Books*, 18 April 1974, 17–24.
36. Box 128, Folder 5. Sontag, *As Consciousness* 438.
37. Box 127, Folder 9.

38. In January 1929, after eight years in Europe, Abbott returned to the United States. She pursued a photographic project on New York, funded by the Federal Art Project and sponsored by the Museum of the City of New York. The result was *Changing New York*, a guidebook to visitors to New York's World Fair, published in 1939 by E. P. Dutton & Co., which included 97 of Abbott's photographs.
39. This is the case of *Stone and William Streets, Manhattan*, May 12, 1936; *City Arabesque, George Washington Bridge, Riverside Drive and 179th Street, Manhattan*, January 17, 1936; but especially *Manhattan Bridge: Looking Up*, November 11, 1936.
40. Berenice Abbott, *Seventh Avenue Looking South from 35th Street*, in Abbott, *Changing New York*.
41. *Changing New York*, Lower East Side: Plate 13.
42. *Changing New York*, Greenwich Village: Plate 10.
43. Berenice Abbott papers, Box 9, Folder 15, Manuscripts and Archives Division, The New York Public Library, Astor, Lenox, and Tilden Foundations.
44. Berenice Abbott papers, Box 9, Folder 15, Manuscripts and Archives Division, The New York Public Library, Astor, Lenox, and Tilden Foundations.
45. Box 128, Folder 8. Sontag, *As Consciousness* 495.
46. For a discussion of these paradoxes, see Armstrong 67. In chapter 4, 'Reform! Bodies, Selves, Politics, Aesthetics', with reference to the body, Armstrong notices that, while it is 'rendered electric or efficient', it also becomes a problem. He identifies a 'contradictory mixture' of nature (Darwin's theories) and pathology (medical discourse on neurasthenia, hyperstimulation etc.) (67). In his turn, Peter Nicholls, in *Modernisms: A Literary Guide*, speaks of the 'ironies of the modern', of the 'sense of splitting and of contradictory impulses at war' within self and society (19), whose most obvious example is perhaps the city seen as 'both dangerous and exhilarating' (17).
47. Box 54, Folder 4.
48. Box 54, Folder 4.
49. Box 128, Folder 6.
50. Box 54, Folder 4. The repression connects with the paradox of a modernity that, while liberating subjective energies, also reduces individuals to cases.
51. Box 149, Folder 5.
52. Box 149, Folder 5. The fascination with Plato comes alive in Sontag's notes. She is especially fascinated with psyche as a source of spontaneous change/activity in all other things as well as with its power to diffuse change of all kinds in the physical world.
53. Demos's words, 'The Soul is freedom', taken down in her notes on Plato, would be echoed, decades later, in the title of her speech 'Literature is Freedom'. The title can be read as a homage, in the mood

of Duchamp's readymade *Apolinère Enameled*. Duchamp's work consists of a metal plate advertising a brand of soap, Sapolin Enamel, in which the letters have been changed to read as a homage to the poet and master (Cabanne 106).

54. Box 148, Folder 5.
55. Box 148, Folder 5.
56. Box 128, Folder 5. Sontag, *As Consciousness* 438.
57. To Mondrian, harmony meant the compenetration of matter and non-matter. His aim was 'to destroy the distinction between figure and ground, between matter and non-matter' (Golding 20).
58. Sontag was familiar with Kandinsky, whom she must have read in 1964 or shortly thereafter. Kandinsky's *The Spiritual in Art* features in a list of titles around that time. Box 125, Folder 1.
59. She explains that with Marx the subject becomes a mode of production, and appears only as a signifying process. The second overcoming is modernism, that is to say, the practice of language and the text by poets who had already discovered the impossibility of a subject present to himself, of 'the subject's impossible coincidence with himself' as Freud too would affirm (Kristeva, *Revolution* 215–16).
60. Box 125, Folder 4. Sontag, *As Consciousness* 171.
61. Box 128, Folder 1.
62. Box 127, Folder 9.
63. Even after she left graduate school (between 1958 and 1959), Sontag went on to teach in philosophy departments at various institutions before becoming a full-time critic and writer. Her syllabi for her courses in the philosophy of religion are impressive and she received letters of appreciation and admiration from her students.
64. Box 128, Folder 1
65. Box 128, Folder 3.
66. Box 128, Folder 8. Sontag, *As Consciousness* 518.
67. Box 128, Folder 8. Sontag, *As Consciousness* 519.
68. Box 128, Folder 3.

Chapter 5

1. The influence they exerted on each other is such that it would not be wrong to think of Sontag and Thek as significant others. In his letters to her, the only side of the correspondence that survives, written for the most part after the high moment of their friendship had passed, the artist recollects a partnership similar in many ways to that of Robert Rauschenberg and Jasper Johns. In the ongoing rediscovery of Thek, Sontag has been acknowledged as 'an intellectual mentor' (Zelevansky 12), and some of the essays in *Against Intepretation* – especially 'Against Interpretation', 'Happenings', 'The Anthropologist

as Hero' and 'The Artist as Exemplary Sufferer' – have been read as proof of an 'intellectual/artistic exchange' between the two (Weibel 39). What went on between them in the first stage of Sontag's career (1959–65) has the nature of an important collaboration which still remains to be written.

2. Derrida to Sontag, 12 February 1965. Box 84, Folder 43.
3. The two articles in question were an early draft of what was to become the first part of the book *Of Grammatology*, 'Writing Before the Letter'.
4. In her beautiful tribute to Thek, 'Beatitudes: Remembering Paul Thek', Ann Wilson writes that his art 'found its guiding principles' in Saint Paul's first letter to the Corinthians, chapter 14, where the Apostle extols the vocation for prophesying and contrasts it with the lower capacity for 'speaking in tongues', to underline Thek's art of moral allegory (116). The connection with Catholicism is crucial to understanding Thek's work. In a letter to Sontag he talks about his religious longings: 'I am a renegade Christian still looking for the Transcendental Experience', and mentions the 'Passion according to Matthew' (24 June 1966) (Sontag Papers, Box 143, Folder 16). Thek maintained a deep connection with the Catholic faith. By 1973 his devotion would include regular retreats to a monastery to meditate and pray (Zelevansky 14). By the late 1970s he was spending increasing amounts of time practising his devotion. In the early 1980s he decided to join a Carthusian monastery. In 1987 he found out he had AIDS, and wrote to a friend that he was on the verge of being accepted by a Benedectine order but that his illness made it impossible (Zelevansky, note 29).

   In another piece, Wilson discusses the adversarial potential of Thek's Catholicism in the context of the art scene of his time. Wilson points out Thek's Catholic rejection of the puritanism of minimalism, offering the example of Donald Judd's installations on the old army base at Marfa, Texas: 'No flesh is there; it is all hard unyielding metal, and neon light' ('Mare Tenebrarum' 231).

   Harald Falckenberg mentions the reception of Thek's work as Catholic. Under the patronage of Opus Dei, the art museum of the archbishopric of Cologne has assembled the largest collection of Thek's work dating from his early period before 1960, but also other important work (Falckenberg, 'Freedom' 22).
5. He would shape life (including sexual experimentation and the use of drugs) into a technique for sensing another reality (Wilson, 'Beatitudes' 117). Comparing him to Bosch, Ann Wilson suggests that Thek was consciously involved in the creation of 'moral allegory' (116).
6. It was begun in New York at the end of 1963 on his return from Italy. He had met the owner of Galleria Trastevere, Topazia Alliata, who had held a private show of his work there and had arranged an exhibition for him at Galleria 88, where he showed *Television Analyzations*. She invited him to Sicily where, near Palermo, he visited the Capuchin catacombs. On his return he started the 'Meat Pieces' (Zelevansky).

I first saw the installation at the Hammer Museum in Los Angeles in 2011, where I was researching in the Susan Sontag archive at UCLA.

7. The original source is Flood (106).
8. Maunsell 61; Susan Sontag Papers, Box 152, Folder 9.
9. Box 124, Folder 6.
10. Box 124, Folder 7.
11. Box 124, Folder 11, September 1963.
12. Box 125, Folder 4.
13. Box 124, Folder 7.
14. Box 125, Folder 1. Sontag, *As Consciousness* 46.
15. Thek to Sontag, 22 June 1965, Box 143, Folder 16. For quotations from Thek's letters to Sontag I am referencing Sontag's papers. However, substantial excerpts are available in Brehm. For Thek's love of nature and his choice to retreat to outlying spots at the edge of the ocean, see Zelevansky.
16. Thek to Sontag, 22 June 1965, Box 143, Folder 16.
17. Thek to Sontag, 22 June 1965, Box 143, Folder 16.
18. Box 128, Folder 6. Sontag, *As Consciousness* 474.
19. The same interest in the body emerges in Sontag's notes. In particular one of the notebooks dated 1965–66 might be called 'the body notebook' because it reads as a long meditation on embodied knowledge. Box 125, Folder 4.
20. Box 125, Folder 4. Sontag, *As Consciousness* 151.
21. Box 125, Folder 4. Sontag, *As Consciousness* 151.
22. Box 143, Folder 16.
23. For discussion of the ways in which Thek's work is 'the product of a concern with one of the central issues of Modernism', that is to say, the autonomy of art, see Weibel 40–2.
24. Paul Thek, *An erotics of art*, c.1980, synthetic polymer on canvas board, 9 3/4 × 12 3/4 in. (25 × 32.5 cm). Private collection. Reproduced in Sussman and Zelevansky, eds, 230, Fig. 252.
25. Paul Thek, *Susan Lecturing on Neitzsche*, 1987, synthetic polymer on canvas board, 12 × 16 15/16 in. (33 × 43 cm). Watermill Center Collection.
26. Box 143, Folder 16, 5 December 1975.
27. Thek to Sontag, 12 March 1987.
28. Rilke united them in a particularly powerful way. Thek died on 10 August 1987 at 1.45 a.m. On 5 August Sontag had gone to see him. Thek asked the other visitors to leave them alone. Sontag said that Thek requested that she read him Rilke's *Duino Elegies*. She went and got a copy and read to everyone from 3.00 to 6.00 p.m. Box 143, Folder 16.
29. Kenneth Burke to Sontag, Box 82, Folder 47.
30. Paul Thek, *Untitled (Diver)*, 1969–70, synthetic polymer and gesso on newspaper, 22 1/4 × 33 3/16 in. (56.5 × 84.3 cm). Collection of Gail and Tony Ganz. Reproduced in Sussman and Zelevansky, eds, 126, Fig. 125.

31. It has been suggested that the source of the painting is the male figure on the cover slab from *The Tomb of the Diver*, unearthed in 1968 in Paestum, Italy, today preserved in the Museo Archeologico Nazionale in Paestum (Zelevansky 10).
32. Although she does not make the connection with Sontag's essay on Pavese, Lynn Zelevansky similarly associates the diver with the artist engaged in his solitary pursuit; the diver, she proposes, is 'a reflection of the contemplative Thek, the artist who sought out moments of private transcendence, intensely idealistic and deeply concerned with matters of the soul' (Zelevansky 10).
33. Box 125, Folder 1.
34. In a thin spiral notebook dated 1960, she draws a list of readings including Heidegger's *Being and Time*, Nietzsche and Wittgenstein. Box 124, Folder 6.
35. Box 128, Folder 1.
36. Box 134, Folder 10.
37. Marie-Rose Logan, conversation with the author, July 2012, Irvine.
38. Between Derrida's letter of 1965 and his lecture at Columbia, Sontag had continued to engage with him in the rawness of the journal form. In 1967 she sees him as on a par with Roland Barthes. She contemplates the 'special application' of his 'semiology' to film, drawing connections between Derrida, Christian Metz and Pasolini (Box 125, Folder 5). His work is on her mind as she writes on photography and conceives her fourth book of essays, *Under the Sign of Saturn*. The title *Margins of Philosophy*, in French, appears on a loose page, as part of a booklist, probably drafted in 1973, together with Foucault's *Birth of the Clinic*, books on photography and a book on Saturn and Melancholy (see Fig. 1). In early October of 1974, in New York, she plans to read Derrida's essay 'Structure, Sign, and Play in the Discourse of the Human Sciences' (Box 127, Folder 9). Derrida's thought accompanies her not only as she sorts out and overcomes her master–disciple relation to Benjamin, but also in her efforts to overcome the Frankfurt School's position on the work of art, in particular Adorno's prohibition of beauty. Derrida's piece 'White Mythology', published in *New Literary History* (1974) features in a reading list that includes Adorno's essay 'Commitment' and work by Hans Robert Jauss, the critic who challenged Adorno.
39. Lynn Zelevansky writes that he identified especially with the early Van Gogh of the Dutch years epitomised by *The Potato Eaters* (1885) (Zelevansky 12).
40. Box 143, Folder 16, 29 August, no year.
41. The exact date when she began to read Benjamin first hand cannot be established with any degree of certainty. In a notebook ostensibly from 1964, but which also contains entries for 1962, there is a Benjamin page. She lists his bibliography taken from *Oeuvres Choisies* (Paris: Juillard, 1959). At the top of the page there is a note to remind herself that in 1928 B. published in German two books, *One-Way Street* and a book

on Baroque Drama. Both the titles are taken down in French (Box 125, Folder 1). At the end of 1964, however, or soon thereafter she probably read Benjamin's *Trauerspiel* book. In a thin spiral notebook from 1964, right after an entry dated 6 December, a page titled 'Read' contains a list of titles which includes 'Walter Benjamin's book on the baroque' (Box 125, Folder 2). For a detailed discussion, see Chapter 7.

42. Box 125, Folder 1.
43. Box 125, Folder 2.
44. Box 124, Folder 11.
45. Box 125, Folder 2.
46. Robert Rauschenberg, *Orphic Ditty* (Salvage Series), 1984, acrylic on canvas, 81½ × 110 in. The Rokkedal Collection, Denmark. See Kotz 51.
47. Mark Ormond, email to the author, September 2004.
48. Achille Bonito Oliva, conversation with the author, 14 November 2004.
49. Construction sites were a favourite with Rauschenberg, evoking his notion of the work of art as an ongoing workshop, a thing in the making.
50. Box 125, Folder 1.
51. The phrase 'summer project' is from a letter that Paul Thek wrote to Sontag on 24 June 1966. Box 143, Folder 16.
52. Box 128, Folder 8.
53. Sayres discusses Sontag's long-standing commitment to 'the self-annulling and irrationalist core of modernist aesthetic' and her struggle with its paradoxes: 'For some fifteen years she committed herself to bringing her particular understanding of this sensibility to terms, and part of the effort had been directed toward curing its transformational delusions' (*Elegiac Modernist* 103).
54. When she breaks up with Nicole Stephane, she is afraid that the end of the relationship is 'my last chance to be first-rate./ (Intellectually, as an artist)'. Box 128, Folder 3.
55. References to Duchamp and Breton crop up in her journals only after she met Johns. During one of her stays at Edisto Beach, she also discovers Schoenberg and reads his letters at midnight. Box 125, Folder 3.
56. Box 125, Folder 4.
57. Box 125, Folder 4.
58. 20 May 1965, Box 125, Folder 3. Sontag, *As Consciousness* 82.
59. Box 125, Folder 4.
60. Box 125, Folder 4.
61. See my discussion of this point in Chapter 7.
62. Box 125, Folder 5.

Chapter 6

1. Box 143, Folder 16, Thek to Sontag.
2. 'The Avant-garde and Contemporary Literature', undated talk. Box 75, Folder 8.

3. Box 75, Folder 8.
4. I am working with the same edition that Sontag read. For more recent English translations, see 'The Work of Art in the Age of Its Technological Reproducibility: Second Version', in Benjamin, *Selected Writings: Vol. 3, 1935–1938*, ed. Howard Eiland and Michael W. Jennings, trans. Edmund Jephcott, Howard Eiland et al. (Cambridge, MA: The Belknap Press of Harvard University Press, 2002), 101–33; and 'The Work of Art in the Age of Its Technological Reproducibility: Third Version', in Benjamin, *Selected Writings: Vol 4, 1938–1940*, ed. Howard Eiland and Michael W. Jennings, trans. Edmund Jephcott et al. (Cambridge, MA: The Belknap Press of Harvard University Press, 2003), 251–83.
5. Karl Marx, 'The Fetishism of Commodities and the Secret Thereof' (qtd. in Jennings 26).
6. Jennings describes the position of Benjamin's spectator as the thinker before an illegible world when he comments on the fact that ambiguity is for Benjamin an epistemological and moral category: 'The cognitive disorientation that results from encounters with the deeply ambiguous world of things prevents the human subject from an adequate moral agency and above all denies her a capacity for resistance and social change' (16).
7. Box 211, Folder 9 (Sontag's Library).
8. Gilles Deleuze's *Difference and Repetition*, which includes a chapter entitled 'The Image of Thought', was originally published in 1968. It was first published in English only in 1994.
9. In their widely used textbook, *Understanding Poetry*, Cleanth Brooks and Robert Penn Warren thus comment on Yeats's 'After Long Silence': 'Wisdom, the power to reach an interpretation, comes only as the body decays' (117). Poetry is associated with youth, vigour and spontaneity; criticism, on the other hand, while representing wisdom, is closely allied to the decay of the body. Criticism is a wisdom, it would seem, that both poem and image can dispense with, just like Yeats's lovers.
10. Found on sheets of paper bearing at the top of the page the logo of San Pellegrino water. See note to the fragment compiled by Giorgio Agamben, Barbara Chitussi and Clemens-Carl Harle, editors of Walter Benjamin, *Charles Baudelaire: Un poeta lirico nell'età del Capitalismo Avanzato* (Vicenza: Neri Pozza, 2011), 26.
11. In the 1937 fragment that I read in this section, Benjamin points to the cinema as a balm for the unbearable loss of the aura ('Che cos'è l'aura?' 26), but, as I have tried to show in the preceding section, the same is true of photography in 'Little History of Photography'.
12. I am working here with two texts: an early essay, 'Ellipsis on Dread and the Specular Seduction', and the rewrite of the ideas from that essay in her book *Intimate Revolt*. I decided to weave references from both the earlier and later versions of Kristeva's ideas on specular seduction, dread and intellectual activity.

13. Adorno credits Benjamin for introducing the aura in 'Little History of Photography' to speak of 'that which moves into the distance and is critical of the ideological superficies of life', but he laments the conflation of auratic and cultic poles in the Art Work essay (*Aesthetic Theory* 72). For Adorno, Benjamin works with a 'simple antithesis between auratic and mass produced work', but in 'Little History' he 'in no way pronounced the antithesis as undialectically as he did five years later in his essay on reproduction' (72). Adorno finds that even the technique of montage, discussed by Benjamin, can be faulted with a 'complaisant irrationalism' for 'adaptation to material that is delivered ready-made from outside the work' (73).
14. Benjamin to Scholem, Paris, 24 October 1935. Benjamin and Scholem 172.
15. Box 128, Folder 8. Sontag, *As Consciousness* 518.
16. Box 128, Folder 3.
17. Box 128, Folder 3.
18. 'Real thinking' is a phrase from Sontag's journals. Box 125, Folder 5.
19. Box 128, Folder 8.
20. One of the traditional sources on the Neapolitan Revolution is Vincenzo Cuoco, *Saggio storico sulla rivoluzione Napoletana*. On Eleonora de Fonseca, see Elena Urgnani, *L'opera letteraria e politica di Eleonora de Fonseca Pimentel*, a study of Fonseca as a woman of letters and of her literary gifts. For a fictional account of Fonseca's life, see Enzo Striano, *II resto di niente* [The remains of nothing]. The novel has been made into a movie, *II resto di niente*, dir. Antonietta De Lillo, perf. Maria de Madeiros, Rosario Sparno, Imma Villa, Enzo Moscato, Istituto Luce, 2004. In an interview, director De Lillo has cited Sontag's *The Volcano Lover* as one of her sources. See Capuani.
21. Her production of Pirandello's *As You Desire Me* (1979) and her play *Alice in Bed* (1991) are perhaps as overt in their feminism as *The Volcano Lover*.

Chapter 7

1. Box 124, Folder 11.
2. Box 125, Folder 1.
3. Box 125, Folder 1. Sontag, *As Consciousness* 19.
4. Box 125, Folder 1. Sontag, *As Consciousness* 19.
5. Box 125, Folder 1.
6. Box 125, Folder 1. Sontag, *As Consciousness* 28.
7. Letter from Benjamin to Adorno (9 December 1938) from his residence in Paris, 10 Rue Dombasle, XVe (Adorno and Benjamin 289–98). Adorno offers his feedback on Benjamin's manuscript 'The Paris of the Second Empire in Baudelaire'. Benjamin replies:

> I believe that speculation can only begin its inevitably audacious flight with some prospect of success if, instead of donning the waxen wings of esotericism, it seeks its source of strength in construction alone. It is the needs of construction which dictated that the second part of my book should consist primarily of philological material. What is involved here is less a case of 'ascetic discipline' than a methodological precaution. Incidentally, this philological part was the only one which could be completed independently – a circumstance which I also had to bear in mind. (291)

In the previous letter (10 November 1938), quoted below, Adorno had expressed concern for Benjamin's 'abstention' from theoretical construction, which only serves to transport subject matter 'into a realm quite opposed to asceticism: a realm where history and magic oscillate' (282).

8. Box 125, Folder 1. The label on this folder says: 'Paris, – London–Paris Aug–Sept 1964. Reading notes and transcription of French lists.'
9. Box 124, Folder 1.
10. Box 125, Folder 1.
11. Adorno was concerned about the spell cast by facticity on the investigator. In the important letter to Benjamin dated 10 November 1938, he refers to his colleague's tendency 'to attribute to mere material enumeration a power of illumination which really belongs to theoretical construction alone rather than to purely pragmatical allusions' (Adorno and Benjamin 284). Adorno reminds Benjamin that the method of dialectical materialism requires the construction of the object in a historical perspective and expresses concern for Benjamin's 'ascetic refusal of interpretation' (282). In his reply of 9 December 1938, Benjamin defends what Adorno had termed his 'wide-eyed presentation of mere facts' (291). He concedes that the spell casts by facticity on the investigator should be dissolved as 'the object is construed in an historical perspective' (292), but, referring to the importance that astonishment has in Adorno's study of Kierkegaard, and amending Adorno's position, proposes that astonishment 'is an outstanding object' of critical inquiry (292).
12. Box 128, Folder 6. Sontag, *As Consciousness* 474.
13. A point emphasised by William Gass in his review. See Gass.
14. In relation to this imaginary construction of the master, it is striking that she calls Adorno a disciple of Benjamin ('Under the Sign of Saturn' 123).
15. For Benjamin, the 'desire of contemporary masses to bring things "closer" spatially and humanly' bears as one of its symptoms a need to surpass uniqueness by accepting a reproduction of an object of reality (*Illuminations* 23).
16. Box 128, Folder 3.

17. Box 128, Folder 3. Sontag, *As Consciousness* 412.
18. Box 128, Folder 3. Sontag's essay on Benjamin was first published in *The New York Times* in 1978 with the title 'The Last Intellectual'. A version of the piece, with notes, was used as the introduction to *One-Way Street and Other Writings* (London: NLB, 1979) and, at last, with the changed title 'Under the Sign of Saturn', was included in the eponymous collection (1980). See Poague and Parsons 237.
19. I borrow the phrase from Lonzi, 'La solitudine' 356.
20. For the notion of an unassimilated avant-garde energy in late modernist writers and, in fact, for the notion of late modernism, I refer the reader to Tyrus Miller's study *Late Modernism*. As defined by Miller, late modernism refers to a cultural network dependent on early twentieth-century innovation, in the sense that it 'deform[s] and change[s] the shape and function of that network' (19). Late modernism may thus be taken to indicate a poetics of response, a set of creative and critical gestures that react to an earlier creative and intellectual network. In the process, it reveals an inalienable bond – Miller speaks of a 'genetic past' (19) – to an undercurrent zone of modernism which Miller calls 'the unassimilated heritage of the avant-garde' (19). Most of the men that Sontag admires are late modernists in this sense: they 'struggle against the apotheosis of form in earlier modernism' (19) and, whether they are creative writers or philosophers, tend to unsettle the formal mastery or craft that had characterised early modernism.
21. Box 128, Folder 3.
22. For a discussion of the same quote, see Hansen (201).
23. 'I've got this onerous charge, this work-obsessed, ambitious writer who bears the same name as I do . . . To write, as Kafka said, you can never be alone enough. But the people you love tend not to appreciate your need to be solitary, to turn your back on them. You have to fend off the others to get your work done. And to appease them – that issue is especially keen if the writer is a woman. Don't be mad, or jealous. I can't help it. You see, *she* writes' ('Singleness' 261).
24. Box 128, Folder 3.
25. I borrow the phrase from Giorgio Agamben's introduction to Walter Benjamin, *Charles Baudelaire: Un poeta lirico nell' età del capitalismo avanzato*, co-edited with Barbara Chitussi and Clemens-Carl Härle. The volume is a fascinating collection of documents through which the editors reconstruct Benjamin's book on Baudelaire.
26. She speaks of 'his reveries' and connects the reverie mode to his need and will to translate materials of interest (especially Baudelaire) into philosophical argument. Benjamin's reveries recall Baudelaire's way of harnessing dreaminess to work ('Under the Sign of Saturn' 126), but Surrealism helped him turn the dreaminess that Baudelaire experienced negatively into 'material needed for work' (127).
27. Box 128, Folder 6. Sontag, *As Consciousness* 474.

28. Box 128, Folder 6. Sontag, *As Consciousness* 474.
29. Box 54, Folder 4.
30. Box 54, Folder 4.
31. Box 128, Folder 6. Sontag, *As Consciousness* 474.
32. Box 128, Folder 6.
33. Box 54, Folder 4.
34. Box 128, Folder 6. Sontag, *As Consciousness* 474.
35. Box 54, Folder 4.
36. Box 54, Folder 4.
37. Box 54, Folder 4.
38. Box 128, Folder 6.
39. Box 128, Folder 6. Sontag, *As Consciousness* 456.
40. Box 128, Folder 6. Sontag, *As Consciousness* 456.
41. Box 128, Folder 6. Sontag, *As Consciousness* 457.
42. Box 128, Folder 8.
43. Box 126, Folder 10. Sontag, *As Consciousness* 368.
44. Box 126, Folder 10.
45. Box 128, Folder 1. Sontag, *As Consciousness* 401.
46. Box 128, Folder 8. Sontag, *As Consciousness* 518.
47. Gershom Scholem's 'Walter Benjamin und Sein Engel', containing the Agesilaus Santander text in the two versions, was published in translation in *Denver Quarterly* in 1974, a year after Sontag had heard Arendt at the party. The original German version appears in *Zur Aktualität Walter Benjamins*, ed. Siegfried Unseld (Frankfurt am Main: Suhrkamp, 1972).
48. Box 128, Folder 5. Sontag, *As Consciousness* 495–6.
49. Tzvetan Todorov calls this simple truth 'personal experience' and specifies that, in the case of the scholar and theorist – of anyone who thinks or studies an object – 'it means neither that confession should replace knowledge nor that they should be construed as parallel' (Todorov 10–11). Nevertheless, the relation of work to life can be one of 'complementarity' (11). Personal experience transforms the scholar's understanding of the world (her way of speaking and writing about an object) (11).
50. Benjamin to Adorno, 9 December 1938. Adorno and Benjamin 290.
51. Box 126, Folder 10.
52. Box 128, Folder 8.
53. The requirement endured in the twentieth century. For Husserl, for example, 'to become a philosopher, a subject has to overcome – by an act of phenomenological reduction – his or her ordinary, "natural" attitude that is dominated by the will to self-preservation, and to take another, phenomenological, truly philosophical attitude beyond an interest in one's own survival in the world' (Groys ix).
54. Benjamin closes the text as follows: 'Just like myself; for scarcely had I seen you for the first time than I returned with you to where I had come from' ('Agesilaus Santander (Second Version)' 715).

55. 'Le lecteur dit à l'ecrivain: "Montre-toi" au moment où celui-ci l'interpelle pour lui dire: "Regarde-moi." Proposition qu'on peut sans doute inverser sans rien y changer de fondamental en faisant dire au lecteur: "Montre *moi*," au moment où il rencontre l'appel de l'écrivain "Regarde toi," en utilisant toutes les ressources polysémiques de ce renversement' (Green 28).

Coda (to the Gentle Reader)

1. 'The World as India', The St. Jerome Lecture on Literary Translation, in *At the Same Time: Essays and Speeches* (New York: Farrar, Strauss, and Giroux, 2007), 156–79.

Bibliography

Abbott, Berenice. *Changing New York*. Intro. Bonnie Yochelson. New York: The New York Press, 1997.

——. 'Changing New York'. *Berenice Abbott, Photographer: A Modern Vision*. Ed. Julia Van Haaften. New York: The New York Public Library, 1989. 24–5.

Adorno, Theodor W. *Aesthetic Theory*. Ed. Gretel Adorno and Rolf Tiedman. Trans. Robert Hullot-Kentor. London: Continuum, 2007. First German edn 1970.

——. *Minima Moralia: Reflections from the Damaged Life*. Trans. E. F. N. Jephcott. London: New Left Books, 1974. First German ed. 1951.

Adorno, Theodor, and Walter Benjamin. *The Complete Correspondence 1932–1940*. Ed. Henry Lonitz. Trans. Nicholas Walker. Cambridge: Polity, 1999.

Agamben, Giorgio. *The Coming Community*. Trans. Michael Hardt. Minneapolis: University of Minnesota Press, 2003. First Italian edn 1990.

Andrew, Dudley. 'A Preface to Disputation'. *The Image in Dispute: Art and Cinema in the Age of Photography*. Ed. Dudley Andrew, with the assistance of Sally Shafto. Austin: University of Texas Press, 1997. vii–xiv.

Arendt, Hannah. 'Introduction. Walter Benjamin: 1892–1940'. *Illuminations*. Ed. Hannah Arendt. Trans. Harry Zohn. New York: Schocken Books, 1969. 1–55.

Argan, Giulio C. 'Ideology and Iconology'. *The Language of Images*. Ed. W. J. T. Mitchell. Chicago: University of Chicago Press, 1980. 15–24.

Armstrong, Tim. *Modernism*. London: Polity, 2005.

Attridge, Derek. '"This Strange Institution Called Literature": An Interview with Jacques Derrida'. *Jacques Derrida: Acts of Literature*. Ed. Derek Attridge. New York and London: Routledge, 1992. 33–75.

Ayers, David. *Modernism: A Short Introduction*. Oxford: Blackwell Publishing, 2004.

Badiou, Alain. *Saint Paul: The Foundations of Universalism*. Trans. Ray Brassier. Stanford: Stanford University Press, 1997.

Barthes, Roland. *Camera Lucida: Reflections on Photography*. Trans. Richard Howard. New York: Hill & Wang, 1981.

Beasley, Rebecca. *Theorists of Modernist Poetry: T. S. Eliot, T. E. Hulme, Ezra Pound*. New York: Routledge, 2007.

Bell, Michael. 'The Metaphysics of Modernism'. *The Cambridge Companion to Modernism*. Ed. Michael Levenson. Cambridge: Cambridge University Press, 1999. 9–32.

Benjamin, Walter. 'Agesilaus Santander (First Version)'. Trans. Rodney Livingstone. *Selected Writings. Vol. 2: 1927–1934*, 712–13.

——. 'Agesilaus Santander (Second Version)'. Trans. Rodney Livingstone. *Selected Writings. Vol. 2: 1927–1934*, 714–16.

——. 'Che cos'è l'aura?' *Charles Baudelaire: un poeta lirico nell'età del capitalismo avanzato*. Ed. Giorgio Agamben, Barbara Chitussi, and Clemens-Carl Härle. Vicenza: Neri Pozza, 2012. 25–6.

——. 'Goethe's Elective Affinities'. Trans. Stanley Corngold. *Selected Writings. Vol. 1: 1913–1926*, 297–360.

——. 'Hashish in Marseilles'. *One-Way Street and Other Writings*. Trans. Edmund Jephcott and Kingsley Shorter. London: NLB, 1979. 215–22.

——. 'Little History of Photography'. Trans. Edmund Jephcott and Kingsley Shorter. *Selected Writings. Vol. 2: 1927–1934*, 507–30.

——. 'On the Mimetic Faculty'. Trans. Edmund Jephcott. *Selected Writings. Vol. 2: 1927–1934*, 720–2.

——. 'On Some Motifs in Baudelaire'. *Illuminations: Essays and Reflections*. Ed. Hannah Arendt. Trans. Harry Zohn. New York: Schocken Books, 1969. 155–200.

——. 'One-Way Street'. Trans. Edmund Jephcott. *Selected Writings. Vol. 1: 1913–1926*, 444–88.

——. *Selected Writings. Vol. 1: 1913–1926*. Ed. Marcus Bullock and Michael W. Jennings. Trans. Edmund Jephcott et al. Cambridge, MA: The Belknap Press of Harvard University Press, 1996.

——. *Selected Writings. Vol. 2: 1927–1934*. Ed. Michael W. Jennings, Howard Eiland, and Gary Smith. Trans. Rodney Livingstone et al. Cambridge, MA: The Belknap Press of Harvard University Press, 1999.

——. 'Theory of Knowledge'. Trans. Rodney Livingstone. *Selected Writings. Vol. 1: 1913–1926*, 276–7.

——. 'The Work of Art in the Age of Mechanical Reproduction'. *Illuminations: Essays and Reflections*. Ed. Hannah Arendt. Trans. Harry Zohn. New York: Schocken Books, 1969. 217–51.

——. 'The Work of Art in the Age of Its Technological Reproducibility: Second Version'. Trans. Edmund Jephcott and Harry Zohn. *Selected Writings: Vol. 3, 1935–1938*. Ed. Howard Eiland and Michael W. Jennings. Trans. Edmund Jephcott et al. Cambridge, MA: The Belknap Press of Harvard University Press, 2002. 101–33

——. 'The Work of Art in the Age of Its Technological Reproducibility: Third Version'. Trans. Harry Zohn and Edmund Jephcott. *Selected Writings: Vol 4, 1938–1940*. Ed. Howard Eiland and Michael W. Jennings. Trans. Edmund Jephcott et al. Cambridge, MA: The Belknap Press of Harvard University Press, 2003. 251–83.

Benjamin, Walter, and Asja Lacis. 'Naples'. Trans. Edmund Jephcott. *Selected Writings. Vol. 1: 1913–1926*. Ed. Marcus Bullock and Michael W. Jennings. Cambridge, MA: The Belknap Press of Harvard University Press, 1996. 414–21.

Benjamin, Walter, and Gershom Scholem. *The Correspondence of Walter Benjamin and Gershom Scholem 1932–1940*. Ed. Gershom Scholem. Trans. Gary Smith and André LeFevere. New York: Schocken Books, 1989.

Benson, Ciarán. *The Absorbed Self: Pragmatism, Psychology and Aesthetic Experience*. New York: Harvester Wheatsheaf, 1993.

Benveniste, Émile. 'Analytical Philosophy and Language'. *Problems in General Linguistics*. Trans. Mar Elizabeth Meek. Coral Gables: University of Miami Press, 1971. 231–8.

Berlant, Lauren. *Cruel Optimism*. Durham, NC: Duke University Press, 2011.

Bollmann, Stefan. *Reading Women*. New York: Merrell Publishers, 2006.

Brehm, Margrit. 'Dear Baby–Dear Sister–Dear Susan: Excerpts from Paul Thek's Letters to Susan Sontag'. *Paul Thek: Artist's Artist*. Ed. Harald Falckenberg and Peter Weibel. ZKM Center for Art and Media Karlsruhe, Germany. Cambridge, MA: MIT Press, 2008. 297–311.

Brightman, Carol, ed. *Writing Dangerously: Mary McCarthy and Her World*. New York: Clarkson, 1992.

Brooks, Cleanth. *The Well Wrought Urn: Studies in the Structure of Poetry*. New York: Harcourt, Brace, 1947.

Brooks, Cleanth, and Robert Penn Warren. *Understanding Poetry: An Anthology for College Students*. New York: Henry Holt, 1951.

Buck-Morss, Susan. *The Dialectics of Seeing: Walter Benjamin and the Arcades Project*. Cambridge, MA: MIT Press, 1991.

Butler, Judith. 'Photography, War, Outrage'. *PMLA* 120.3 (2005): 822–7.

——. 'Torture and the Ethics of Photography: Thinking with Sontag'. *Frames of War: When Is Life Grievable?* London: Verso, 2009. 63–100.

Cabanne, Pierre. *Duchamp & Co*. Paris: Éditions Pierre Terrail, 1997.

Capuani, Monica. 'La rivoluzione di Napoli dagli occhi di donna'. Review of *Il Resto di Niente*. Dir. Antonietta De Lillo. http://www.espressonline.it. Accessed 28 January 2016.

Cartier-Bresson, Henri. *The Europeans*. New York: Simon and Schuster, 1955.

Castle, Terry. 'Desperately Seeking Susan'. *London Review of Books* 27.6 (2005). http:/www.lrb.co.uk/v27/n06/terry-castle/desperately-seeking-susan. Accessed 28 January 2016.

Ching, Barbara. '"Not Even a New Yorker": Susan Sontag in America'. *The Scandal of Susan Sontag*. Ed. Barbara Ching and Jennifer A. Wagner-Lawlor. New York: Columbia University Press, 2009. 52–77.

Copeland, Roger. 'The Habits of Consciousness'. *Conversations with Susan Sontag*. Ed. Leland Poague. Jackson: University Press of Mississippi, 1995. 183–91.

Cotter, Holland. 'On Sontag: Essayist As Metaphor and Muse'. *The New York Times* 18 April 2006. Weekend Arts section, K. www.nytimes.com/2006/08/18/arts/design/18sont.html. Accessed 28 January 2016.

Crescentini, Claudio. *Melancolico De Chirico 1905–1935*. Rome: Lithos, 2000.

Cuoco, Vincenzo. *Saggio storico sulla rivoluzione Napoletana*. Turin: Unione Tipografico-Editrice Torinese, 1975.

De Lillo, Antonietta, dir. *Il resto di niente*. Perf. Maria de Madeiros, Rosario Sparno, Imma Villa, Enzo Moscato. Istituto Luce, 2004.

Derrida, Jacques. 'Force and Signification'. *Writing and Difference*. Chicago: University of Chicago Press, 1978. 3–30.

——. *Of Grammatology*. Trans. Gayatri Chakravorty Spivak. Baltimore: Johns Hopkins University Press, 1976.

——. *Positions*. Trans. Alan Bass. Chicago: University of Chicago Press, 1981.

——. 'Restitutions of Truth in Pointure'. *A Derrida Reader: Between the Blinds*. Ed. Peggy Kamuf. New York: Columbia University Press, 1991. 277–309.

——. 'Signature Event Context'. *Margins of Philosophy*. Trans. Alan Bass. Chicago: University of Chicago Press, 1982. 307–30.

——. 'The Theater of Cruelty and the Closure of Representation'. *Writing and Difference*. Chicago: University of Chicago Press, 1978. 232–50.

Derrida, Jacques, and Eric Prenovitz. 'Archive Fever: A Freudian Impression'. *Diacritics* 25.2 (1995): 9–63.

Dimock, Wai Chee, 'Weak Theory: Henry James, Colm Tóibín, and W. B. Yeats'. *Critical Inquiry* 39.4 (2013): 732–53.

Esposito, Roberto. 'Melanconia e Comunità'. *Termini della politica: Comunità, immunità, biopolitica*. Milan: Mimesis, 2008.

Etzioni, Amitai, and Alyssa Bowoditch, eds. *Public Intellectuals: An Endangered Species?* Lanham, MD: Rowman & Littlefield, 2006.

Fagiolo Dell'Arco, Maurizio. *L'Opera completa di De Chirico, 1908–1924*. Milan: Rizzoli, 1984.

Falckenberg, Harald. 'Freedom is First of all Freedom from Identification'. *Paul Thek: Artist's Artist*. Ed. Harald Falckenberg and Peter Weibel. ZKM Center for Art and Media Karlsruhe, Germany. Cambridge, MA: MIT Press, 2011. 16–37.

——. 'Why?! . . . wondering what we're actually doing'. A conversation in Berlin, with Harald Falckenberg, Julian Heynen and Luc Tuymans, 26 April 2012. *Paul Thek Luc Tuymans*: *Why?!* Galerie Isabelle Czarnowska. Berlin: Distanz, 2013. 43–69.

Flood, Richard. 'Paul Thek: Real Misunderstanding'. *Paul Thek: The Wonderful World That Almost Was*. By Paul Thek, Anke Bangma, Barbera van Kooij, and Louise Neri. Rotterdam: Witte de With, Center for Contemporary Art, 1995. 104–12. First published in *Artforum* 20.2 (1981): 48–523.

Foucault, Michel. *The Archaeology of Knowledge and the Discourse on Language*. Trans. A. M. Sheridan Smith. New York: Pantheon Books, 1972.

Friedman, Susan Stanford. 'Planetarity: Musing Modernist Studies'. *Modernism/modernity* 17.3 (2010): 471–99.

——. 'Theory'. *Modernism and Theory: A Critical Debate*. Ed. Stephen Ross. New York: Routledge, 2009. 237–45.

Gadamer, Hans-Georg. 'Aesthetics and Hermeneutics'. *Philosophical Hermeneutics*. Trans. and ed. David E. Linge. Berkeley: University of California Press, 1977. 95–104.

Gass, William. 'On Photography'. *The New York Times Review of Books* 18 December 1977. http://www.nytimes.com/1977/12/18/books/booksspecial/sontag-photo.html?_r=0. Accessed 28 January 2016.

Golding, John. *Paths to the Absolute: Mondrian, Malevich, Kandinsky, Pollock, Newman, Rothko, and Still*. Washington, DC: Thames and Hudson, 2000.

Gombrich, Ernst H. *Symbolic Images: Studies in the Art of the Renaissance*. London: Phaidon, 1972.

Green, André. *La Déliaison: Psychoanalyse, anthropologie et littérature*. Paris: Les Belles Lettres, 1992.

Groys, Boris. *Introduction to Antiphilosophy*. Trans. David Fernbach. London: Verso, 2012.

Hansen, Miriam B. 'Benjamin, Cinema, and Experience: "The Blue Flower in the Land of Technology"'. *New German Critique* 40 (1987): 179–224.

Heller, Dana. 'Absolute Seriousness: Susan Sontag in American Popular Culture'. *The Scandal of Susan Sontag*. Ed. Barbara Ching and Jennifer A. Wagner-Lawlor. New York: Columbia University Press, 2009. 32–51.

Henry, Michel. *Incarnazione: Una filosofia della carne*. Turin: Società Internazionale Editoriale, 2001.

Horowitz, Daniel. 'Sexuality and a New Sensibility'. *Consuming Pleasures: Intellectuals and Popular Culture in the Postwar World*. Philadelphia: University of Pennsylvania Press, 2012. 307–34.

Jankélévitch, Vladimir. *Il non-so-che e il quasi-niente* [*Le Je-ne-sais-quoi et le presque-rien*]. Trans. Carlo Bonadies. Turin: Einaudi, 2011.

Jarvis, Simon. *Adorno: A Critical Introduction*. Cambridge: Polity, 1998.

Jauss, Hans Robert. *Aesthetic Experience and Literary Hermeneutics*. Trans. Michael Snow. Minneapolis: University of Minnesota Press, 1982.

Jennings, Michael. 'Walter Benjamin and the European Avant-garde'. *The Cambridge Companion to Walter Benjamin*. Ed. David S. Ferris. Cambridge: Cambridge University Press, 2004. 18–34.

Kaplan, Ann E. 'Sontag, Modernity, Cinema'. *The Scandal of Susan Sontag*. Ed. Barbara Ching and Jennifer A. Wagner-Lawlor. New York: Columbia University Press, 2009. 106–27.

Kennedy, Liam. *Susan Sontag: Mind as Passion*. Manchester: Manchester University Press, 1995.

Klibansky, Raymond, Erwin Panofsky and Fritz Saxl. *Saturn and Melancholy: Studies in the History of Natural Philosophy, Religion and Art*. Cambridge: Thomas Nelson, 1964.

Koestenbaum, Wayne. 'Susan Sontag, Cosmophage'. *The Scandal of Susan Sontag*. Ed. Barbara Ching and Jennifer A. Wagner-Lawlor. New York: Columbia University Press, 2009. 236–42.

Kotz, Mary Lynn. *Rauschenberg/Art and Life*. New York: Harry N. Abrams, 2004.

Krauss, Rosalind. 'Robert Rauschenberg and the Materialized Image' (1974). *Robert Rauschenberg*. Ed. Branden W. Joseph. Cambridge, MA: MIT Press, 2002. 39–55.

Kristeva, Julia. 'Ellipsis on Dread and the Specular Seduction'. *Narrative, Apparatus, Ideology: A Film Theory Reader*. Ed. Philip Rosen. New York: Columbia University Press, 1986. 236–43

——. *Intimate Revolt: The Powers and Limits of Psychoanalysis*. Trans. Jeanine Herman. New York: Columbia University Press, 2002.

——. 'A New Type of Intellectual: The Dissident'. Trans. Seán Hand. *The Kristeva Reader*. Ed. Toril Moi. New York: Columbia University Press, 1986. 292–300.

——. *Revolution in Poetic Language*. New York: Columbia University Press, 1984.

Krupnick, Mark. 'Jewish Intellectuals and the "Deep Places of the Imagination"'. *The New York Public Intellectuals and Beyond: Exploring Liberal Humanism, Jewish Identity, and the American Protest Tradition*. Ed. Ethan Goffman and Daniel Morris. West Lafayette: Purdue University Press, 2009. 60–77.

Lacan, Jacques. 'Function and Field of Speech and Language'. *Ecrits: A Selection*. Trans. Alan Sheridan. New York: W.W. Norton, 1977. 30–113.

Leyden, Anne M., ed. *Paul Strand: Photographs from the J. Paul Getty Museum*. Los Angeles: J. Paul Getty Museum, 2005.

Liska, Vivian. 'Kafka, Modernism, and Literary Theory'. *A Handbook of Modernism Studies*. Ed. Jean-Michel Rabaté. Chichester: Wiley, 2013. 75–86.

Lonzi, Carla. 'La critica è potere'. *Scritti Sull'Arte*. Milan: et al-/Edizioni, 2012. 647–50.

——. 'La solitudine del critico'. *Scritti Sull'Arte*. Milan: et al-/Edizioni, 2012. 353–6.

——. *Sputiamo su Hegel*. Milan: et al-/Edizioni, 2010. First published 1970.

Loock, Ulrich. 'Paul Thek Luc Tuymans: Why?!' *Paul Thek Luc Tuymans: Why?!*. Galerie Isabelle Czarnowska. Berlin: Distanz, 2013. 6–7.

Lopate, Phillip. *Notes on Sontag*. Princeton: Princeton University Press, 2009.

Lyons, Deborah. *Gender and Immortality: Heroines in Ancient Greek Myth and Cult*. Princeton: Princeton University Press, 1997.

Makdisi, Saree. 'Edward Said and the Style of the Public Intellectual'. *Edward Said: The Legacy of a Public Intellectual*. Ed. Ned Curthoys and Debjani Ganguly. Carlton, Victoria: Melbourne University Press, 2007. 21–35.

Maunsell, Jerome Boyd. *Susan Sontag*. London: Reaktion, 2014.

McLeod, Glen. 'The Visual Arts'. *The Cambridge Companion to Modernism*. Ed. Michael Levenson. Cambridge: Cambridge University Press, 1999. 194–216.

McQuade, Molly. 'A Gluttonous Reader: Susan Sontag'. *Conversations with Susan Sontag*. Ed. Leland Poague. Jackson: University of Mississippi Press, 1995. 271–8.

Miller, J. Hillis. 'Forum'. *Public Intellectuals: An Endangered Species?*. Ed. Amitai Etzioni and Alyssa Bowoditch. Lanham: Rowman & Littlefield, 2006. 195–7.

Miller, Tyrus. *Late Modernism: Politics, Fiction, and the Arts Between the World Wars*. Berkeley: University of California Press, 1999.

Mondrian, Piet. *The New Art—The New Life: The Collected Writings of Piet Mondrian*. Ed. and trans. Harry Holtzman and Martin S. James. Boston: G.K. Hall, 1986.

Montale, Eugenio. 'Mediterraneo'. *Tutte le poesie*. Ed. Giorgio Zampa. Milan: Mondadori, 1984. 51–61.

Naldi, Giovanna, ed. *Italy: One Hundred Years of Photograph*. Texts by Cesare Colombo and Susan Sontag. Florence: Fratelli Alinari, 1988.

Nancy, Jean-Luc. *Corpus*. Trans. Antonella Moscati. Naples: Cronopio, 2004. 3rd edn. First French edn 1992.

Nelson, Cary. 'Soliciting Self-Knowledge: The Rhetoric of Susan Sontag's Criticism'. *Critical Inquiry* 6.4 (1980): 706–26.

——. 'Susan Sontag and the Practice of Modernism'. *American Literary History* 1.3 (1989): 593–611.

Ngai, Sianne. *Our Aesthetic Categories: Zany, Cute, Interesting*. Cambridge, MA: Harvard University Press, 2012.

Nicholls, Peter. *Modernisms: A Literary Guide*. London: Macmillan, 1995.

Nietzsche, Friedrich. *Thus Spoke Zarathustra*. Ed. Adrian Del Caro and Robert B. Pippin. Trans. Adrian Del Caro. Cambridge: Cambridge University Press, 2006.

Novick, Peter. 'Discussion Forum'. *The New York Public Intellectuals and Beyond*. Ed. Ethan Goffman and Daniel Morris. West Lafayette: Purdue University Press, 2009. 154–8.

Ormond, Mark. 'Introduction'. *Robert Rauschenberg: Works from the Salvage Series*. Sarasota, FL: The John and Mable Ringling Museum of Art Foundation, 1985.

Ortese, Anna Maria. 'Da Moby Dick all'Orsa Bianca'. *Da Moby Dick all'Orsa Bianca*. Milan: Adelphi, 2011. 97–102.

Paldam, Camilla Skovbjerg. 'The Materiality of a Contemporary Avant-Garde? Legacies of Surrealist Collage'. *The Aesthetics of Matter: Modernism, the Avant-Garde and Material Exchange*. Ed. Sarah Posman, Anne Reversau, David Ayers, Sascha Bru, and Benedikt Hjartarson. Berlin: De Gruyter, 2013. 167–79.

Panofsky, Erwin. *Albrecht Dürer*. 2 vols. Princeton: Princeton University Press, 1948. First published 1943.
——. *The Life and Art of Albrecht Dürer*. Princeton, NJ: Princeton University Press, 1955.
——. *Three Essays on Style*. Ed. Irving Lavin. Cambridge, MA: MIT Press, 1995.
Panofsky, Erwin, and Fritz Saxl, *Dürers 'Melancholia I'. Eine quellen- und typengeschichtlichen Untersuchung*. Leipzig: Teubner, 1923.
Parker, Andrew, and Eve K. Sedgwick. 'Introduction: Performativity and Performance'. *Performativity and Performance*. Ed. Andrew Parker and Eve K. Sedgwick. London: Routledge, 1995. 1–18.
Pasolini, Pier Paolo. 'La terra di lavoro'. *Le Ceneri di Gramsci*. Milan: Garzanti, 2003. 100–5.
Petrucciani, Stefano. *Introduzione ad Adorno*. Rome: Laterza, 2007.
Peucker, Brigitte. 'Looking and Touching: Spectacle and Collection in Sontag's *Volcano Lover*'. *The Yale Journal of Criticism* 11.1 (1998): 159–65.
Poague, Leland, and Kathy Parsons. *Susan Sontag: An Annotated Bibliography 1948–1992*. New York: Garland Publishing, 2000.
Poggioli, Renato. *Theory of the Avant-Garde*. Trans. Gerald Fitzgerald. Cambridge, MA: The Belknap Press of Harvard University Press, 1968. First Italian edn 1962.
Posner, Richard. *Public Intellectuals: A Study of Decline*. Cambridge, MA: Harvard University Press, 2001.
Richie, Donald. *The Japan Journals: 1947–2004*. Berkeley: Stone Bridge Press, 2005.
Ricoeur, Paul. *Memory, History, Forgetting*. Trans. Kathleen Blamey and David Pellauer. Chicago: University of Chicago Press, 2006.
Ross, Andrew. *No Respect: Intellectuals and Popular Culture*. New York and London: Routledge, 1989.
Ross, Stephen. 'Introduction: The Missing Link'. *Modernism and Theory: A Critical Debate*. Ed. Stephen Ross. London: Routledge, 2009. 1–22.
Said, Edward. 'The Public Role of Writers and Intellectuals'. *The Public Intellectual*. Ed. Helen Small. Oxford: Blackwell Publishers, 2002. 19–39.
——. *Representations of the Intellectual*. The 1993 Reith Lectures. New York: Vintage, 1996.
Sayres, Sohnya. 'Susan Sontag and the Practice of Modernism'. *American Literary History* 1.3 (1989): 593–601.
——. *Susan Sontag: The Elegiac Modernist*. New York and London: Routledge, 1990.
Scholem, Gershom. 'Walter Benjamin'. The Leo Baeck Memorial Lecture 8. New York: The Leo Baeck Institute, 1965.
——. 'Walter Benjamin and His Angel'. *On Walter Benjamin: Critical Essays and Recollections*. Ed. Gary Smith. Cambridge, MA: MIT Press, 1988. 51–89.

——. 'Walter Benjamin und Sein Engel' (1972). *Walter Benjamin Und Sein Engel*. Frankfurt am Main: Suhrkampf Verlag, 1983. 35–72.
Schreiber, Daniel. *Susan Sontag: A Biography*. Evanston: Northwestern University Press, 2014.
Sedgwick, Eve Kosofsky, *A Dialogue on Love*. Boston: Beacon, 2000.
——. 'Paranoid Reading and Reparative Reading, or, You Probably Think This Essay Is About You'. *Touching Feeling: Affect, Pedagogy, Performativity*. Durham, NC: Duke University Press, 2003. 123–52.
Shklovsky, Victor. 'Art as Technique'. *Modern Criticism and Theory: A Reader*. Ed. David Lodge. London: Longman, 1988. 16–30.
Showalter, Elaine. 'Writing Well is the Best Revenge: Susan Sontag'. *Inventing Herself: Claiming a Feminist Intellectual Heritage*. New York: Scribner, 2001. 225–46.
Shusterman, Richard. *Pragmatist Aesthetics: Living Beauty, Rethinking Art*. Lanham: Rowman & Littlefield, 2000.
Small, Helen, ed. *The Public Intellectual*. Oxford: Blackwell Publishers, 2002.
Sontag, Susan. 'About Hodgkin'. *Where the Stress Falls*, 151–60.
——. 'The Aesthetics of Silence'. *Styles of Radical Will*, 3–34.
——. *Against Interpretation*. New York: Picador, 2001. First published 1966.
——. 'Against Interpretation'. *Against Interpretation*, 3–14.
——. 'The Anthropologist as Hero'. *Against Interpretation*, 69–81.
——. 'Artaud'. *Antonin Artaud: Selected Writings*. Intro. Susan Sontag. Trans. Helen Weaver. Berkeley: University of California Press, 1976. xvii–lix.
——. 'The Artist as Exemplary Sufferer'. *Against Interpretation*, 39–48.
——. *As Consciousness is Harnessed to Flesh: Journals & Notebooks 1964–1980*. Ed. David Rieff. New York: Farrar, Straus, and Giroux, 2012.
——. 'At the Same Time: The Novelist and Moral Reasoning'. *At the Same Time: Essays and Speeches*. 210–30.
——. *At the Same Time: Essays and Speeches*. Ed. Paolo Dilonardo and Anne Jump. New York: Farrar, Straus, and Giroux, 2007.
——. 'Certain Mapplethorpes'. *Where the Stress Falls*, 233–7.
——. 'The Double Standard of Aging'. *Saturday Review* 23 September 1972. 29–38
——. 'Fascinating Fascism'. *Under the Sign of Saturn*, 73–105.
——. 'Fragments of an Aesthetic of Melancholy'. '*Veruschka*': *Transfigurations*. Ed. Holger Trülzsch and Vera Lehndorff. Boston: Little, Brown, 1986. 6–12.
——. 'Godard.' *Styles of Radical Will*, 147–89.
——. 'The Idea of Europe (One More Elegy)'. *Where the Stress Falls*, 285–9.
——. *In America*. New York: Farrar, Straus, and Giroux, 2000.
——. 'In Memory of Their Feelings'. *Where The Stress Falls*, 178–86.
——. 'Is The Reader Necessary'. *Partisan Review* 30 (1963): 260–8.

——. 'The Last Intellectual'. *The New York Review of Books* 12 October 1978. 75–82.

——. 'The Literary Criticism of Georg Lukács'. *Against Interpretation*, 82–92.

——. 'Marat/Sade/Artaud'. *Against Interpretation*, 163–74.

——. 'Mind as Passion'. *Under the Sign of Saturn*, 181–204.

——. 'Nathalie Sarraute and the Novel'. *Against Interpretation*. 100–11.

——. 'Notes on "Camp"'. *Against Interpretation*, 275–92.

——. 'On Paul Goodman'. *Under the Sign of Saturn*, 3–10.

——. *On Photography*. London: Penguin, 2002. First published 1977.

——. 'On Style'. *Against Interpretation*, 15–36.

——. 'One Hundred Years of Italian Photography'. *Where the Stress Falls*, 216–22.

——. 'Photography: The Beauty Treatment'. *The New York Review of Books* 28 November 1974. 35–9.

——. *Reborn: Journals & Notebooks 1947–1963*. Ed. David Rieff. New York: Farrar, Straus, and Giroux, 2008.

——. *Regarding the Pain of Others*. New York: Farrar, Straus, and Giroux, 2003.

——. 'Remembering Barthes'. *Under the Sign of Saturn*, 169–77.

——. 'The Salmagundi Interview'. *A Susan Sontag Reader*. Ed. Elizabeth Hardwick. New York: Farrar, Straus, and Giroux, 1982. 327–46.

——. 'Shooting America'. *The New York Review of Books* 18 April 1974. 17–24.

——. 'Singleness'. *Where the Stress Falls*, 259–62.

——. 'Spiritual Style in the Films of Robert Bresson'. *Against Interpretation*, 177–95.

——. *Styles of Radical Will*. New York: Picador, 2002. First published 1969.

——. 'Syberberg's Hitler'. *Under the Sign of Saturn*, 137–65.

——. '"Thinking Against Oneself": Reflections on Cioran'. *Styles of Radical Will*, 74–95.

——. 'The Third World of Women'. *Partisan Review* 40 (1973): 181–206.

——. 'Trip to Hanoi'. *Styles of Radical Will*, 205–74.

——. *Under the Sign of Saturn*. New York: Writers and Readers Publishing, 1983. First published 1980.

——. 'Under the Sign of Saturn'. *Under the Sign of Saturn*, 109–34.

——. *The Volcano Lover*. New York: Vintage, 1992.

——. 'Wagner's Fluids'. *London Review of Books* 10 December 1987. 8–9.

——. 'Waiting for Godot in Sarajevo'. *Where the Stress Falls*, 299–322.

——. *Where the Stress Falls*. New York: Vintage, 2003.

——. 'The World as India'. *Where the Stress Falls*, 156–79.

——. 'Writing as Reading'. *Where the Stress Falls*, 263–7.

Stein, Gertrude. *The Autobiography of Alice B. Toklas*. *Selected Writings of Gertrude Stein*. Ed. Carl Van Vechten. New York: Vintage 1990. 3–237.

Steinem, Gloria. 'Letter to the *Saturday Evening Post*, 20 Sept. 1956'. Gloria Steinem Papers. Sophia Smith Collection. Smith College

Striano, Enzo. *Il Resto di niente* [*The remains of nothing*]. Milan: Mondadori, 2005.

Sussman, Elisabeth, and Lynn Zelevansky. 'Introduction'. *Paul Thek: Diver. A Retrospective*. Ed. Elisabeth Sussman and Lynn Zelevansky. Whitney Museum of American Art, New York, Carnegie Museum of Art, Pittsburgh. New Haven, CT: Yale University Press, 2010. 8–27.

Sussman, Elisabeth and Lynn Zelevansky, eds. *Paul Thek: Diver. A Retrospective*. Whitney Museum of American Art, New York, Carnegie Museum of Art, Pittsburgh. New Haven, CT: Yale University Press, 2010.

Szondi, Peter. *Introduction to Literary Hermeneutics*. Trans. Martha Woodmansee. Cambridge: Cambridge University Press, 1995. First German edn 1975.

Thek, Paul, Anke Bangma, Barbera van Kooij, and Louise Neri. *Paul Thek: The Wonderful World That Almost Was*. Rotterdam: Witte de With, Center for Contemporary Art, 1995.

Todorov, Tzvetan. *Gli altri vivono in noi e noi viviamo in loro: Saggi 1983–2008*. Trans. Emanuele Lana. Milan: Garzanti, 2011.

Tytell, John. *The Living Theatre: Art, Exile and Outrage*. New York: Grove Press, 1995.

Urgnani, Elena. *L'opera letteraria e politica di Eleonora de Fonseca Pimentel*. Naples: Edizioni del Sole, Istituto per gli Studi Filosofici, 1998.

Van Haaften, Julia, ed. *Berenice Abbott, Photographer: A Modern Vision*. New York: The New York Public Library, 1989.

Waddel, Helen. *The Desert Fathers*. London: Constable, 1936.

Weibel, Peter. 'Art (Re)forms and (Re)forms of Life'. *Paul Thek: Artist's Artist*. Ed. Harald Falckenberg and Peter Weibel. ZKM Center for Art and Media Karlsruhe, Germany. Cambridge, MA: MIT Press, 2008. 39–56.

Wellek, René. *A History of Modern Criticism: 1750–1950*. Vol. 6: *American Criticism, 1900–1950*. New Haven, CT: Yale University Press, 1986.

——. *Storia della critica moderna*. Vol. 7: *Germania, Russia, ed Europa orientale 1900–1950*. Trans. Agostino Lombardo. Bologna: Il Mulino, 1995.

Wellek, René, and Austin Warren. *Theory of Literature*. New York: Harcourt, Brace & World, 1956. 3rd edn.

Wilson, Ann. 'Beatitudes: Remembering Paul Thek'. *Paul Thek: Diver. A Retrospective*. Ed. Elisabeth Sussman and Lynn Zelevansky. Whitney Museum of American Art, New York, Carnegie Museum of Art, Pittsburgh. New Haven, CT: Yale University Press, 2010. 116–19.

——. 'Mare Tenebrarum: Sea of Darkness'. *Paul Thek: Artist's Artist*. Ed. Harald Falckenberg and Peter Weibel. ZKM Center for Art and Media Karlsruhe, Germany. Cambridge, MA: MIT Press, 2011. First printing 2008. 231–8.

——. 'Voices from the Era'. *Paul Thek: The Wonderful World that Almost Was*. By Paul Thek, Anke Bangma, Barbera van Kooij, and Louise Neri. Rotterdam: Witte de With, Center for Contemporary Art, 1995. 57–82.

Wiseman, Susan. 'Femininity and the Intellectual in Sontag and Cixous'. *The Body and the Text: Hélène Cixous, Reading and Teaching*. Ed. Helen Wilcox et al. New York: Harvester Wheatsheaf, 1990. 98–113.

Woolf, Virginia. 'A Sketch of the Past'. *Moments of Being*. Ed. Jeanne Schulkind. San Diego: Harcourt, Brace, 1985. 61–160.

Yochelson, Bonnie. 'Introduction: A "Fantastic Passion" for New York'. *Changing New York*. New York: The New York Press, 1997. 9–34.

Zelevansky, Lynn. 'Life Is Just a Bowl of Cherries: The Life and Art of Paul Thek'. *Paul Thek: Diver. A Retrospective*. Ed. Elisabeth Sussman and Lynn Zelevansky. Whitney Museum of American Art, New York, Carnegie Museum of Art, Pittsburgh. New Haven, CT: Yale University Press, 2010. 12–13.

Index